A Teach
COMMENTARY
on First and Second
CORINTHIANS

Dan R. Owen, Ph. D.

ISBN 978-1-63885-995-6 (Paperback)
ISBN 978-1-63814-545-5 (Hardcover)
ISBN 978-1-63814-546-2 (Digital)

Covenant Books, Inc.
11661 Hwy 707
Murrells Inlet, SC 29576
www.covenantbooks.com

A TEACHER'S COMMENTARY ON FIRST CORINTHIANS

FIRST CORINTHIANS IN THE LIFE OF PAUL

After Paul's conversion, he began preaching in the city of Damascus about the risen Jesus. After a short time, he left Damascus and went away into Arabia. Then he returned to Damascus. Three years after his conversion, he went to Jerusalem and spent fifteen days visiting with Peter and James. He then returned to his home in Tarsus of Cilicia and stayed there until Barnabas came and brought him to help with the newly established work in Antioch of Syria. From Antioch, Paul and Barnabas went East and North, spending about fourteen years establishing and strengthening the churches of Galatia. After their return to Antioch of Syria, they went up to the conference in Jerusalem where they argued convincingly that one does not need to be circumcised and keep Moses's law in order to be saved. Not long after the great conference, Paul made his way to Macedonia where he founded the churches in Philippi, Thessalonica, and Berea. Then he traveled south to Athens and finally to Corinth. There he proclaimed the Gospel of Christ, first to the Jews in the synagogue and soon after to the pagans (Acts 9–18; Galatians 1–2).

When Luke describes Paul's initial stay in Corinth, he names Gallio as the current proconsul of Achaia. Luke says, "While Gallio was proconsul of Achaia, the Jews made a united attack on Paul and brought him into court" (Acts 18:12). The famous Gallio inscription from nearby Delphi confirms that Gallio was, indeed, the proconsul in A.D. 52 during the reign of Claudius.

Here is a translation of the inscription, line by line, very similar to a number of others. The lacking portions are due to the fragmented stone on which the inscription was found.

> Tiber[ius Claudius Cae]sar Augustus Ge[r-manicus, invested with tribunician po]wer [for the 12th time, acclaimed Imperator for t]he 26th time, F[ather of the Fa]ther[land…]. For a l[ong time have I been not onl]y [well-disposed towards t]he ci[ty] of Delph[i, but also solicitous for its pro]sperity, and I have always guard[ed th]e cul[t of t]he [Pythian] Apol[lo. But] now [since] it is said to be desti[tu]te of [citi]zens, as [L. Jun]ius Gallio, my fri[end] an[d procon]sul, [recently reported to me, and being desirous that Delphi] should retain [inta]ct its for[mer rank, I] ord[er you (pl.) to in]vite well-born people also from [ot]her cities [to Delphi as new inhabitants" (O'Conner, p. 161).

Given a date of 52 AD for the Delphi inscription, the fact that Paul was in Corinth around that time and the fact that Paul stayed in Corinth for at least a year and a half before moving on, the writing of First Corinthians could have taken place as early as A.D. 53–54 or perhaps as late as A.D. 57. Paul sends greetings at the end of 1 Corinthians from the churches in Asia where he spent three years teaching and preaching after leaving Corinth (Acts 20:31). During his stay in Asia, he received news from the household of Chloe about the Corinthian church (1 Corinthians 1:11ff). This news revealed that the Corinthian church was plagued with division and strife over a number of issues. To heal this division and get the Corinthian Christians back on the same page both in belief and practice, Paul wrote this letter (1 Corinthians 1:10; 4:16; 16:15).

The Environment in Ancient Corinth

Corinth was located on a strategic waterway for first-century travelers, merchants, and mariners going from the Ionian Sea to the Aegean Sea. The sailing distance could be greatly cut down if instead of sailing all the way around southern Greece, mariners sailed from the Ionian Sea into the waterway transecting southern Greece, then allowed their ships to be pulled on great rollers across a small isthmus of land to the port of Cenchrea, which launched them into the Aegean. Corinth was located on the southwestern side of this isthmus and was a convenient and attractive place for mariners and other travelers to stop.

According to Strabo's geography, the great temple of Aphrodite with its many cult prostitutes attracted many to come and spend their money in that city. It is no surprise that there is much discussion in Paul's letter about fornication and idolatry, and how Christians must flee from both (1 Corinthians 5–7; 6:18; 10:14). Strabo says:

> The temple of Aphrodite [in Korinthos in the days of the tyrant Kypselos] was so rich that it owned more than a thousand temple slaves, courtesans, whom both men and women had dedicated to the goddess. And therefore it was also on account of these women that the city was crowded with people and grew rich; for instance, the ship captains freely squandered their money, and hence the proverb, "Not for every man is the voyage to Korinthos." Now the summit [of the Akrokorinthos] has a small temple of Aphrodite; and below the summit is the spring Peirene. At any rate, Euripides says, "I am come, having left Akrokorinthos that

is washed on all sides, the sacred hill-city of Aphrodite." (Geography 8.6.20)

Later, Strabo continues:

> Korinthos, there, on account of the multitude of courtesans, who were sacred to Aphrodite, outsiders resorted in great numbers and kept holiday. And the merchants and soldiers who went there squandered all their money so that the following proverb arose in reference to them: 'Not for every man is the voyage to Korinthos.' (Geography 12.4.36)

There were other pagan temples in ancient Corinth as well with plenty of sacrificial meat available. The second-century geographer Pausanias says:

> The things worthy of mention in the city include the extant remains of antiquity, but the greater number of them belong to the period of its second ascendancy. On the market-place, where most of the sanctuaries are, stand Artemis surnamed Ephesian and wooden images of Dionysus, which are covered with gold with the exception of their faces; these are ornamented with red paint. They are called Lysius and Baccheus. (Descriptions of Greece 2.2.6)

He later says:

> In the middle of the market-place is a bronze Athena, on the pedestal of which are

wrought in relief figures of the Muses. Above
the market-place is a temple of Octavia the sister
of Augustus… The Acrocorinthus is a moun-
tain peak above the city, assigned to Helius
by Briareos when he acted as adjudicator, and
handed over, the Corinthians say, by Helius to
Aphrodite. As you go up this Acrocorinthus
you see two precincts of Isis, one of Isis sur-
named Pelagian (Marine) and the other of
Egyptian Isis, and two of Serapis, one of them
being of Serapis called "in Canopus… On the
summit of the Acrocorinthus is a temple of
Aphrodite. The images are Aphrodite armed,
Helius, and Eros with a bow. (Descriptions of
Greece, 2.3.1–2.4.6)

The Corinthian social and economic culture was based in
idolatry, its temples, the fornication it involved, and the eating
of meals comprised of sacrificial meat. The second-century orator
Aristides gives us a snapshot of this kind of thing as he relates a
dream that he had in which the god Asclepius commanded, "After
this [it was necessary] to go to the temple to sacrifice a full-grown
animal to Asclepius and to place sacred bowls and to distribute
the sacred shares among all my fellow pilgrims" (Aelius Aristides,
Hieroi Logoi, 2.27). Paul addressed these pagan meals and the
temptations that surrounded them in 1 Corinthians 8–10.

The following are examples from the *Oxyrhynchus Papyri* of
invitations to sacrificial meals involving the worship of these and
other gods. While these ancient quotes may not be specific references to activity in Corinth, they certainly shed some cultural
light on the struggles of the ancient Christians over whether or not
to eat meat that had been sacrificed to the various gods in their
respective cities (see 1 Corinthians 8–10).

"Chaeremon asks you to dine at a table of the lord Sarapis in the Sarapian [temple] tomorrow, which is the 15th, from the 9th hour" (P. Oxy. 110).

"Apollonius asks you to dine at a table of the lord Sarapis on the occasion of the coming of age of his brothers in the Thoerian [temple]" (P. Oxy. 1484).

"Antonius, [son] of Ptolemaeus, asks you to dine with him at a table of the lord Sarapis in the [house] of Claudius Sarapion on the 16th from the 9th hour" (P. Oxy. 523).

The Corinthian epistles provide a unique insight into the kind of issues involved for ancient people, particularly those converted from paganism to Christianity as they tried to fight temptation and live Christian lives. They also provide major insight into the struggles of those who tried to minister to such people, teach them the truth, and continue to encourage them in true Christian conduct. As a result, they provide many powerful insights for people today who struggle to be Christians surrounded by the pressures of ungodly culture, false religion, and modern philosophical challenges to the faith.

The Text of 1 Corinthians

The translation of 1 Corinthians presented below is my own translation of the *UBS Greek* text and sometimes of *Nestle-Aland 28th Edition*. To be sure, the translation is imperfect, and the reader is admonished to compare it and criticize it where warranted, but it is my best attempt to translate what Paul wrote in the way it was meant to be understood by Paul himself. Since 1975, I have had a close daily relationship with the Greek Text of the New Testament, constantly reading it and learning the nuances of various New Testament writers. Each reader of this commentary should compare my translation with other more literal translations like the NASB, ESV, ASV, and even the NIV 1984 edition if you can find it. This will help the reader in his/her understanding. Also, in many of my comments, I have explained to the reader why I translated it the way I did. Where *I have added words in parentheses,* they are my own words designed to better explain what I think the text is trying to say. They are words that need to be supplied for meaning to be complete, but they are *not* part of the Greek text.

1

First Corinthians Text and Commentary

First Corinthians 1:1–3

> Paul, a called apostle of Jesus Christ by the
> will of God, and Sosthenes the brother, to the
> assembly of God which is at Corinth, to those
> sanctified in Christ Jesus, to the called saints,
> along with all who call on the name of our Lord
> Jesus Christ in every place. Grace and peace to
> you from God our Father and the Lord Jesus
> Christ.

As stated in Galatians 1:1, Paul's apostleship was not by man or
through man, but he was chosen directly by Jesus Christ and accepted
as an equal by the Jerusalem apostles (Galatians 2:8–10). This letter
is to God's congregation or assembly at Corinth. There were other
ekklesiai or assemblies at Corinth that did not belong to God as there
were in all other locations. The assembly of people to which Paul
wrote, like the one in Thessalonica, was "in God the Father and our
Lord Jesus Christ (1 Thessalonians 1:1–2). The assembly of God at
Corinth was made up of those who are sanctified in Christ Jesus, the
"called saints" or "invited saints." They were invited by the gospel

into the fellowship of Christ (1 Corinthians 1:9; 2 Thessalonians 2:14). This letter was addressed to this special group of people along with all who call upon the name of our Lord Jesus Christ. This is a group of baptized believers (Acts 18:8; 22:16). They "call upon" or trust in the Lord Jesus Christ and his redemptive work. The letter is not just from Paul but from God the Father and Jesus Christ as well. As stated later in the letter, the things Paul wrote were the Lord's commands (1 Corinthians 14:37).

First Corinthians 1:4–7

> I thank my God always for you, for the grace of God which was given to you in Christ Jesus, because you were made rich in every way in him, in all word and in all knowledge, just as the mystery of Christ was established among you, so that you might not be lacking in any spiritual gift as you eagerly await the revelation of our Lord Jesus Christ.

Paul's love and concern for the Corinthians is evident in this thanksgiving as well as in other statements. He opened his heart to this group of people in spite of their difficulties (2 Corinthians 6:11–13; 7:2ff). The phrase, "the grace of God which was given to you," likely has reference to the spiritual gifts that had been given by God to this group of Christians. Paul uses the same phrase to describe his own gift of apostleship as well as other spiritual gifts (Romans 12:3, 6; 2 Corinthians 8:1; Galatians 2:9; Ephesians 3:2, 7, 8; 4:7). Paul mentions here the gifts of utterance and knowledge, perhaps meaning prophecy and knowledge, gifts mentioned in 1 Corinthians 12:8–10 and 1 Corinthians 13:8–9. They had been enriched by God so that they would not lack any spiritual gift needed to carry on the ministries of Christ (see 1 Corinthians

12:4–7, 11, 18). Paul mentions here the *Parousia* or second coming of Christ as he does in many other places. This was a core element in the expectation of every Christian (1 Corinthians 15:19ff; 1 Thessalonians 4:13–18).

First Corinthians 1:8–9

> Who will also establish you unto the end,
> blameless in the day of our Lord Jesus Christ.
> God is faithful by whom you were invited into
> the fellowship of his son Jesus Christ our Lord.

Paul wants them to know that God has given them everything they need in order to serve him faithfully until the end. God is trustworthy or faithful. He upholds his part of the covenant between himself and those in Christ. Paul mentions here "the day of our Lord Jesus Christ," most likely a reference to the *Parousia* of Christ and the judgment to follow (see 1 Corinthians 15:20ff). All who have heard, understood, and obeyed the gospel have been called or invited by God into the fellowship of Christ. John later said that the reason we share the gospel with the lost is that "they might have fellowship with us and our fellowship is with the Father and his Son Jesus Christ" (1 John 1:3). The invitation to fellowship comes to all through the gospel of Christ (2 Thessalonians 2:14).

First Corinthians 1:10

> And I urge you, brothers, through the
> name of our Lord Jesus Christ, that you all
> speak the same thing, and that there be no divisions among you, and you be knit together in
> the same mind and in the same understanding.

This is one of three passages in the book where Paul uses the petition word *parakalo*. This word indicates that what is said is central to what Paul wants to ask them in his letter. This is what he really desires from them. The other two formal petition passages are 1 Corinthians 4:16 and 1 Corinthians 16:15, both of which are connected with the request for unity in this passage. Paul wants the divided Corinthian church to be united, to be on the same page, and to act in unity. Notice that he wants them to speak the same things. This is only possible if people are "knit together in the same mind and the same understanding." This sameness of mind was impossible unless the Corinthians could all accept the same objective standard of authority. This is why Paul begins the discussion of human wisdom versus divine wisdom. He explains that only the divine revelation given to the apostles provides divine wisdom and unifies God's people (1 Corinthians 2:6–13).

First Corinthians 1:11–13

> For it was shown to me about you, my brothers, by those of Chloe's household, that there are factions among you. I say this, that each of you says, I am of Paul, I am of Apollos, I am of Cephas, and I am of Christ! Is Christ split into parts? Paul wasn't crucified for you was he? And you were not baptized into the name of Paul, were you?

The source of Paul's understanding of the present condition in the Corinthian church was a letter from the family of Chloe. Evidently, Paul trusted the source enough to address the issues raised. Of course, what he heard was carefully compared with what Paul already knew based on his eighteen months of personal experience with the Corinthian disciples. The people were divided into factions, claiming allegiance to one leader or another. We learn from 1 Corinthians 4:6 that they were really following local people deemed to be leaders of some kind, and Paul was using his name and the name of Apollos to spare their feelings while getting his point across. As stated in 1 Corinthians 4:6, they were arrogant or "puffed up" on behalf of one person against another. They were, as stated in his second letter, "measuring themselves by themselves and comparing themselves with themselves," (2 Corinthians 10:12).

Paul reminds them here that Christ is not divided, but he did his redemptive work to create the unity of the Spirit in the bond of peace (Ephesians 2:14–18; 4:4). It was no human leader who died for them but Christ. They were not baptized in the name of any human being but in the name of Jesus Christ. Paul converted people to Christ, not to Paul. He later wrote, "We do not preach ourselves, but Christ Jesus as Lord and ourselves as your servants for Jesus' sake" (2 Corinthians 4:5).

First Corinthians 1:14–17

> I thank God that I baptized no one except Crispus and Gaius. So that no one might say you were baptized into my name! And I also baptized the household of Stephanus. And as for the rest I don't know if I baptized any other. For Christ did not send me to baptize, but to preach the gospel, not in wisdom of words, so that the cross of Christ might not be made useless.

The reason Paul is glad he did not personally baptize many of them is because he did not want them claiming to be his disciples. He was their father in the gospel (1 Corinthians 4:15), but they were disciples of Christ. He mentions Crispus who was likely the ruler of the synagogue mentioned in Acts 18:8. He also mentions Gaius and the household of Stephanus. The latter were the first of his converts in Achaia according to 1 Corinthians 16:15. Paul did not keep track of those whom he personally baptized. His role was to preach the gospel of Christ. His mission was to tell the message of Jesus. It was the responsibility of the hearers to be baptized. It did not matter who baptized them if they were baptized as a legitimate response to the gospel of Christ. What counted was that each person "obeyed from the heart that symbolic representation of the teaching which was delivered" (Romans 6:17). It is God who causes the spiritual growth and transformation, not the preacher (1 Corinthians 3:5–6).

The Choice Between Trusting Human Wisdom or Divine Wisdom

First Corinthians 1:18–20

> For the message of the cross is foolishness to those who are perishing, but to those who are being saved, it is the power of God. For it is written, "I will destroy the wisdom of the wise ones, and will nullify the understanding of the intelligent ones." Where is the wise person? Where is the scribe? Where is the debater of this age? Hasn't God made foolish the wisdom of the world?

Much as he does in 2 Corinthians 2:15, Paul divides humanity into two parts: those who are being saved and those who are perishing. The different groups tend to view the content of the gospel in different ways. One group sees the message of Christ dying on the cross as complete foolishness, while the other group sees the same message as the power of God (Romans 1:16). Those who are perishing do not respect divinely revealed wisdom (1 Corinthians 2:6). God's revealed wisdom is not like the wisdom of man. It is comprised of things "no eye has seen, things no ear has heard, things which never entered the mind of man" (1 Corinthians 2:9). Paul quotes Isaiah 29:14 where God is disparaging those who live by "rules taught by man." Such wisdom will be proven useless by the Almighty. The people viewed as wise, intelligent, and capable debaters by the world are often ignorant of the things revealed by God. The wisdom of the world does not hold the secrets of eternal salvation. Worldly wisdom cannot lead man to be reconciled with God! It is very likely that an exaggerated respect for worldly wisdom in some Achaian believers was helping to cause the divisions in Corinth.

First Corinthians 1:21

> For since in the wisdom of God, the
> world, through its wisdom, did not know God,
> God was pleased, through the "foolishness" of
> what was preached, to save them that believe!

Paul clearly taught that some things could be known about God from his creation (Romans 1:19–20). The creation certainly proclaims that there is a God and that he is everlastingly powerful and divine. But beyond that, human reasoning and human research cannot lead man to a relationship with God. We cannot know God through human wisdom. We cannot know his character, what he loves, and what he hates apart from divine revelation. Paul is sarcastically referring to the "foolishness of what was preached" because that was the way many in southern Greece viewed the gospel. Paul did not preach based on public opinion but based on the revelation of God. Those who consider the redemptive work of Christ to be foolishness are "those who are perishing" (1 Corinthians 1:18). Later, he calls them "natural" people as opposed to "spiritual" and "carnal" as opposed to "mature" (1 Corinthians 2:6, 14, 15; 3:1).

First Corinthians 1:22–24

> And even though the Jews ask for signs and the Greeks are seeking wisdom, we are preaching Christ crucified, to the Jews an occasion of stumbling, and to the gentiles, foolishness, but to those who are invited, both Jews and Greeks, Christ, the power of God and the wisdom of God!

Those from different cultures asked for different things as proof for the gospel. The Jewish culture asked for signs, and Paul gave them signs (1 Corinthians 2:4–5; 2 Corinthians 12:12). The pagan culture wanted the gospel presented to them in the language of the Greek philosophers who argued their cases on Mars Hill in Athens. The idea of God incarnate being crucified for man was a deal breaker for the Jews because their idea of a Messianic King did not allow for his humiliation and his sacrificial death. Paul did not present the gospel to the Corinthians "with excellency of speech or of wisdom," so many people with a Greek mindset rejected him (1 Corinthians 2:1–2). The verb *kaleo*, means call, or, in its noun form, *kletos,* it means called or invited. It carries the idea of someone who hears an invitation and accepts it. This is the word group used for the invitation extended for the great banquet in Luke 14 and the parallel passage in Matthew. When people hear the invitation of God in the gospel and accept that invitation to come into a relationship with God, they then are classified as the "called" or "invited" of God (1 Corinthians 1:2, 9; 2 Thessalonians 2:14). For these people, Christ and his redemptive work represent the power and wisdom of God working on their behalf.

First Corinthians 1:25

> Because the foolishness of God is wiser than men, and the weakness of God is stronger than men.

If there is any sense in which anyone could use the word foolishness with reference to God, God's most foolish point is wiser than man's wisest point. There is as much distance between God and man "as the heavens are higher than the earth" (Isaiah 55:8–9). The very weakest point in the Almighty is stronger than all mankind combined. Nothing is impossible with God (Matthew 19:26; Luke 1:37).

First Corinthians 1:26–29

> Look at your calling, brothers, that not many wise according to the flesh, not many powerful, not many noble born are called! But God chose the foolish things of the world, so that he might put the wise to shame, and God chose the weak things of the world, so that he might put the strong to shame, and God chose the lowborn of the world and the things that are despised, even the things that are not, so that he might nullify the things that are, so that no flesh may boast before God.

Our "calling" or vocation is Christianity. Fewer of those who consider themselves "wise according to the flesh" are Christians because they are trusting in human wisdom for their answers. Fewer of the "powerful" are Christians because they trust in their own power instead God's power. The gospel is God's power to save, not man's power (Romans 1:16). The highborn trust in their noble family heritage and don't feel the need for God as much as the lowborn. Jesus was born in a stable and laid in a manger. He did not live his life among the mighty but among the masses. He died for all people, not a few. Because the power and wisdom of God are revealed in Christ, it shames the wise, the powerful, and the noble born because they are all powerless to save man from sin and death. No person, high or low, can reconcile himself/herself to God. In the great judgment, John sees "the great and the small standing before the throne" (Revelation 20:11–13). All are sinners, separated from God. The ground is level at the foot of the cross!

First Corinthians 1:30–31

> It is from him that you are in Christ Jesus, who was made for us wisdom from God, and righteousness, and sanctification, and redemption, so that just as it is written, "He who boasts, let him boast in the Lord!"

When Paul says it is "from him" or "of him" that we are in Christ, he means that it is not from ourselves or from our own efforts or power or position. It is as a result of the redemptive work of God that we stand justified and reconciled in Christ (Romans 5:6–11; Ephesians 2:6–10). Christ became our wisdom when God revealed his plan to reconcile man through his redemptive death (1 Corinthians 2:6–11). Christ became righteousness for us because only in the gospel of Christ is the righteousness of God revealed, a righteousness that comes to us apart from works of law, a righteousness that is given to us as a free gift (Romans 1:17; 3:21; 5:17). Christ became sanctification for us because he shows us how to live a sanctified life and helps us to follow his footsteps. Christ became redemption for us because he paid the price to purchase us out of slavery to sin and death (Acts 20:28; 1 Corinthians 6:19–20; 1 Peter 1:18; Revelation 5:9–10). As a result, no person can boast in his/her own power, position, or efforts. We can only boast in the goodness and grace of God (see also 2 Corinthians 10:17–18).

Reflections on Chapter 1

1. Find passages in chapter one where the word "called" or "invited" is used and talk about their meaning.
2. Discuss the importance of Paul's petition in 1 Corinthians 1:10 for the Corinthian church and for churches today.
3. Why did Paul say he was glad he only baptized a very few of the Corinthians personally?
4. Does 1 Corinthians 1:17 diminish the importance of baptism? Why or why not?
5. What exactly was a stumbling block to the Jews and considered "foolishness" to the Greeks according to Paul?
6. What social/educational strata made up most of the Christian population in Corinth according to 1 Corinthians 1:26ff? Why do you think this was true?
7. What effect does individual boasting and pride have on unity in the church? See 1 Corinthians 1:29, 31.

2

First Corinthians 2:1

> And I brothers, when I came to you, did
> not come with excellency of speech or wis-
> dom proclaiming to you the mystery of God.
> For I decided not to know anything among
> you except Jesus Christ and him crucified.
> And I was with you in weakness and in fear
> and in much trembling. And my speech and
> my preaching were not in persuasive words of
> wisdom, but with demonstration of Spirit and
> power, so that your faith might not be in the
> wisdom of men but in the power of God!

The wisdom and speech Paul mentions in this passage are the worldly wisdom and rhetoric of Athens, the worldly wisdom discussed in 1 Corinthians 1:18–25. Paul did not approach the Corinthians with the argumentation of Mars Hill philosophers or the style of the pagan debaters (1 Corinthians 1:26). He brought them a message about things that had actually happened: the death and resurrection of Christ. He explained to them the meaning and implications of those events. He told them a story of events, past, present, and future. He explained what God had accomplished for them through the redemptive events and how they could take advantage of Gods saving work. As he stated earlier, "We preach

Christ crucified" (1 Corinthians 1:22–23). Paul did not claim human erudition or prowess as he brought this message. He was with the Corinthians in weakness and trembling. As he states in his second letter, he and others like him carried the gospel treasure in clay jars (2 Corinthians 4:7). He was just a weak man, but the message he carried in the fragile jar of humanity was the pearl of great price! He did not want the Corinthians placing their faith in human wisdom or expertise but in the power of God! For this reason, Paul preached the simple message and confirmed it with "the signs of an apostle" (2 Corinthians 12:12). The signs of an apostle confirmed the message as Gods word (Mark 16:20; Hebrews 2:4).

First Corinthians 2:6–8

> We speak wisdom among the mature, yet a wisdom not of this age nor of the rulers of this age who are being nullified. But we speak Gods wisdom in a mystery, which was hidden, which God foreordained before the ages for our glory, which none of the rulers of this age knew. For if they had had known it, they would not have crucified the Lord of glory.

Christ is the wisdom of God for us (1 Corinthians 1:30). It is the spiritually mature who accept this divinely revealed wisdom. Paul later calls the mature Christians the "spiritual" people in 1 Corinthians 2:15 and 1 Corinthians 3:1. These are contrasted with the "natural" and "carnal" people who do not respect the things revealed by God to the apostles (1 Corinthians 2:14; 3:1–2). The revelation of God's redemptive plan in Christ was a mystery because it was hidden from mankind for long ages. Paul describes this mystery as that "Which in other generations was not made known to the sons of men, as now it has been revealed to his holy apostles and prophets by the Spirit" (Ephesians 3:5). This recently revealed mystery of Christ was foreordained by God before the ages. It is part of God's eternal purpose, which he purposed in Christ (Ephesians 1:10–11; 3:9–10). The powerful people of Paul's day did not understand the plan of God in Christ. Perhaps this was necessary because if they had known it, they would not have crucified Christ. But it was necessary that the Christ should suffer (Luke 24:46). His death was part of the "determinate counsel and foreknowledge of God" (Acts 2:22). It was only after the fact of his death that it was time to reveal the meaning of his death in the preaching of the gospel.

First Corinthians 2:9–11

> But just as it is written, "Things no eye has seen, and no ear has heard, and have never arisen in the mind of man, things God prepared for those who love him." But to us God revealed them through the Spirit. For the Spirit searches all things, even the deep things of God. For who among men knows the things of a man except the spirit of the man that is in him. In the same way no one knows the things of God except the Spirit of God.

Man's reason does not lead to God's redemptive plan. Empirical research and verification through the five senses will not lead one to figure out God's redemptive purpose. The only way one could come to know the eternal plan of God is through divine revelation. Paul said he did not receive it from man nor was he taught it, but it came to him by revelation from Jesus Christ (Galatians 1:12; Ephesians 3:3). In verse 9, Paul is not talking about the afterlife per se, but is talking about God's eternal plan to save mankind. The only one who knows what is in God's mind is God himself. We never know exactly what is in another person's mind unless that person discloses it. The same is true with God. Only God can reveal the deep and secret things of his mind to mankind (Daniel 2:20–21). The Spirit of God searches the deep things of God and reveals them to his apostles and prophets (Ephesians 3:5). We could not know what God loves and what he hates and the reasons why he has done what he has done without divine revelation. We could not know what God has ordained to do in the future without divine revelation. The Christian faith rests on the acts of God and the divine revelations of God.

First Corinthians 2:12

> But we have not received the spirit of the world, but the Spirit which is from God, so that we might know the things freely given to us by God. Which things also we speak, not in words taught by human wisdom, but in (words) taught by the Spirit, explaining spiritual things to spiritual (people).

Paul believed that both the demons and the Spirit of God were trying to speak to people in the world. The seducing spirits with their demonic doctrines were always spreading their lies (1 Timothy 4:1ff). The god of this world was always trying to "blind the minds of the unbelievers" (2 Corinthians 4:4). The prince of this world and his ministers are trying to build fortresses around the minds of men and women to block out the knowledge of God and his Son (2 Corinthians 10:3–5). The word of God seeks to tear down those walls made out of the reasoning and arguments of unbelievers. Paul claims to be a recipient of the Holy Spirit and the divine revelations given by him. The teaching of Paul to the

Corinthians is "the Lord's command" (1 Corinthians 14:37). He spoke words to them and others which had not been taught by human wisdom but by direct revelation from the Spirit (Galatians 1:12). The last part of 1 Corinthians 2:13 is a little difficult to translate. The phrase is *pneumatikois pneumatika sugkrinontes.* The verb *sugkrino* means to bring things together or to explain or to compare (Kittel, *Theological Dictionary of the New Testament*, III, 953). Paul is talking about divine revelations. He is saying that through his teaching to the Corinthians, he is "explaining spiritual things." These spiritual things, *pneumatika*, are the things he has received directly from God. The difficulty comes when we attempt to understand the dative *pneumatikois*. It can be translated "to spiritual" or "with spiritual" or "by spiritual" or "in spiritual." So, Paul either intends to say that he is explaining spiritual things in, with, or by "spiritual *words*," or that he is explaining spiritual things to "spiritual *people*." He has already explained that the words he is sharing are taught by the Holy Spirit. However, he has begun to explain that these spiritual things are only respected by a certain group of people that he formerly called the "*teleiois*" or "the mature." The very next phrase after this problematic ending of verse 13 states that "the natural man does not receive the things of the Spirit of God" (1 Corinthians 2:14). He contrasts this natural man who does not respect divine revelation with "he that is spiritual" in 1 Corinthians 2:15. For these reasons, I believe the right contextual meaning of the last phrase in 1 Corinthians 2:13 is "explaining spiritual things to spiritual *people.*" The spiritual people he has in mind are mentioned again in 1 Corinthians 2:15 and 1 Corinthians 3:1. The spiritual people are those who accept divine wisdom over human wisdom. They are the spiritually mature people of 1 Corinthians 2:6.

First Corinthians 2:14–15

> But the natural man does not receive the
> things of the Spirit of God, for they are foolish-
> ness to him, and he cannot understand them,
> because they are spiritually discerned. But he
> that is spiritual discerns all things, and he is not
> understood by anyone.

The natural man stands in stark contrast to the spiritual man. It is the natural or carnal man (cf. 1 Corinthians 3:1) who does not welcome the things revealed by God to the apostles. He does not welcome them because he has too much regard for human reason and human intelligence. It is difficult for him to accept something that human beings have not been able to figure out and verify with their senses and experience. The "spiritual things" of verse 13 are "foolishness" to the natural man. These spiritual things include the message of the cross (1 Corinthians 1:18) and the whole message of the redemptive work of Christ (1 Corinthians 1:21, 23, 25). The natural man is the one who welcomes the wisdom of this age which is nullified by the wisdom of God (1 Corinthians 1:19, 27). The one who is spiritual is a stark contrast to the natural man. The spiritual person accepts and respects the things revealed by God. The spiritual person trusts in divine wisdom, knowing that the way of man is not in himself (Jeremiah 10:23). The spiritual person "discerns" or gains insight into all things, including spiritual things because he/she is open and thoughtful about such things. The spiritual person allows the revealed wisdom of God to "cast down arguments and every high thing that exalts itself against the knowledge of God" and to "bring every thought into captivity unto the obedience of Christ" (2 Corinthians 10:3–5). At the same time, others who have a natural or carnal outlook on the world cannot understand the spiritual person and his/her thinking.

First Corinthians 2:16

> For who has known the mind of the Lord
> and who has given him advice? But we have the
> mind of Christ!

These questions are rhetorical. As he explains in 1 Corinthians 2:9, no human being has ever known the mind of God. Nobody knows the things of God, except the Spirit of God (1 Corinthians 2:11). But Paul and the other apostles had received direct divine revelation (1 Corinthians 2:13; Galatians 1:12). They "received from the Lord" what they passed on to the Corinthians and others (1 Corinthians 11:23; 15:3). So they possessed the mind of Christ because Christ had revealed it to them supernaturally (John 14:26; 16:7–8, 13).

Reflections on Chapter 2

1. What was the primary emphasis of Paul's preaching in Corinth according to 1 Corinthians 2:1–3?
2. What was it that confirmed the conviction of the Corinthians that Paul's message was from God (1 Corinthians 2:4–5)?
3. What are the people called who seemed to accept Paul's message as divinely revealed wisdom? See 1 Corinthians 2:6, 15.
4. What does 1 Corinthians 2:9 say about the chances of human beings arriving at God's plan without divine revelation?
5. According to 1 Corinthians 2:13, Paul did not speak to the Corinthians in _____ taught by human wisdom but those taught by the _____.
6. The one who refuses to accept the revelations given to Paul and the apostles is called the _____ man (1 Corinthians 2:14).

3

First Corinthians 3:1

> And I, brothers, was not able to speak to
> you as to spiritual (people), but as to carnal
> (people), as to babes in Christ. I gave you milk
> to drink, not meat, because you were not yet
> able, and you are still not able! For you are still
> carnal! For whereas there is jealousy and strife
> among you, are you not still carnal and walking
> according to (the ways of) mankind?

Paul now plainly scolds the Corinthians because they are not yet mature (1 Corinthians 2:6) or spiritual (1 Corinthians 2:15), but are still natural (1 Corinthians 2:14) or carnal (1 Corinthians 3:1). The reason he could not speak to them as to spiritual people was because they still lacked the proper respect toward divine revelation and they were thinking and behaving like the rest of humanity who do not know God. He was giving them milk to drink, the very basic things of the gospel because they were not grounded enough to accept meat. Part of that grounding is accepting the fact that divine revelation as given to the apostles and prophets is the basis for our faith and practice. The jealousy and strife that was evident among them reflected the division reported by Chloe's household (1 Corinthians 1:10–11). This division existed because they did not have the same mindset or the same judgment. Those who

DAN R. OWEN

gave too much credence to worldly wisdom would always differ from those who only trusted in the wisdom of God revealed to Paul and the other apostles. Therefore, Paul was still trying to give them the gospel milk, trying again to lay the foundation of the redemptive work of Christ and the reign of Christ as Lord over all things. The jealousy and strife in Corinth did not reflect the "unity of the Spirit and bond of peace" created by God (Ephesians 2:14–18; 4:3). Christians can drift back into ways of thinking that subvert their faith (Colossians 2:8). This seems to have been the case with the Corinthians because they were "puffed up" or "arrogant" on behalf of one person and against another (1 Corinthians 4:6).

First Corinthians 3:4–5

> For whenever someone says, "I am of Paul," and another, "I am of Apollos," are you not human beings? What, then, is Apollos? And what is Paul? They are servants (ministers) through whom you believed, and to each as the Lord gave him *gifts*.

The word *anthropoi* does not mean males but people, human beings. The people were divided into factions (1 Corinthians 1:10–15). These factions were aligning themselves, not with Paul and Apollos specifically, but with local leaders claiming some superior viewpoint or insight. Paul explains that he was only using his own name and that of Apollos as examples to spare their feelings (1 Corinthians 4:6). Paul and Apollos were only *diakonoi*, servants or ministers. God grants various people different spiritual gifts to use in their ministries (Ephesians 4:11–12). The word *gifts* is supplied in the translation above because it seems to fit the context of what different ministers have (1 Corinthians 1:5–8). Different ministers have different gifts, but only whatever God has given them (Ephesians 4:11). Still, it is God who works through each one in his/her unique way. God is the one whose power works in redemption and whose power is unleashed in ministry of various kinds (Acts 14:26–27; Philippians 2:13).

First Corinthians 3:6–8

> I planted. Apollos watered. But God made it grow! So then, neither is the one who plants anything, nor the one who waters, but God who makes it grow! He who plants and he who waters are the same. Each one shall receive his own reward according to his own labor.

Some ministers are good planters. They can go in and lay a foundation. Some ministers water the seed, encouraging and facilitating its growth. But the seed is the word of God (Luke 8:11). The rule of God in the lives of human beings has always started and grown through the word of God. Jesus's stories of the soils, the wheat and the tares, and the mustard seed all illustrate this principle in one way or another (Matthew 13). The story of the growing seed in Mark 4:27–28 illustrates that the seed works independently of the sower. It works, *automate*, "all by itself." It is through this divine seed that a new being is conceived and made to develop (1 Peter 1:23; 1 John 3:9). The transformation continues as the word of God works with the indwelling Spirit to produce more and more fruits of sanctification (Galatians 5:22–23). Through every stage of growth God is doing the work. The human beings are just facilitators.

First Corinthians 3:9–11

> For we are God's fellow workers. You are God's field, God's building. According to the

grace of God which was given to me as a wise architect, I laid a foundation, and another builds on it. Let each one be careful how he builds on it. For no other foundation can be laid than that which was laid, which is Jesus Christ.

This passage is interesting because Paul makes a distinction between those who are evangelizing and teaching and those who are recipients of that teaching. "We" is contrasted with "you." The teachers and evangelists are God's fellow workers, cooperating with God in getting the kingdom seed into the minds of human beings and creating an optimal environment for growth. The people receiving the seed are God's field, God's building. The concept of being the field in which the divine seed is planted and cultivated is developed in 1 Corinthians 3:6–8. The concept of the church as God's building is developed in 1 Corinthians 3:10ff. In 1 Corinthians 3:10, Paul uses this phrase "the grace of God which was given to me" referring to a divine gift given by God (see Romans 12:3, 6; 1 Corinthians 3:10; 2 Corinthians 8:1, 6–7; Galatians 2:9; Ephesians 3:2,7,8; 4:7). As a select person given the gift of apostleship, Paul was made an architect or master builder, *architekton*, of God's temple, the church. God gave Paul and the other apostles the plans for his spiritual temple. These plans called for a particular foundation, Jesus Christ. Paul based this on Isaiah 28:16 where the ancient prophet talked about a particular foundation stone chosen by God, a stone in which one could place one's trust and never be disappointed. God himself has laid the stone around which the entire building is built. It is a stone which the "builders," the religious leaders of Jesus's day, rejected, but God chose that stone as the foundation of his building (Psalm 118:22; Matthew 16:18; 21:42ff; Acts 4:11; 1 Peter 2:4–9).

Paul began to build the Corinthian church on the preaching of Christ and his redemptive work (1 Corinthians 1:18–25; 2:1–

5). That core preaching should be the foundation of the church today! With reference to others who might come along and teach in Corinth after him, Paul says they should be very careful how they build on the foundation he had already laid. In other words, they should be careful not to build anything that is not squarely founded upon Jesus Christ, his redemptive work, and his Lordship (2 Corinthians 11:1–5).

First Corinthians 3:12

> If anyone builds on that foundation gold, silver, precious stones, wood, grass, and straw, then the work of each one shall become evident, for the Day shall show it (clearly) because it will be revealed by fire. And the same fire will test the work of each one.

Now the work of sharing the gospel and growing the church is compared to the building of a building. "Each one" is each teacher/preacher who shares the gospel and brings people into God's church. "The Day" or "the day of the Lord" is an expression used throughout Scripture to describe a time of great trial or judgment when great suffering occurs. It can refer to the final judgment but often refers to great events of temporal suffering as well. In this passage, various converts will bear up under the fires of suffering with greater or lesser endurance. Wood, grass, and straw are easily and quickly consumed in the fire, while it is much more difficult to burn up gold, silver, and precious stones. Some Christians will remain faithful through the fiery trials (1 Peter 1:5–7). Others will be destroyed by them. The "work" of each preacher/teacher will be tested over the lifetime of each convert. Ultimately, we who evangelize are only facilitating the work of God. "We are his workmanship" (Ephesians 2:10). The trials of life will test the souls of all Christians to see if they will continue to trust him and his word or fall into unfaithfulness. Paul spoke in terms of fire burning against God's spiritual building. Jesus spoke in terms of rain, wind, and floods assaulting the house built on the Rock or the sand (Matthew 7:24–28).

First Corinthians 3:14–15

> If anyone's work remains which he built upon it, he will receive a reward. If anyone's work shall be burned up, he will suffer loss, but he himself will be saved, in the same manner as through fire.

Each preacher/teacher is building living souls onto the foundation of Christ. We are helping to found the lives of people on Jesus, his teaching, and his redemptive work. If our converts' faith is destroyed by the fires of life's trials and temptations, we will suffer loss because we will be filled with sadness and regret (2 Corinthians 11:28–29). We who teach and preach are fellow workers or fellow builders, but we are also souls built on to the foundation just like all others who come to Christ. If our converts falter, we will feel their loss, but we can still be saved if we can survive the fires of trial ourselves. So just as weather and pests and many other factors make it challenging for planted seeds to grow to maturity in God's field, so the fires of this world's trials make it difficult for the materials in God's spiritual building to endure. Perhaps Paul wanted to make it clear that these "fires" of trial brought on by Satan and human lusts, were burning against the Corinthian church in an attempt to destroy what Paul had tried to build.

First Corinthians 3:16

> Do you not know that you are a temple of
> God and the Spirit of God lives in you? If any-
> one destroys the temple of God, God destroys
> this person because God's temple is holy and
> that is what you are.

Elsewhere, Paul tells the Asian Christians that they are "built together for a dwelling place of God in the Spirit" (Ephesians 2:22). It was by his death and resurrection that Jesus destroyed the Old Testament temple and built a spiritual house of living stones (John 2:18–22; 1 Peter 2:4–9). The Holy Spirit lives in the bodies of all who are baptized into Christ (1 Corinthians 6:18–19; 12:13). Collectively, he dwells in a group of redeemed people. The personal pronoun *you* in this passage is plural. All of the Christians collectively make up the temple or dwelling place of God. Because some people were selfish and factious in Corinth, he warns them severely about God's wrath to be poured out on anyone who would destroy God's temple, his church. Through Christ's redemptive work, God created "the unity of the Spirit in the bond of peace" (Ephesians 2:14–18; 4:3). God wants that unity maintained, not destroyed (1 Corinthians 1:10). When Paul says the temple of God is "holy," he is saying that it has been designated and set apart by God himself. It is the "church of God" (1 Corinthians 1:2). Because it is distinct and divinely designated, set apart from all other groups, it deserves the respect and consideration that God expects for all things holy.

First Corinthians 3:18

> Let no one deceive himself! If anyone
> thinks he is wise in this age, let him become

a fool, so that he might become wise. For the wisdom of this world is foolishness with God. For it is written, "He catches the wise in their craftiness," and again, "The Lord knows the arguments of the wise, that they are useless."

The two quotes are from Job 5:13 and Psalm 94:11 respectively. Job 5:13 is part of the speech of Eliphaz the Temanite. He is replying to Job's speech about how God is mistreating him. Eliphaz is trying to communicate that no human being can know more than God or be justified in his reasoning against God. The Psalmist in Psalm 94:11 is talking about the arrogant words of the wicked. He calls them fools who need to become wise by listening to God and insists that their arrogant thoughts and words are futile or useless. Paul seems to be blaming those in Corinth who boast about human wisdom for the division and destruction in the church (1 Corinthians 1:26–30).

First Corinthians 3:21

So, then, let no one boast in men. For all things are yours, whether Paul, or Apollos, or Cephas, or the world, or life, or death, or things present, or things to come, all things are yours, and you are Christ's and Christ is God's.

In 1 Corinthians 3:5, Paul says that the ministers or servants of God are just God's facilitators who have received all that they have from God. They have received the message of reconciliation and the gifts necessary for sharing it. For this reason, there is no room for anyone to boast about personal wisdom or erudition (1 Corinthians 1:30–31; 3:21; 2 Corinthians 10:17–18). Every spiritual resource is ours for the asking, because it all belongs to our God, the gracious Giver!

Reflections on Chapter 3

1. Why exactly does Paul say the Corinthians are not spiritual people but carnal (1 Corinthians 3:1–2)?

2. What were the roles of people like Paul and Apollos in God's field? And what is the role of God (1 Corinthians 3:5–8)?

3. The teachers and preachers of God's word are God's _____ according to 1 Corinthians 3:9, and the rest are called God's _____ and God's _____.

4. What role did Paul claim for himself in the construction of God's spiritual building (1 Corinthians 3:10)?

5. What is the foundation of God's building (1 Corinthians 3:11)?

6. List the different kinds of material (people) that are added to God's building, and explain what is different about them (1 Corinthians 3:12–15)?

7. What warning is given to those who would destroy God's church by causing division and disunity (1 Corinthians 3:17)?

8. How does the warning of 1 Corinthians 3:21 figure into the problem of division in the church?

4

First Corinthians 4:1–2

> So, let a person think of us as Christ's helpers, and administrators of God's mysteries. Moreover, in the end, it is required of administrators that a person is found trustworthy.

The word *uperetas* means a helper, an assistant. It is one that carries out the directions of another. The steward or administrator or dispenser, *oikonomos*, is the one who distributes or administers that which belongs to another (Ephesians 3:2, 7, 8). The gospel is a treasure belonging to God (2 Corinthians 4:7). This treasure is administered by human beings to other human beings. Because of divine revelation, the apostles and prophets were entrusted with this message (1 Corinthians 2:6–13; Ephesians 3:3–5). Evangelists like Timothy were entrusted with the message passed along to them by the apostles. As we who teach today hold to the apostolic revelations, sharing just what we received from them, we become faithful administrators of the gospel. Like Paul, who taught only what he had received by revelation, we are faithful stewards if we share only what the apostles have left us in the New Testament. Another important point in this passage is that an administrator cannot keep to himself the possessions with which he has been entrusted. He must administer those possessions to the people who need them. The gospel must be shared with the lost if we are to be faithful stewards.

First Corinthians 4:3

> To me it is a matter of small import that
> I should be judged by you, or by any human
> day (in court). I do not even pass judgment on
> myself. I am not conscious of anything against
> myself, but I am not justified by this. The Lord
> is the one who judges me!

The word *hemera*, "day," cannot stand alone and convey Paul's meaning. He seems to mean a day of adjudication or judgment of some kind, like a court date. The word *anakrino* means to examine for judgment, to call one into account, to determine guilt or innocence through careful examination. Christ is the one who has that role. The implication here is that some in Corinth were trying to criticize or judge Paul, perhaps with the assertion that they possessed greater worldly wisdom which qualified them to judge. This is much more clearly seen in 2 Corinthians where there is clearly some comparing going on between a group of Judaizers and Paul (2 Corinthians 3:1–2; 10:12). Perhaps something similar was going on with the leaders of the various factions in Corinth at the time of 1 Corinthians. God is the Judge, and God's revealed wisdom is the standard of that judgment. Paul was much more concerned about God's assessment of him than he was about the assessment of people who operated under worldly standards.

First Corinthians 4:5

> So then, do not judge anything before (it
> is) time, when the Lord shall come and shed
> light on the secret things of darkness, and make
> clear the counsels of the hearts. And then, each
> one shall have his praise from God!

One gets the feeling from reading this that some were praising themselves or boasting in their own qualifications, accomplishments, and wisdom. Paul insists that God's approval is the approval we should seek (2 Corinthians 10:17–18). The only one who knows the thoughts and intentions of all human beings is God. God knows every hidden thought and every hidden act of every human being (Psalm 139). It seems clear that various would-be leaders of the Corinthian factions were competing with one another and probably with Paul as well. This would have been their motivation for their criticisms or judgments against Paul. As 1 Corinthians 4:6 clearly states, they were "puffed up" or arrogant on behalf of one person and against another. This was a certain recipe for division.

First Corinthians 4:6

> And these things, brothers, I have portrayed using myself and Apollos for your sakes, so that in us (as illustrations) you might learn not to go beyond what is written, so that none of you should be puffed up on behalf of one person and against another.

Paul uses the word *metaskematizo* here and also in 2 Corinthians 11:13–15. There, he uses the word three times to refer to someone who is masquerading as someone else, or trying to portray themselves as someone else. In this passage, he seems to use the word in a more figurative sense. In this letter, he is speaking as if the factions in Corinth were divided because some were following Paul, others were following Apollos, etc. In reality, it was not Paul or Apollos they were following, but other individuals in the Corinthian church. Paul was not using the names of the leaders of the various factions because he wanted to spare their feelings and to be more diplomatic in his approach. Still, he has been making his point about people who are truly servants and helpers, trusting completely in Christ, versus those who are boastful and proud, trusting in their own abilities and their own wisdom. Servants of Christ only trust the divine wisdom that has been written in holy Scripture, the things transmitted by God's apostles and prophets. To go beyond this revelation into the realm of human philosophy and opinion pits people against one another and causes division. The word *phusiao* is used several times in the Corinthian epistles to describe people that are arrogant and self-important in their attitudes (1 Corinthians 4:18–19; 5:2, etc.). Most trouble in the church today comes down to people pitted against other people, often over things that have little to do with biblical teaching.

First Corinthians 4:7–8

> Who makes distinctions (between you)? And what do you have that you did not receive? And if you received it, why do you boast as if you did not receive it? You are already filled! You have already become rich! You have already come to reign without us! And Oh, that you did reign, so that we might reign together with you!

Paul already explained to them that preachers and teachers are only helpers, assistants, and servants given whatever gifts God decides to give them (1 Corinthians 3:5; 4:1). It is God who causes the growth of the kingdom seed and does the redemptive work in the lives of people. The Corinthians were emphasizing differences in qualifications and worldly wisdom, and by doing this, they were making the divisions worse in Corinth. The word *kauchaomai* or "boast" is used along with the verb *phusiao*, "be arrogant," to describe the self-promoting attitudes and actions of the leaders of the various factions in Corinth (1 Corinthians 1:30–31; 4:18–19; 5:2). Some of the Corinthians seemed to feel that they had everything they needed without the apostles, their divine revelation, and their Spirit power. Paul wants them to see the fallacy of this kind of thinking. God sent Christ to redeem the world, and Christ sent the apostles to proclaim God's plan of salvation and sanctification!

First Corinthians 4:9

> For I think God put us apostles on display last of all, as those condemned to death, so that we might become a spectacle to the world, to angels, and to men. We are fools for Christ's sake, but you are wise in Christ! We are weak, but you are strong! You are glorious and we are dishonored! From the beginning unto this very hour we hunger and thirst and are naked and beaten and homeless.

Verse 9 is very important in the flow of this book because it identifies the apostles as the group Paul is talking about when he says "We" or "Us." Earlier he said, "We preach Christ crucified" (1 Corinthians 1:22–23); and "We speak wisdom among those who are mature" (1 Corinthians 2:6); and "which things we speak, not in words which man's wisdom teaches, but which the Spirit teaches" (1 Corinthians 2:13); and "We have the mind of Christ" (1 Corinthians 2:16). It is to Paul and the other apostles of Christ that divine revelation was given. These possessed the mind of Christ, the wisdom that comes from above (John 14:26; 16:13). Their teaching alone formed the basis of faith and unity in the ancient church. They bound on earth what had been bound in heaven (Matthew 16:19; 18:18). Until people recognized the authority of these ambassadors from Christ, there could be no unity.

Yet Paul often felt that he and the other apostles were "on display" as a "spectacle" for others who despised them and their mission. The apostles of Christ were persecuted for their dogged determination to evangelize the world. In this letter and his second letter, Paul talks about his great tribulation in Asia when he was sentenced to death and fought with the wild beasts at Ephesus (1 Corinthians 15:32; 2 Corinthians 1:7–9). Heaven and earth watched the drama as the gospel was preached and God's ambassadors were persecuted. They were often despised by the very people they sought to save. Paul sarcastically refers to the puffed-up Corinthians as wise, strong, and glorious while the apostles were considered foolish, weak, and dishonored. He acknowledges their frequent hunger, thirst, nakedness, and homelessness as they sought to share the saving message with ungrateful people (2 Corinthians 6:3ff; 11:22–29).

First Corinthians 4:12

> And we labor, working with our own hands. When we are reviled, we bless. When we are persecuted, we forbear. When we are defamed, we encourage. We have become like the dirt scrubbed from the world, the off-scouring of all things even until now.

Paul later speaks in some detail about his decision to work with the Corinthians without any monetary support (1 Corinthians 9:1–16). He demonstrated his pure motives by continuing to support himself while working hard to share the gospel (2 Corinthians 7:2; 11:7–11). His sincerity and dedication could not be questioned. Still, people often spoke against him and denigrated him for one reason or another. He prayed for such people. People defamed his character unjustly, but he encouraged in return. He was often treated like the dirt washed from people's pots and pans, though he was a chosen apostle of Jesus Christ. The people he loved and sought to save often hurt him in return, but still, Paul persisted as a father persists in loving his children.

First Corinthians 4:14–16

> It is not for shaming you that I write these things, but to instruct you as my beloved children. For even if you have ten thousand mentors in Christ, still, you do not have many fathers, for in Christ Jesus I fathered you through the gospel! Therefore, I beg you, be imitators of me!

The apostle has spoken sarcastically in 1 Corinthians 4:7–13 about the self-sufficiency, arrogance, and pride of some of the Corinthians who thought they did not need the direction of God's apostles. They seem to have believed they possessed sufficient wisdom without Paul's divinely revealed teaching. Much of Paul's argument in the first four chapters is to turn them away from this notion. Divine wisdom is revealed by God to the apostles. Christian unity is found only in following the teaching of the apostles (Matthew 16:19; 18:18; John 13:20; 17:20; Acts 2:42; 1 Corinthians 14:37; Ephesians 2:20; 3:3–5; 2 Thessalonians 2:15). There may be others who water the seed or build on the foundation Paul laid, but they must respect the divine revelation given to the apostles (1 Corinthians 3:5–17). Paul begat or fathered the Corinthians by sharing the gospel revealed to him by the risen Christ and the Holy Spirit (1 Corinthians 2:6–13; Galatians 1:10–12). Paul planted the divine seed of the word in the hearts of the Corinthians. He uses the formal petition word *parakalo*, "I beseech you," three times in this letter (1 Corinthians 1:10; 4:16; 16:15). These three formal petitions are very much related. The first is that there be no divisions, and they all speak the same things (1 Corinthians 1:10). The second is that they be imitators of Paul, following his teaching and his example (1 Corinthians 4:16). The third is that they follow local leaders who are doing as Paul has taught them to do (1 Corinthians 16:15). All three petitions form Paul's path to unity.

First Corinthians 4:17

> For this reason, I have sent Timothy to you, who is my beloved and faithful child in the Lord, who will remind you of my ways in Christ Jesus, just as I always teach in every church!

Paul told Timothy to pass on to others what Timothy had learned from Paul (2 Timothy 2:2). The divine revelation given to the apostles was the standard of thought and behavior for all Christians and all congregations. As a faithful evangelist, Timothy would convey these things to the Corinthians, helping them to see what Christ's ambassador wanted them to do (2 Corinthians 5:20). This passage shows that there was a consistent body of teaching delivered in every church. Galatians 2:1–10 shows that the Jerusalem apostles and Paul were preaching the same gospel in various locations.

First Corinthians 4:18

> Some are arrogant as though I were not coming to you. But I will come to you quickly if the Lord wills, and I will know not the word,

but the power of those who are arrogant. For the rule of God is not just in word but in power. What do you wish? Shall I come to you with a stick, or with a spirit of love and gentleness?

The word *phusiao*, meaning "to be arrogant" or "to be puffed up," is used periodically in this letter along with *kaukaomai*, "boast," to reflect the attitude of those who trusted in their own wisdom and sought the approval and accolades of other people. These words describe the self-exalting attitudes of some who were leading various factions in Corinth, causing division and preventing unity. Paul meant to come and confront these people personally, but ended up being diverted to another mission (2 Corinthians 2:12). He also later decided not to come because he didn't want to cause the Corinthians more sorrow as he had done by writing the first epistle (2 Corinthians 2:1). Some in Corinth eventually accused Paul of not keeping his word because of this. By the time he wrote the second letter, a group of factious teachers were entrenched in the Corinthian church. At the writing of this first letter, it seems likely that the church was plagued by the bad leadership of some who questioned the apostolic authority of Paul and respected worldly wisdom over divine revelation. Paul did not want to be harsh with the Corinthians, but he assured them he would not shrink from it if it became necessary. At this point in the Corinthian letter, the foundation has been laid for all the rest. It is only through divine wisdom revealed by God to his apostles and prophets that the church of Christ can find unity. They can all speak the same things only if they are committed to the same divine revelation which is spoken and written down by the chosen apostles of Christ.

Reflections on Chapter Four

1. How does Paul want the church at Corinth to view him according to 1 Corinthians 4:1?

2. Discuss the word translated "steward" or "administrator" and how that helps us think of the role of teachers and preachers.

3. What does 1 Corinthians 4:6 tell us about the identity of the actual leaders of the factions in Corinth?

4. What does the last part of 1 Corinthians 4:6 tell us about the dynamics of the division in Corinth? How does the warning in 1 Corinthians 3:21 help us see the problem?

5. What are some things mentioned in 1 Corinthians 4:9–13 that should have given great credibility to the apostles in the eyes of the Corinthians?

6. How did Paul contrast himself with other would-be teachers in the eyes of the Corinthians (1 Corinthians 3:15–16)?

7. Look through chapters 1–4 and find passages where Paul talks about people being arrogant or puffed up or boastful and talk about how this informs us about the divisions in Corinth.

5

Divine Wisdom Regarding Fornication

First Corinthians 5:1–2

> It is actually being reported that there is
> fornication among you, and such fornication as
> is not even among the Gentiles, that a man has
> his father's wife. And you are arrogant, and did
> not rather mourn, that the one who has done
> this deed might be taken out of your midst.

Fornication, *porneia*, is sexual intercourse with someone other than one's divinely recognized husband or wife (Leviticus 18; Hebrews 13:4). Fornication includes all kinds of premarital heterosexual relations as well as homosexual relations. It also includes sexual congress between married people with others to whom they are not married. Adultery and homosexual relations are subcategories of fornication. Paul is rebuking the Corinthians for permitting those in the church to commit fornication without censure. According to Paul, even the pagans in Corinth would not condone a son taking his father's wife. It was not only obvious to the Jewish Christians that this was wrong, but the conscience of the Greeks would not even permit it (Leviticus 18:7–8). Somehow, the arrogance of those involved in the various factions in Corinth was preventing the church coming together to discipline this blatant fornicator. Perhaps the pride and arrogance of family leaders would not permit them to admit that their son was guilty of sin and needed to be put out of the church. The phrase "taken out of your midst" is actually an allusion to the phrase quoted at the close of the chapter, "put away the evil that is among you" (1 Corinthians 5:13; Deuteronomy 17:7; 19:19; 22:21, 24; 24:7). In Deuteronomy, this phrase is Moses's repeated warning for the Israelites not to permit idolatry and lawlessness to exist among them unchecked, lest it lead the rest of God's people away into sin.

First Corinthians 5:3–5

> For I, though absent in body, yet present in spirit, have already passed judgment as though present on the one who has committed this deed. In the name of our Lord Jesus, when you are gathered together, along with my spirit and the power of the Lord Jesus, deliver such a person to Satan for the destruction of the flesh, so that the spirit might be saved in the day of the Lord.

This passage shows that what is sinful is always sinful. Paul did not need to know all the circumstances and struggles of the fornicator's life to know that this conduct is against the will of God. He was simply judging the actions of this person as against the written revelation of God and against the sayings of Jesus. Fornication is always wrong. As an ambassador of Christ, Paul spoke "in the name of our Lord Jesus" (1 Corinthians 1:10; 5:4). He was conveying the will of Jesus. The excommunication of this impenitent person was to be done during the assembly of the

Christians. Paul would be present with them in spirit when they did as Christ commanded. They would do this thing with the authority and power of Christ behind them. The offender would be put out of the church so that he would see the error of his ways and repent. The object of the discipline, at least in part, was the repentance and ultimate salvation of the offender. The phrase "deliver unto Satan" is also used by Paul to describe his discipline of false teachers who would not turn from their error (1 Timothy 1:20).

When we are called by the gospel into the fellowship of Christ and other Christians, we are "delivered out of the power of darkness" (1 Corinthians 1:9; Colossians 1:13; 2 Thessalonians 2:14). When the church recognizes the rebellion of an unrepentant sinner who is sinning a sin that leads to death, the church recognizes that this person has chosen to go back under the rule of Satan and has separated himself/herself from God (1 John 5:16). Such a person is in a lost state where the only thing that remains for them is "a certain, fearful expectation of judgment and the fierceness of fire which shall devour the adversary" (Hebrews 10:26–27).

First Corinthians 5:6–7

> Your boasting is not good! Don't you know that a little yeast leavens the whole lump of dough? Clean out the old leaven, so that you may be a new lump, just as you are unleavened. For Christ, our Passover, has been sacrificed.

The boasting here is the same as the arrogance of 1 Corinthians 5:2. In some way, the arrogance and self-promotion of these who were trying to be leaders was causing them to allow this fornication to continue. A little yeast will permeate the whole lump of dough. One bad apple or one rotten potato will spoil all the rest.

Besides the separation of the offender from God, continued sin in the church can spoil the attitudes of the others toward sin and can even lead others into sin. Just as the Jews were commanded to rid their homes of all leaven before the feast of the Passover, so Christians are supposed to turn away from sin in order to serve Christ. Paul sees Christ as the Lamb of God (John 1:29, 35; 19:36; 1 Peter 1:18). Since he has been sacrificed, it is time for us to turn away from sin, not embrace it and cause the destruction of the church. Israel and Judah allowed the leaven of sin to corrupt their entire nation. As a result, God cast them out of his presence (2 Kings 17:18; 23:27; 24:3).

First Corinthians 5:8

> Let us observe the feast, not with the old leaven, nor with the leaven of wickedness and evil, but with the unleavened bread of sincerity and truth.

We must eat the feast according to God's mandates. The Feast of Unleavened Bread required the removal of all leaven. To eat the spiritual Passover, in Paul's illustration, is to live for Christ, our paschal lamb. If we live sincerely for Christ, we will not deny the teaching of Christ and his apostolic ambassadors by embracing what Christ taught us to shun. We cannot sincerely follow Christ if we do not try to walk in his teachings. There must be genuine repentance (Romans 6:1–2, 11; 12:1–2; Ephesians 4:22–24). Only some paganized pretense for Christianity would allow fornication, not to mention incest, as an accepted practice (see 1 Corinthians 6:9–11, 18). Yet, today, the church is plagued with fornication from all sides with the unmarried, the homosexuals, the adulterers, and even those who are involved in incest. The culture around us is reluctant to call such things sinful and to help people turn away from those sins. Faithful preachers and teachers will continue to teach the truth on this and other matters and call for conformity to apostolic teaching.

First Corinthians 5:9

> I wrote to you in the epistle not to min-
> gle with fornicators, not at all meaning with
> the fornicators of the world, or with the greedy,
> or with thieves or with idolaters, for then you
> would be obligated to go out of the world.

Some have concluded from this passage that Paul had written an earlier letter to the Corinthians, which is no longer extant. This is possible, but he may also be referring to what he already wrote a few verses earlier. The word *sunanamignumi* means to mix together, to mingle, to associate. Marriage is God's ordained plan for sexuality (Genesis 2:24; Matthew 19:3–6; Hebrews 13:4). We can, like Jesus, eat with tax collectors and sinners in order to influence them for good, but we cannot be "yoked together" with unbelievers in relationships that weaken us (2 Corinthians 6:14). Close association with fornicators who call themselves Christians does not match the expectation of Christ for his people. Paul's instructions in this chapter have nothing to do with people outside of the church (1 Corinthians 5:12). Paul's instructions have to do with God's church teaching the conduct expected of Christians. His instructions are not just for Christian fornicators but all Christians who live willfully in sinful behavior.

First Corinthians 5:11

> Now I wrote to you not to associate if any-
> one who is named a brother is a fornicator, or

greedy, or an idolater, or a reviler, or a drunk-
ard, or a thief. With such a person you should
not even eat!

The same letter in view in 1 Corinthians 5:9 is also in view
here. For our purposes, it is the instruction given in 1 Corinthians
5:3–4 because we are unaware of any other letter written by Paul.
Even if there was another letter, this letter gives the same instruction. The word *adelphos*, or "brother," is used in the sense of a
fellow member of the church. Christ is the firstborn among many
brothers (Romans 8:29). Christ is not ashamed to call us "brothers" (Hebrews 2:11). We are "holy brothers, partakers of a heavenly calling" (Hebrews 3:1). Onesimus the slave is now a beloved
brother in Christ (Colossians 4:9; Philemon 16). Christian slaves
should not despise their masters, even if their master is a brother
(1 Timothy 6:2). Paul uses the term in this passage the same way,
clearly indicating a fellow Christian, a member of the church of
Christ. Paul's mandate is that the church must not continue normal fellowship with fellow members of the body who are willfully
continuing in sin. This applies to all fornicators. This also applies
to those who live in selfish greed instead of using their wealth to do
God's will (Matthew 25:14ff; Luke 12, 16; 1 Timothy 6:10–18).
We are not to continue in fellowship with those who insist on participating in paganism of any kind (Exodus 20:1–4; 1 Corinthians
10:14). A reviler who continues to hatefully destroy others by
his/her words must not be tolerated in the church (Ephesians
4:29–31). Those who persist in drunkenness must not be allowed
to continue in the church (Galatians 5:19–21). God condemns
thieves but commands everyone to work at something honorable
and support themselves (Ephesians 4:28; 2 Thessalonians 3:10).
Paul says that when one is "delivered unto Satan," we should not
even eat with such a person. What does he mean by this?

In another place, he says, "Treat him not as an enemy, but admonish him as a brother" (2 Thessalonians 3:14f). So does Paul mean that we should not under any circumstances share a meal with one who is excommunicated? Would this teaching include husbands eating with wives or parents eating with children? Perhaps, but there may be another way to understand this given what is discussed in Corinthians. Does he mean, alternatively, that we should not eat the Lord's Supper with such a one? Certainly, the Lord's Supper is a demonstration of fellowship (1 Corinthians 10:16–17). It is designed for those who have been baptized into the body of Christ and share in its blessings (1 Corinthians 12:13). So when the church puts one out of fellowship, it stands to reason that the one excommunicated should not be accepted as part of the meal which demonstrates fellowship. In chapter 11, Paul argues for complete inclusion of every member of the body in the Lord's Supper. Surely, delivering one unto Satan would demand exclusion from the same.

First Corinthians 5:12

> What (concern) is it for me to judge those
> on the outside? Do you not judge those on the
> inside? God judges those on the outside! Cast
> out the evil from among yourselves!

The law of Christ is not understood by those "on the outside." Those on the outside are those in the realm of Satan, those who are not in the body of Christ. In daily commerce, work, and education, we deal with those on the outside who are ignorant of the ways of Christ. They are all condemned without Jesus, but we want to show them kindness and lead them toward Christ (Romans 2:12–16; 3:20–23). Christians have a spiritual responsibility to other Christians. We are accountable to God and to one another in the body of Christ. It is our task to restore brothers and sisters who stray (Galatians 6:1–2; Matthew 18:15–18; 1 Timothy 5:18–20). The final admonition is a recurring quote from Deuteronomy, reminding the new generation of Israelites not to tolerate idolaters, false prophets, and other transgressions which would corrupt them and deter their obedience to God's laws. This is a constant theme in the Hebrew Bible. Allowing sin to remain unchallenged in the church would be like the corrupt kings of Israel and Judah refusing to destroy the idolatrous high places in their territory, thereby allowing the infection of paganism to persist among the people (1 Kings 13:32; 2 Kings 12:3; 14:4; 15:4, 35; 17:10). Both Hezekiah and Josiah tried to remove the high places and cut out the cancer from Judah, but other rulers turned a blind eye and corrupted the people, bringing them to destruction (2 Kings 17:18; 23:3). Are we holding Christians accountable in today's church?

Reflections on Chapter Five

1. What kind of fornication was being tolerated in the Corinthian church?

2. The arrogance and boasting mentioned in 1 Corinthians 5:2, 6 seems to connect with earlier mentions of boasting or being "puffed up." Find verses where these things are mentioned earlier and list them.

3. Under what circumstances did Paul instruct the congregation to publicly deliver the man to Satan?

4. Paul compared putting the sinful man out of the church to putting away the _____ during the feast of the _____.

5. What are two specific reasons given by Paul for putting the fornicator out of the fellowship of the church?

6. Paul makes it clear that his instructions apply to those _____ the church and not to those _____ the church.

7. See if you can locate some of the places in Deuteronomy where Moses commands the Israelites to "put away the evil from among you!"

6

First Corinthians 6:1

> Dare any of you, having a matter (of dispute) against another, go to judgment before the unrighteous, and not before the saints?

The word *krino*, to judge or decide or adjudicate, is used three times in 1 Corinthians 5:12–13 and is immediately used again in 1 Corinthians 6:1–4, 6. Paul has instructed the church to "judge" those on the inside of the church. Matters involving the moral and spiritual conduct of church members should be decided by those who know the mandates of God regarding the conduct of God's people. The flow of thought suggests that perhaps this case of the man living with his father's wife was being taken outside the church to worldly judges to decide the matters involved. Paul sees this as a shame for many different reasons (1 Corinthians 6:5). This is another indication that some respected the opinions and judgments of respected Greeks more than the mandates of God's apostles. The word translated "dare" in the first verse suggests a degree of audacity and goes well with the behavior described as arrogance and boasting among the various leaders of the factions in Corinth (1 Corinthians 3:21; 4:18, 19; 5:2, 6).

First Corinthians 6:2

> Or do you not know that the saints shall
> judge the world? And if the world will be
> judged by you, are you unworthy for judging
> the smallest matters?

It is unclear exactly how the saints shall judge the world.
The apostles were told that in "the regeneration," they would sit
on twelve thrones judging the twelve tribes of Israel (Matthew
19:28). This passage seems to refer to what will happen when
Christ returns. Compare "when the Son of Man sits on his glorious throne" in Matthew 19:28 to the same phrase in Matthew
25:31. So in some way, the apostles are going to "judge" the people
of God. We know from Paul that everyone will appear before the
tribunal of Christ (Romans 2:16; 2 Corinthians 5:10; 2 Timothy
4:1). Does this mean that we will somehow participate in the reign
of Christ and in his judgment (Revelation 3:21)? Scripture does
not fully explain these matters but leaves us wondering. At any
rate, it is clear that God expects his people, informed by his word,
to be able to decide the right and wrong of human conduct. But
to decide requires taking a stand, and that requires accepting the
consequences of that stand. Some people will likely not be happy
with the decisions made based on Christ's teaching.

First Corinthians 6:3

> Don't you know that we shall judge
> angels, not to mention mundane matters? But
> if you have lawsuits over mundane matters,
> why do you seat (as judges) those despised by
> the church? I say this to you for shame! Is there
> not one wise person among you who is able

to render a decision between his brother (and others)?

If it is unclear how we shall judge the world, it is certainly unclear how we shall participate in the judgment of angels. Perhaps Paul is referring to those angels that sinned (2 Peter 2:4; Jude 6–7). Perhaps he is speaking of those who fought against Michael and his angels after the death and resurrection of Jesus and were cast out of heaven to the earth (Revelation 12:7–10). What is clear is that Paul is ashamed and horrified that Christians are having public lawsuits with one another and asking the spiritually uninformed to be the judges between them. It may have been, if we read between the lines, that the one who was living with his father's wife was at the root of these disputes and that he and those who defended him were seeking decisions from worldly people, those who are despised by the church. Verse 1 seems to indicate that the ones chosen as judges in these disputes were not among the saints at all, but among the lost pagans of the city, perhaps pagans respected by those who revered worldly wisdom. This is confirmed in 1 Corinthians 6:6. When Paul asks whether they can find one wise person, he surely means one who is versed in the divinely revealed wisdom of God, that which came by direct revelation to God's apostles (1 Corinthians 2:6–15). The wise person of 1 Corinthians 6:5 is the same as the "mature" person of 1 Corinthians 2:6 and the "spiritual" person of 1 Corinthians 2:15.

First Corinthians 6:6

But, brother goes to judgment with brother, and this before unbelievers! It is already a defeat for you that you have lawsuits with one another! Why not rather be treated unjustly? Why not rather be defrauded? But

> you do injustice and you defraud and this to
> your own brothers!

To turn to unbelievers for spiritual judgment is a total defeat for God's people. It destroys the fundamental allegiance we are supposed to have to the revealed word of God! God's word must be the basis for our decisions in the church! It would be better for a Christian to suffer the wrong done to him/her by another Christian than to parade those things before the world and defame the church in the process. Paul told Timothy that the conduct of church members and especially church leaders is "the pillar and ground of the truth" (1 Timothy 3:15). Our conduct must support the divine truth that we teach. In the case of the Corinthians involved in these court cases, they were wronging and defrauding others in direct violation of God's law, and were despising the authority of God's law by seeking judgments based on worldly, ungodly law. Many in the church today are more influenced by what is currently legal and acceptable in the world than they are by the revealed will of God in the New Testament. What is legal in the eyes of men is often clearly immoral in the eyes of God.

First Corinthians 6:9

> Or do you not know that the unrighteous
> will not inherit the kingdom of God?

The unrighteous here are the very ones the Corinthians were choosing to judge between brothers in Christ (1 Corinthians 6:1, 6). It makes no sense to have the lost, who have no relationship with God, making decisions about things involving the people of God and the word of God.

First Corinthians 6:9b

> Do not be deceived! Neither fornicators, nor idolaters, nor adulterers, nor effeminate, nor men who have intercourse with men, nor thieves, nor greedy, nor drunkards, nor those who hurl insults, nor robbers will inherit the kingdom of God.

This list is similar but not identical to the list in 1 Corinthians 5:11. People who live this way will be lost. They will not hear the words, "Come, you blessed of my Father, inherit the kingdom that was prepared for you from the foundation of the world" (Matthew 25:34). Consider this list of behaviors. First we have *pornoi*, fornicators, those who have sex outside the confines of God-ordained marriage (Hebrews 13:4). Then we have *eidololatrai*, those who are practitioners of paganism, who worship and serve other beings besides the Creator (1 Corinthians 10:14, 20–21). A great deal of illicit sexual activity was involved in Corinthian idolatry. Next in the list is *moichoi*, adulterers, those who have sex that violates a marriage contract. This is a subcategory of fornication, a type of fornication in which one or both parties is married to someone other than the one with whom they are having intercourse. This precisely describes the person who was to be excommunicated in 1 Corinthians 5:4ff. The next word is *malakoi*, meaning soft or effeminate. These are men who are trying to present themselves as women or as feminine in nature. Many of the male cult prostitutes in Corinth likely presented themselves in this way as do many homosexual men today. Deuteronomy 22:5 prohibits men dressing as women or women dressing as men. Gender roles are part of God's creative order and are not to be confused by us. Men are to act and dress as men, and women are to act and dress as women. Then we see in the list is a very graphic word, *arsenokoitai*. It is a two-part word which literally describes males who have sexual intercourse with males or male homosexuals. This is the one who was to receive the death penalty in Leviticus 20:13.

Followed by *kleptai* or thieves. Next are *pleonektai* or greedy people who are driven to possess more and more with selfish intent. The list continues with *methusoi*, "drunkards." These are those who drink to the point of intoxication. The word means to be full of alcohol. Ephesians 5:18 forbids this behavior to those who have put off the old sinful man and put on the new man created in God's image. *Loidoroi* are revilers or people who hurl insults at others. They are placed beside drunkards in both 1 Corinthians 5:11 and here, perhaps because when people get drunk, they tend to defame and insult others with much more abandon, having lost their inhibitions. The last group in the list is *harpages*. This word can refer to robbers. It is literally someone who grabs or snatches something and takes it away. The word is certainly used here in a negative sense so is translated something like robber or thief or extortioner. None of the people who live these lifestyles will inherit the kingdom of God. Why then would the Corinthians want those who live these lifestyles to decide spiritual matters for them unless they did not trust in divinely revealed wisdom? Paul is not saying there is no forgiveness for these things, but that one cannot continue these lifestyles and be a Christian. This is very obvious because of what comes next.

First Corinthians 6:11

> And some of you were these very things. But...you were washed, you were sanctified, you were made righteous by the name of our Lord Jesus Christ and by the Spirit of our God!

The guilt of these past lifestyles was gone for those who had trusted and obeyed the gospel of Christ. They were washed in the blood of the Lamb (Hebrews 9:22; 10:22; Revelation 1:5; 7:14; 12:10–11). They were sanctified or set apart from those who live those sinful lifestyles and welcomed into a group that lives according to a different law (1 Corinthians 1:2). They were made righteous freely, by his blood, through the redemption that is in Christ Jesus (Romans 3:24; 1 Corinthians 1:30). This meant that their sins of the past were forgiven, and the sinful behaviors of the past had been exchanged for a new godly lifestyle. People who are washed, sanctified, and justified cannot continue those old lifestyles and still have God's grace. This is the whole point of the discussion since 1 Corinthians 5:1.

First Corinthians 6:12

> "All things are lawful for me" but not all things are beneficial. "All things are lawful for me" but I will not be brought under the authority of any. "Meat is for the belly, and the belly is for meat," but God will destroy both it and these. The body is not for fornication, but for the Lord, and the Lord for the body.

These little sayings like "all things are lawful for me" and "meat for the belly and the belly for meat" seem to have been cultural mantras for the people in Achaia in Paul's day. These sayings reflect how they viewed the satisfaction of fleshly desires. It was simply expected that people would satisfy these desires because they were natural and basic to all human beings. Paul seeks to counter these cultural sayings by replying, "But not all things are beneficial" and saying, "The body is not for fornication, but for the Lord, and the Lord for the body." Christ calls people to be guided by Him, not by the baser desires of the flesh. God calls us to say, "Not my will, but yours be done." Just because we have the urge to do something does not mean that we should do it. In fact, Christ calls us to discipline all of our desires and to direct them in certain ways. The topic in chapters 5–7 is fornication and how one deals with the urge, the act, and the aftermath. The topic in chapters 8–10 is the eating of meat, and more specifically, sacrificial meat. The first consideration in both areas is not what one desires to do, but what God desires that we do.

First Corinthians 6:14

> And God both raised up the Lord and will raise you up through his power. Do you not know that your bodies are members of Christ? So, then, shall I cause the members of Christ to become members of a prostitute? May it never be! Don't you know that he who is joined closely with a prostitute is one body, for it says, "The two shall be into one flesh."

That Christians are members of the body of Christ is made clear in later discussions (1 Corinthians 10:16; 12:12–13, 18). The body is destined for greater things than this physical life. The body will one day be raised from the dead and transformed into an incorruptible body, eternal in the heavens (1 Corinthians 15:50–58; 2 Corinthians 5:1–5). When thinking of what we do with our bodies now, we should consider God's long-term purpose for our body and spirit. God wants only legitimately married couples to be joined in fleshly sexual union (Genesis 2:24). Jesus cited these same passages in his teaching on marriage. God does not want Christians joining in that way with anyone other than their committed marriage partner. Sex should only occur between those whom God has joined together (Matthew 19:6). He does not want the sexual relationship viewed casually or taken lightly (1 Thessalonians 4:3ff; Hebrews 13:4). In Corinth, many were sexually joined to various cult prostitutes and others in the course of pagan worship. This was never sanctioned by God and was always detestable to God (Numbers 25).

First Corinthians 6:17

He who is joined to the Lord is one spirit.

The word *kollomenos* means to join closely with or be connected with. It is the same word in verses 16 and 17. Just as we connect with human beings sexually, the committed Christian connects with God, who is a Spirit, spiritually. It is a spirit to spirit connection, deep and personal. It is a sacred bond often compared to the marriage bond in Scripture (Ephesians 5:23–30). Since the Christian is "joined together" with the Lord Jesus, we must not allow ourselves to be illicitly joined together with others besides our God-ordained mate.

First Corinthians 6:18–20

Flee from fornication! Every sin which a man might do is outside of the body, but the one who commits fornication is sinning in his own body. Or do you not know that your body is a temple of the Holy Spirit which is in you, which you have from God, and you are not your own! You were bought for a price! Glorify God with your body!

A similar command is "Flee from idolatry" in 1 Corinthians 10:14. The word *flee* has vast implications. This is more than abstinence from an act. This is directing one's life away from fornication purposefully. This means avoiding people and situations that might lead to fornication and building protective structures in one's life to shield one from fornication. Fleeing is the opposite of flirting! There is something about the joining of bodies in sexual congress that is different from other sins. The text says that we who are joined to the Lord also have his Spirit indwelling our bodies. We are not the proprietors of our own bodies. We have been purchased with the blood of Christ (Acts 20:28; 1 Peter 1:18; Revelation 5:9–10). The physical body with which one might commit fornication is the dwelling place of God's Spirit. We must use our physical bodies for his purposes, not for our own self-gratification. To glorify God with our bodies in this passage would be to live in sexual purity and fidelity, honoring marriage, including our own marriage and the marriages of others. Glorifying God in one's body means living a decent and disciplined life. It means presenting our bodies as a living, holy, acceptable sacrifice (Romans 12:1–2). It means presenting the members of our bodies to God as instruments of righteousness (Romans 6:12–13). It means using our bodies to do good, not evil.

Reflections on Chapter 6

1. How do the last two verses of chapter 5 fit with Paul's directives in the beginning of chapter 6?
2. Why does it make no sense for Christians to go to secular courts to determine issues involving spiritual matters?
3. Discuss each of the sins listed in 1 Corinthians 6:9–10 to understand exactly what they are.
4. Read 1 Corinthians 6:11. What does this verse suggest to us about how we should treat Christians with very sinful backgrounds?
5. Discuss thoroughly what is involved when a person is fleeing from fornication. How does one actually accomplish this?
6. How should we properly apply the admonition "glorify God in your bodies"? Consider the context.

71

7

First Corinthians 7:1

> Now concerning what you wrote about,
> "It is good for a man not to touch a woman."
> But because of fornication, let each man have
> his own wife, and let each woman have her
> own husband.

There are two ways to look at this statement, "It is good for a man not to touch a woman." One way is to take this as Paul's own blessing of celibacy as a way of life. This is possible because he says in 1 Corinthians 7:7 that he wishes everyone could be like him, content to live as a single man. However, since the subject since early in chapter 5 has been fornication, how to deal with it, and how we are to flee from it, it seems likely that this is not Paul's recommendation for everyone. In fact, in his very next sentence, he says that God's way of avoiding fornication is to be sexually active within God-ordained marriage. Paul may simply mean that it is not a bad thing if one can remain single. Later he says this would be preferable because of some present distress about which he does not elaborate (1 Corinthians 7:26). Asceticism is not mentioned in the Corinthian epistles as it is in Colossians 2:18ff, but it is possible that some in Corinth were offering it as an alternative to sexual activity. In any case, Paul goes on to explain that God's plan for sexual expression is marriage.

First Corinthians 7:3–5

> Let the husband give his wife what he owes
> her, and in the same way let the wife give to
> her husband (what she owes him). The woman
> does not have power over her own body, but
> the man. Likewise, the man does not have
> power over his own body, but the woman. Do
> not withhold (what is owed) from one another,
> unless it be by mutual agreement for a time, so
> that you may dedicate yourself to prayer, then
> become one again, so that Satan may not tempt
> you because of your lack of self-control.

The clear teaching here is that sexual attention is a marital obligation. The word *opheile,* signifies a debt or obligation or duty. This is something that is owed by one party to another. It is God's design that partners in marriage provide sexual release to their spouse. Because sexual activity is a duty or obligation, one party does not have the divine right to keep denying the other partner. In this sense, the body of the husband belongs to the wife and vice versa. This teaching is certainly tempered by the commands to love one's spouse, to nourish and cherish one's spouse, and to live with one another in an understanding way (Ephesians 5:25–30; 1 Peter 3:7). The word translated "defraud," *apostereo*, can literally mean to rob or steal. When a spouse denies his/her mate a sexual partner habitually, one is both disobeying God and setting both partners up for a heightened vulnerability to sexual temptation from outside the marriage. It is acceptable for a couple to mutually agree to a short period of abstinence in order to devote themselves to prayer and spiritual pursuits, but they are clearly instructed to "become one again." This seems to be based on Genesis 2:24. Otherwise, Satan will tempt one or both parties to commit fornication because of a lack of self-control. Satan will enhance the desire and provide the opportunity to satisfy sexual desires outside of the sacred union of marriage (James 1:14–15).

First Corinthians 7:6

> This I say as a concession and not as a command. And I wish all men to be as I am, but each one has his own gift from God, one in this way and the other in another way.

Paul, inspired by the Spirit, freely acknowledged that his wish that everyone could live celibate lives is not a command. It was God's advice at that time, considering the impending circumstances (1 Corinthians 7:26). He later recommends that fathers withhold permission for their daughters to marry unless such a refusal would put the daughter in an untenable position because of a lack of self-control (1 Corinthians 7:37). Not everyone has the gift of being able to live a celibate life. This is why God directs young widows to marry, because they may not be able to keep a commitment to remain celibate (1 Timothy 5:11ff). While the teaching of Jesus on marriage and divorce does result in some having to live their lives in celibacy, God has a plan that gives people a sexual outlet and preserves his design for marriage (Matthew 19:12; Romans 7:1–4).

First Corinthians 7:8–9

> I say to the unmarried and to the widows, it is good for them if they remain as I am. But if they cannot control themselves, let them marry, for it is better for them to marry than to burn (with passion).

The unmarried here are those who have never married. This is obvious because the divorced are to "remain unmarried" (1 Corinthians 7:11) while this group is permitted to marry. The widows are addressed further in 1 Corinthians 7:39 and permitted to marry "only in the Lord." Paul recommends that they all stay single, likely because of the present distress mentioned in 1 Corinthians 7:26. We do not know what these stressful circumstances were, but Paul's recommendation does seem to have been situational in nature. It is clear that the unmarried and the widows would need to exercise lots of self-control over their sexual urges. If they could not do this, they were advised by Paul to marry rather than to "burn." This seems to mean burning with sexual lust or passion. We see the same idea expressed in Romans 1:27.

First Corinthians 7:10

> To the married I command, not I but the Lord, that a woman not divorce from her husband. But if she should divorce, let her remain unmarried or be reconciled to the husband, and a husband should not leave his wife.

This is the teaching of the Lord Jesus in Matthew 5:32; 19:9; Mark 10:11–12; Luke 16:18. Paul repeats this same teaching in Romans 7:2–3. I justify the translation of *chorizo* as "divorce" because Paul clearly references the teaching of the Lord Jesus, and it was this verb, *chorizo*, that Jesus used in his answer to the Pharisees in Matthew 19:6. Jesus said that man should not put asunder or separate that which God has joined. If people divorce when God has joined them, then they must remain unmarried or be reconciled to one another. The only exception given by Jesus is fornication. If one of the parties in the marriage has been unfaithful, then the other has the right to remarry without committing adultery. Paul's teaching here is the exact teaching one finds in Mark 10:11–12; Luke 16:18; and Romans 7:2–3.

First Corinthians 7:12

> For the rest, I say, not the Lord. If any brother has an unbelieving wife and she is content to live together with him, let him not leave her. And if any woman has an unbelieving husband, and he is content to live together with her, let her not leave the husband.

"The rest" in this passage are believers who are married to unbelievers. When Paul came to Corinth and preached the gospel, "many of the Corinthians, hearing, believed, and were baptized" (Acts 18:8). Among them, however, there were certainly some who obeyed the gospel when their spouses did not. The law of Moses prohibited Israelites from intermarrying with the indigenous people of Canaan because of their idolatry (Exodus 34:11–16; Deuteronomy 7:3–6). God said, "You shall make no covenant with them, nor with their gods" (Exodus 23:32). Marriage is certainly a covenant (Malachi 2:14). Ignoring these commands is clearly given as a main reason for the apostasy in the book of Judges (Judges 3:6). The same reason is given for the unfaithfulness of Solomon (1 Kings 11:1–8). The people who came back from Babylonian captivity had intermarried with foreign women, and when they read the law of God, they repented and put away their foreign wives and children (Ezra 9:1–12; 10:3, 11). All of this is probably the basis for the concern of the Corinthians about the acceptability of being married to an unbeliever. However, Paul instructed them not to leave their unbelieving mates.

First Corinthians 7:14

> For the unbelieving husband is sanctified by the wife, and the unbelieving wife is sanctified by the brother. Otherwise, your children would be unclean, but now they are holy.

Paul explains that both the marriage and the children born to the marriage are seen as holy and are not considered "unclean" or unacceptable the way they were in the stipulations of the Old Covenant.

First Corinthians 7:15

> But if the unbeliever divorces, let him divorce. The brother or the sister is not enslaved by such people, and God has called us in peace.

The same word, *chorizo*, is used here as was used in 1 Corinthians 7:10–11. If the unbeliever does what Jesus commanded should not be done in Matthew 19:6, the brother or sister has no control over that. The brother or sister is not enslaved to the unbeliever but to Christ. It is the will of Christ, not the will of the unbeliever, that has precedence. The word that many translators render as "bound" in verse 15 is actually the verb *douloo*, which means to be enslaved. The perfect tense, *dedoulotai*, is used, meaning that the brother or sister was not enslaved in the past nor is he/she enslaved in the present to the unbeliever. This word is not the same as the word for the marriage bond used in 1 Corinthians 7:27, 39. That word is the verb *deo*, which means to tie or bind something together. *Deo* is also used in Romans 7:2–3 to describe the marriage bond. In 1 Corinthians 7:15, Paul does not give the brother or sister permission to remarry. He has already spoken to that in 1 Corinthians 7:11. He is simply saying that one cannot control what the unbeliever does, and that Christians are given to peace, not perpetual conflict.

First Corinthians 7:16

> For how do you know, O woman, if you
> might save the husband, or how do you know,
> o man, if you might save the wife.

Here lies one of the main motivations for staying with one's unbelieving husband or wife. Certainly, the avoidance of fornication is one motivation for staying in the marriage (1 Corinthians 7:1–2). In addition, there is a strong possibility that through a good example and through kind and loving treatment of one's spouse, that spouse could be won over to Christianity. Peter says virtually the same thing in 1 Peter 3:1–2.

First Corinthians 7:17

> Except as the Lord has called each one,
> as God has called (each one), so let (each one)
> walk. And so I command in all the churches.

Verse 15 says God has called us "in peace." If a person is called by the gospel into the fellowship of Christ (1 Corinthians 1:9), one should remain with one's spouse whether or not the spouse responds to the gospel. This is Paul's point. This does not, in our view, mean that one should remain with one's spouse regardless of previous divorces for unscriptural causes. He is simply saying that one should not desert one's spouse because the spouse is not a Christian (1 Corinthians 7:12–14).

First Corinthians 7:18–20

> Was anyone called who is circumcised?
> Let him not seek to be uncircumcised. Was any
> called in uncircumcision? Let him not seek to
> be circumcised. Circumcision is nothing and
> uncircumcision is nothing, but keeping God's
> commands! Each one in the state in which he
> was called, in this let each one remain.

Notice what matters, according to the apostle, is the keeping of God's commands. Jesus told the apostles to teach people to observe "whatever I have commanded you" (Matthew 28:19–20). Keeping Jesus's commands about divorce and remarriage and about all other matters is the most important thing for Christians. Being married to an unbeliever does not violate any of Christ's commands nor did Christ legislate on whether or not one should be circumcised.

First Corinthians 7:21

> Were you called as a slave? Don't worry
> about it! But if you are able to be free, that is
> much better. For whoever is called as a slave is
> the Lord's freedman. Were you called as a free
> person? You are Christ's slave!

Again, being slave or free does not cause one to be at odds with the commands of Christ. One can be a Christian in either state. First Corinthians 7:15 indicates that married people are not slaves to one another but to Christ. Their allegiance to Christ comes first, so they must do his will, even if an unbelieving spouse exerts pressure to do otherwise.

First Corinthians 7:23

> You were bought with a price! Do not be
> slaves of men! Each in which he was called,
> brothers, in that state let him remain with God!

The fact that we have been purchased is repeated from 1 Corinthians 6:20. Because of this, we are slaves of Christ who purchased us with his blood. We must glorify him with our bodies, and we must not be enslaved to people. According to 1 Corinthians 7:12–16, Christ wants us to stay with our legitimate mates, whether or not they are Christians, so that we may avoid fornication and perhaps save their souls. In doing this, we remain in that state or relationship in which we were called into Christian fellowship (1 Corinthians 1:9). This statement, repeated in various ways in 1 Corinthians 7:17, 20, 24, does not suggest that we remain in relationships that are contrary to God's law! We must not ignore what precedes this admonition in 1 Corinthians 7:8–16! The uncertainty among the Corinthians was whether they should stay married to people who were not part of the body of Christ!

First Corinthians 7:25

> Concerning virgins, I have no command
> from the Lord, but I give my judgment as one
> who has been given mercy by the Lord to be
> considered faithful. I think therefore, that it is
> good because of the present necessity, for a man
> to be as I am.

When Paul says he has no commandment from the Lord Jesus, he means simply that Jesus did not speak to this issue. He says the same in 1 Corinthians 7:12 where he indicates that Jesus did not address the matter of believers who are married to unbelievers. Paul is an apostle who has the gift of divine revelation and gives his judgment informed by that revelation. In this passage, he says clearly that the advice he gives is circumstantial, "because of the present necessity." We do not know to what circumstances Paul was referring, but we do not need to know to discern that his admonition for people to stay single, if possible, was related to certain adverse circumstances.

First Corinthians 7:27

> Are you bound to a wife? Do not seek to
> be loosed! Are you loosed from a wife? Do not
> seek a wife! But if you should marry, it is not
> a sin, and if the virgin should marry, she has
> not sinned. These shall have tribulation in the
> flesh, and I would spare you.

The directives given here do not contradict those given earlier in the discussion. They are given in consideration of two things. First, they are given in consideration of God's divine revelation. Secondly, they are given in consideration of the circumstances to which Paul referred. Paul clearly states that those who marry can expect to endure more affliction, tribulation, or suffering in these circumstances. It is not against God's command to marry, but it may cause them difficulty they could otherwise avoid.

First Corinthians 7:29

> This I say, brothers! The time is here, finally,
> that those who have wives will be like those who
> do not have them, and those who weep like

> those who do not weep, and those who rejoice
> as those who do not rejoice, and those who buy
> as those who possess nothing, and those who use
> the world as those who do not use it, for the
> form of this world is passing away!

The circumstance to which Paul is referring is difficult to ascertain. We are aware of nothing in the historical records that would enlighten us. Paul refers to this difficult time as "the present necessity" (1 Corinthians 7:26). He then seems to suggest that these difficult circumstances are soon to be coming upon his readers (1 Corinthians 7:29). Paul told the Thessalonians that Christ would not come again until the man of lawlessness was revealed (2 Thessalonians 2:1–9). The great Roman persecution foretold by Daniel had not yet taken place (Daniel 7:1–25). Perhaps Paul is looking forward into the latter decades of the first century and the first decade of the second century when Domitian and Trajan were persecuting Christians. It is impossible to know the actual circumstances to which he had reference. All we can say is that circumstances were coming in which Paul said it would be much more difficult to be married.

First Corinthians 7:32

> But I wish you to be without worry! The
> unmarried man is concerned about the things
> of the Lord, how he might please the Lord. But
> the married man is concerned about the things
> of the world, how he might please his wife, and
> he is divided! And the unmarried woman and the
> virgin are concerned with the things of the Lord,
> that she might be holy in body and in spirit. But
> the married woman is concerned about the things
> of the world, how she might please her husband.

While this was much more true in the circumstances that were present or soon to be coming upon the Corinthians, it is also true, to some degree, for us today. One who is unmarried and focused on God can devote one's self much more completely to God's work. Paul chose to be single and found that he could concentrate more fully on God's work without worrying about a wife and children (1 Corinthians 7:6–7). Paul also told Timothy that only Ephesian widows over sixty who agreed never to marry were to be supported as full-time workers in the church for the rest of their lives (1 Timothy 5:1–15).

First Corinthians 7:35

> I say this for your benefit! Not that I may place a burden on you, so that you might be properly devoted to the Lord without distraction!

The mentality of Paul is strange to many modern-day readers! He is most concerned about the circumstances that will allow one to serve the Lord most effectively. One who does not have a spouse is much less distracted by worldly concerns, provided that person can control the lusts of the flesh (1 Corinthians 7:8–9). If one cannot control those lusts, one is still distracted to the detriment of his/her Christian service. In those cases, "it is better to marry than to burn with passion" (1 Corinthians 7:9).

First Corinthians 7:36–38

> If anyone thinks he is acting in an inappropriate way toward his virgin, if she is past her prime, and so he feels an obligation, let him do what he wants to do. He does not sin. Let

> them marry! But whoever stands steadfast in
> his mind, not having a necessity, and he has
> power over his own will, and he has decided in
> his own heart, to keep his own virgin (single),
> he shall do well. So then, the one who permits
> his virgin to marry does well, and the one who
> does not permit her to marry does better!

It seems best to understand this section as apostolic advice given primarily to the fathers of young ladies. The fathers of the young ladies either gave their permission for their daughters to marry or did not. Paul makes it clear that the wise thing to do depends on the circumstances. He uses the word *huperakmos*, which basically means "past marriageable age" or "past one's prime." If a father saw that his daughter may not have an opportunity to marry, and such an opportunity arose, he may have felt obligated, for the sake of his daughter, to allow her to marry rather than see her become an old maid. On the other hand, if a father has a younger daughter and feels no such obligation because she will be desired as a marriage partner for many years to come, Paul says it is better if he keeps her single a while longer. Again, this advice was circumstantial, based on difficult circumstances which Paul calls "the present necessity" or "present distress" (1 Corinthians 7:26). Neither the father who allows his daughter to marry or the father who refuses to allow it sins. But Paul's advice is clearly that being single would be better under the circumstances he saw coming.

First Corinthians 7:39–40

> A woman is bound for however long a
> time that her husband lives, but if the husband
> dies, she is free to be married to whomever she
> wishes, only in the Lord.

This teaching is the same as in Romans 7:2–3. The word *bound* here is *dedetai*, which means to be tied to something or someone. This tie is only broken by death or by divorce when the spouse has committed adultery. The widow is free to marry whomever she wishes to marry "only in the Lord." This phrase may mean that she is only free to marry a Christian. This, however, seems strange in light of the teaching of 1 Corinthians 7:12–16 that believers should remain with their unbelieving spouses. Some would cite 2 Corinthians 6:14 to counter this, but in 2 Corinthians 6:14, Paul is actually talking about the Corinthians' continued association with false teachers who were trying to bind the law of Moses on them. The other possibility in this passage is that "only in the Lord" means "only according to the Lord's teaching" on marriage and divorce. If this is true, Paul is using the phrase "in the Lord" like he uses it in Ephesians 6:1.

Reflections on Chapter 7

1. How do the admonitions in 1 Corinthians 7:1–5 fit in with the command to "flee from fornication" in 1 Corinthians 6:18?
2. Discuss the marital obligation of sexual fulfillment in 1 Corinthians 7:3–5.
3. If married couples do abstain from sex for a time, what are the rules according to 1 Corinthians 7:5?
4. How do we reconcile what is said in 1 Corinthians 7:1–2 with what Paul says in 1 Corinthians 7:6–7?
5. What group is included in 1 Corinthians 7:8–9? And how do you know?
6. What is the difference between the "unmarried" in 1 Corinthians 7:8 and the "unmarried" in 1 Corinthians 7:11?
7. To what group is Paul speaking in 1 Corinthians 7:12–16 whose issue Jesus did not directly address in his teaching?
8. What is the repeated command given to the group in 1 Corinthians 7:12ff?
9. In the context of Paul's admonition to remain with one's unbelieving husband or wife, what does he mean in 1 Corinthians 7:17ff when he says, "Let everyone remain in the state in which he was called"?
10. Why does Paul encourage fathers to keep their virgin daughters single for the time being?
11. When Paul tells widows to marry "only in the Lord," what are two possibilities for his meaning?

8

First Corinthians 8:1

> Now concerning things offered to idols, we
> know that we all have knowledge. Knowledge
> makes (people) arrogant, but love builds (peo-
> ple) up. If anyone thinks he knows something,
> he does not yet know as he ought to know. If
> anyone loves God, he will be known by Him.

The introductory words, "Now concerning," *peri de,* indicate that the apostle is addressing yet another of the matters about
which the Corinthians had written him (1 Corinthians 7:1). This
time, it is the matter of sacrificial meals. Participation in pagan
sacrificial meals was a social fact of life for Corinthian people. To
the Christian, it presented many potential conflicts, especially for
those who obeyed the apostolic command to "flee from idolatry"
(1 Corinthians 10:14). This discussion of the appropriateness of
eating sacrificial meat consumes the apostle in 1 Corinthians 8–10.
One does not grasp his inspired pronouncements on the matter
unless one digests the entire discussion. In this matter of sacrificial
meat, some were "puffed up," *phusioi,* because they felt that their
knowledge and superior wisdom enabled them to eat this meat
without any culpability. They were likely the same people who
were "boasting" in their own wisdom (1 Corinthians 1:29, 31).
They were likely the same people who were reluctant to accept the

things revealed to the apostles by the Spirit (1 Corinthians 2:14; 3:1). They were probably the same ones who were "puffed up" and saying Paul would not be coming (1 Corinthians 4:18–19). They were probably the same ones who were "puffed up" in their own wisdom, and for this reason, they were confident in their inaction over the fornicator in their midst (1 Corinthians 5:2). These people thought they were too wise, too intelligent to be tempted through the eating of sacrificial meat. They were not walking in love because they were more concerned about their own rights, *exousiai*, than they were about the effect of their actions on the faith of others (1 Corinthians 8:9, 13). What Paul wanted them to know, which they did not yet seem to know, was how much God values the souls of men far above any one person's perceived "rights."

First Corinthians 8:4–6

> Therefore, concerning food offered to idols, we know that an idol is nothing in the world because there is no God but one. For even if there are many who are called gods, whether in heaven or on earth, just as there are many gods and many lords, in contrast, there is one God the Father, from whom are all things and we (exist) for him, and one Lord Jesus Christ, through whom are all things and we (exist) through him.

Biblically, we know that idols are only images, forbidden by the commandments (Exodus 20:1–3; Romans 1:19–24). There is but one Creator, Yahweh, the one God of the Hebrew Bible (Deuteronomy 6:4). That being said, Paul understands that there are "gods" or demonic powers behind the pagan cults (1 Corinthians 10:20–21). There are "many gods and many lords."

These are the "spiritual hosts of wickedness in the heavenly realms" (Ephesians 1:20–21; 3:9–10; 6:12). We may be assured in our minds that there is one Creator, but the Satanic spiritual entities compete for the souls of men and women, and one way they do it is through the allure of paganism. Paganism was an extremely powerful cultural pull on the people who lived in the world of ancient Corinth. It remains very powerful in many less secularized cultures of today, including Latin America, the African continent, the Caribbean Islands, among the Native American cultures, and in many Asian cultures as well.

First Corinthians 8:7

> But this knowledge is not in everyone. But some, even until now, thinking about the idol, eat as if for an idol, and their conscience which is weak, is defiled. But food does not commend us to God. For we are no worse off if we do not eat, neither are we better off if we do eat. Be careful, lest by any means your right (to eat) should become an occasion of stumbling for the weak.

Those who were puffed up in their "knowledge" needed to realize that not everyone had sufficient knowledge to participate in eating sacrificial meat without violating his/her conscience. These people could not help thinking about the pagan deities when they ate. They could not help feeling the connection between themselves and the spiritual entity with whom they had once had fellowship (1 Corinthians 10:20). While it is true that meat is just meat, participation in this sacrificial meat could cause others to sin because their conscience was weak and they could not disconnect the meat from the demonic powers of the pagan cult.

First Corinthians 8:10–11

> If anyone should see you, who have knowl-
> edge, sitting down to eat in an idol's temple,
> will not his conscience, being weak, be encour-
> aged to eat what is sacrificed to idols? Then, by
> your knowledge, the weak brother for whom
> Christ died is destroyed.

The one who claims to have knowledge may be bold enough
to actually eat a meal with pagan friends in the environs of the
pagan temple. This was spiritually risky, not only because of the
clear association with the pagan deity, but because of the other
activities common in the temple environs, including fornication
with cult prostitutes. In the scenario Paul paints, whether this meal
is in a place on the temple grounds or is in a private home, dedicated to one of the gods, the presence of a Christian brother or sister at such a meal could encourage other weaker Christians also to
be present. Those weaker Christians might eat with offense and be
lured back into paganism by the example of the supposedly stronger Christian. This is not loving behavior. The demanding of one's
"rights," *exousiai*, to eat, could well end up spiritually destroying a
person for whom Christ died. In this case, the supposedly "stronger" Christian by his/her behavior was encouraging the weaker
Christian to sin against God. The same principle could be applied
to discussions about social drinking, some kinds of dancing, and
other issues as well.

First Corinthians 8:12

> In this way, sinning against the broth-
> ers and wounding their weak conscience, you
> sin against Christ! Wherefore, if meat causes

> my brother to stumble, I will never, ever, eat
> meat, so that I might not cause my brother to
> stumble.

The person who was demanding his/her rights and insisting on participating in sacrificial meals was taking the risk of destroying fellow Christians. The example of an influential Christian encourages others to follow his/her behavior, whether the influential Christian intends it or not. One cannot simply look at the technical rightness or wrongness of a behavior but must also think carefully about the potential of that behavior to lead others into sin. This is why Paul says at the beginning of the chapter that "knowledge" makes people arrogant, often to the detriment of others, while love makes sure to build up others spiritually.

Reflections on Chapter 8

1. According to 1 Corinthians 8:1–2, what is the effect when people make claims of superior knowledge, versus when people act in love?
2. In 1 Corinthians 8:4–6, is Paul saying that other gods do not exist? Or is he saying that there is but one Creator? Discuss.
3. What does Paul mean when he says in 1 Corinthians 8:7, "This knowledge is not in everyone"? Is he speaking of different degrees of faith and understanding among Christians? Discuss.
4. Is it wrong to violate one's conscience? Discuss.
5. In 1 Corinthians 8:9, Paul warns that demanding our "rights" can possibly have what evil outcome?
6. Can you give other examples of things which in themselves may not be sinful but can become sins against Christ and others in some circumstances?

9

First Corinthians 9:1

> Am I not free? Am I not an apostle? Have
> I not seen Jesus our Lord? If to others I am not
> an apostle, surely I am to you! For you are the
> seal of my apostleship in the Lord!

Paul now sets about to use himself as an example as one who has the right to do certain things, but chooses to give up that right for the spiritual good of others. Paul's bona fides were evident to those who knew him. He had come to the Corinthians in demonstration of the Spirit and power (1 Corinthians 2:4). He had done "the signs of an apostle" among them (2 Corinthians 12:12). It was obvious to other apostles that God was working in Paul as an apostle to the Gentiles (Galatians 2:9–10). The Corinthians and their changed lives were a living letter attesting to God's redemptive work through Paul (2 Corinthians 3:1–3). Paul was the real deal and the Corinthians knew it!

1 Corinthians 9:3

> My defense to those who judge me is this.
> Do we not have the right to eat and drink? Do
> we not have the right to lead about a wife who
> is a sister, as also Cephas, and the rest of the

apostles and the Lord's brothers do? Or do only
Barnabas and I not have the right not to work?

Some of the Corinthians were claiming their "right," *exousia,*
to eat meat, regardless of whether or not it had been sacrificed to
idols (1 Corinthians 8:9). Paul uses the same word, *exousia,* and
suggests that he has the same right to eat and drink whatever he
chooses (1 Timothy 4:4–5). Not only that, but he has the right
to be married if he chooses. The other apostles were married, but
Paul chose not to be married (1 Corinthians 7:6–7). Paul also had
the right to receive compensation from the church for his work
in the gospel (1 Corinthians 9:16). But like these other rights he
chose to forego, he chose to forego his right to financial support in
the city of Corinth. Just because we may technically have the right
to do something does not mean we should take advantage of that
right in all circumstances.

First Corinthians 9:7–8

What soldier serves paying his own wages?
Who plants a vineyard and does not eat the
fruit of it? Who tends a flock and does not eat
the milk from the flock? I am not saying these
things only according to human *values*! Doesn't
the law say the same thing?

Paul centered his example of giving up his rights on the matter
of financial support for his preaching. He now gives some examples
from the culture to show that it is a widely accepted principle that
people should earn their living from their work. Soldiers expect to be
paid for their services. Those who plant and tend vineyards expect to
eat the fruit and drink the wine. Those who tend flocks expect to eat
the curds and drink the milk from the flock! This is not just a cultural

expectation. The law of God says the same thing! Paul is a farmer in God's field, a soldier in God's army, and a shepherd of God's flock. Therefore, he has a right to be paid.

First Corinthians 9:9–12a

> For in the law of Moses it is written, 'You shall not muzzle the ox while he is threshing.' It is not just for oxen that God is concerned, is it? Or does he not say it always for us? For our sakes it was written, that he that plows ought to plow in hope, and he that threshes ought to thresh in hope of partaking! If we sowed spiritual things to you, is it a great matter if we reap your fleshly things? If others partook of this right from you, should not rather we (*do the same*)?

Paul cites the same passage of Scripture, Deuteronomy 25:4, in 1 Timothy 5:18 along with the saying of Jesus from Luke 10:7. In his letter to Timothy, he is legitimizing the financial support of preaching elders. Here, he cites the passage to show that those who preach the gospel have a right to make their living from the gospel. This passage lays down a basic principle that people have a right to make their living from their labors. Those who labor in the work of preaching the gospel of God have that same right. Just as the ones who plow and harvest the fields make their living from the crops, those who plant the seed of the kingdom and water it have a right to make their living from their labors. Paul shared spiritual things with the Corinthians, and it was only right that they should share their fleshly goods with him. As he told the Galatian churches, "Let him that is taught share with him that teaches in all good things" (Galatians 6:6).

First Corinthians 9:12b–13

> But we have not made use of this right,
> but we bear all things so that we might give no
> hindrance to the gospel of Christ! Don't you
> know that those who work among the holy
> things, eat the things from the temple? Those
> who serve at the altar, share in (the sacrifices
> of) the altar!

Paul had the same rights as did the spiritual leaders of the Mosaic covenant. Paul had the right to take support, but he chose to forego that right. He did the same thing with his right to marry and his right to eat any food he chose. He gave up his rights from time to time for the good of others for the salvation of souls. To further emphasize his right for financial support, he reminds his readers that the priests in the temple were given portions of the sacrifices brought to the temple. They ate from the holy things, including sacrificial meat and the bread of the presence (Leviticus 24:5–8; 1 Samuel 1:1–6; Matthew 12:3–4). They sustained themselves by their work for the Lord.

First Corinthians 9:14

> In the same way, also, the Lord com-
> manded that those who proclaim the gospel
> should live from the gospel! But I did not make
> use of any of these things! And I did not write
> these things so that it might be so with me! For
> it would be better for me to die than for my
> boasting to become empty!

Paul knew that he had a right to make his living from the gospel, but he chose not to do this among the Corinthians. Paul later explained that he did not want the Corinthians to have any excuse to question his love or sincerity toward them. He "boasted" before them that he preached to them out of purely altruistic motives, wanting nothing from them but the salvation of their souls. The Corinthians knew this. They knew the sacrifices Paul had made to preach the gospel to them and nurture them spiritually (2 Corinthians 11:7–11). He held this fact over the heads of the Corinthians whenever they questioned his sincerity.

First Corinthians 9:16–18

> For even if I preach the gospel, I have nothing to boast about! For necessity is laid upon me! But woe to me if I do not preach the gospel! For if I willingly do this, I have a reward. And even if I do it unwillingly, I have been entrusted with a stewardship! What then is my reward? That I might offer the gospel free of charge, so that I might not make use of my right in the gospel!

Christ personally commissioned Paul to preach the gospel to the Gentiles (Acts 9:15; 26:15–18). Paul had been commanded by Christ to do this work. Therefore, he had no choice if he was going to obey God. He took his stewardship of the gospel seriously and tried his best to discharge his duty as a good steward should (Ephesians 3:2, 7, 8). His joy was to do this from time to time without charge as a willing service to the Lord from which he gained nothing! While we are not directly commissioned as Paul was, we also have a responsibility to share the gospel once it has been entrusted to us by faithful teachers! Paul was very clear about this to Timothy (2 Timothy 1:6–7; 4:1–5). Still, the overall point of this whole discussion is that we sometimes should decide not to use our rights for the good of others!

First Corinthians 9:19

> For even though I am free from all people, I have made myself a slave to all, so that I might gain more (people). To the Jews I became like the Jews so that I might gain Jews. To those under law, I became as those under law (not that I myself am under law), so I might gain those under law. To those without law I became as one without law (not that I was without the law of God but within the law of Christ), so that I might gain those without the law. To the weak I became like the weak, so I might gain the weak. I became all things to all people so that in every possible way I might save some.

When Paul speaks of those without law, he is speaking of the Gentiles who are a law unto themselves (Romans 2:12–16). Those under law are the Jews who serve the letter of the Hebrew Scriptures and are not yet enlightened by the spiritual meaning of the law as it is realized in Christ (2 Corinthians 3:6ff). Paul ate and dressed and worked according to the culture in which he was functioning so that he could relate to both Jews and Gentiles, and not create barriers to the gospel. Paul mentions the "weak" several times in 1 Corinthians 8:7–11. This is the person whose conscience is defiled by eating sacrificial meat. In respect to such people, Paul readily gave up his right to eat meat so that he would not cause them to sin and so that his good influence over those people might be preserved! More of us today need to be ready and willing to give up our "right" to do things that might lead others into sin. Some claim to have the "right" to drink socially, or to dance with people other than their spouses, or to use certain semilegal drugs, or to frequent places where questionable activities often take place. These people need to think carefully about what exercising these "rights" might do to other people!

First Corinthians 9:23

> I do everything for the sake of the gospel,
> so that I might be a partner with Him.

This powerful statement sets a very high bar! Paul's decisions about his activities were based solely on how he might be a good partner, a good steward, a good helper for the Lord Jesus Christ in the spreading and nurturing of the gospel. This is the mentality of great evangelists and great servants of the Lord!

First Corinthians 9:24–27

> Do you not know that those who run in the 185-meter race all run, but only one receives the prize. Run in such a way as to receive the prize! Everyone who competes exercises self-discipline in all things. They do it so they might receive a corruptible wreath, but we (do it to receive an) incorruptible (wreath). I run in such a manner as not aimlessly. I box not as one hitting the air! But I beat on my own body and make it my slave, so that after having preached to others, I myself might not be disqualified!

The apostle is urging his readers to be more serious about the salvation of souls. He is urging them to be more dedicated, disciplined, and unselfish in their pursuit of souls. He is implying that some of them are "running" the Christian race in a haphazard, undisciplined way. Such people are not "in training" or in a strict program of discipline as they train to run this race. They are self-indulgent and lazy, not truly dedicated. Paul says we need to run or compete like those who intend to win. Such people are serious and willing to give up much in order to obtain the fleshly wreath of victory! Paul has a definite goal in mind. He wants to win souls for Jesus! He is willing to give up much to achieve that goal, including his own rights! He is not running the Christian race aimlessly!

Are we running aimlessly? Or are we really trying to achieve the spiritual goals God has put before us? We cannot achieve great things for God without exercising self-control! Paul did not want to be rejected from the Christian race after teaching others to join the race and endure the race. The word *adikimos* in the last verse means to be tested and fail the test. Those who are serious about the Christian race will discipline themselves. In the context of this discussion, this speaks directly to those who did not have enough self-discipline to abstain from sacrificial meat and the environment that surrounded it.

Reflections on Chapter 9

1. Paul gives three examples of things he had the right to do. What are these three things?
2. Which of the three examples takes up most of his discussion?
3. Did Paul exercise his rights in these three cases? Why or why not?
4. How did Paul make himself a slave to all people so that he might win more (1 Corinthians 9:19–22)?
5. When discussing a willingness to give up one's rights, why does Paul bring up the illustration of athletes in training (1 Corinthians 9:24–27)?
6. What rights of yours are you willing to give up for the good of the souls around you? Examples?

10

F irst Corinthians 10:1ff

> I do not want you to be ignorant brothers,
> that our fathers were all under the cloud and
> they all passed through the sea. And they were
> all baptized into Moses in the cloud and in the
> sea, and all of them ate the same spiritual food
> and drank the same spiritual drink. For they
> drank from the spiritual rock following (them),
> and the rock was Christ.

The entire discussion of chapters 8–10 concerns food and drink and the ramifications of partaking in food and drink under different circumstances. The food and drink of the Israelites is called "spiritual" food and drink, though it was actual food and drink. It was spiritual because it was clearly connected with their relationship to God. They were "baptized into Moses" spiritually or figuratively. God gave them the manna and quail, and God made the water come out of the rock (Exodus 16–17; Numbers 20). The rock "followed them" because they got water from the rock at Rephidim before they came to Mount Sinai, and they also got water from a rock years later at Kadesh long after Sinai. So, though it was in a different location years later, it was as if the water-giving rock was following them wherever they went. Of course, it was actually the presence of God that was with them, giving them food and water (Deuteronomy 8:3–5). It was God or "Christ" who was with them in the desert.

First Corinthians 10:5–6

> But with most of them God was not pleased, for they were destroyed in the desert! These things happened as examples for us, so that we might not lust after evil things as they also lusted.

Paul's warning is to those who demand their right to eat food sacrificed to idols. He calls the people to remember these full-fledged, bona fide, baptized Israelites who shared in the same spiritual food and drink and still died in the desert because they dared to flirt with idolatry! They became unfaithful to the God who redeemed them. While we are not under the law of the Israelites nor are we part of the covenant God made with Israel, the example of their behavior and its consequences is still a powerful warning for us! The writer of Hebrews makes a very similar argument in Hebrews 3:7–4:11. He warns his readers of hardening their hearts, straying in their hearts, and having unfaithful hearts in falling away from the living God. The example of unfaithfulness is the example of Israel, who failed to enter God's rest in the land of Canaan. The desire for things that would take us from God has been the spiritual downfall of many!

First Corinthians 10:7

> Neither let us be idolaters as some of them were, just as it is written, "*The people sat down to eat and to drink, and they got up to play.*"

The quotation is from Exodus 32:6. The word *paizein* means to have fun or amuse oneself in whatever manner the context demands. In this case, it refers to the sexual play of the idolaters who eat and drink and fornicate before the fertility gods. Later in the text of Exodus, Moses and Joshua descended from Sinai, and they "saw the calf and the dancing" (Exodus 32:19). The Hebrew word *cHul* means to dance, whirl around, or writhe according to Brown, Driver, and Briggs. In Exodus 32, it describes the kind of dancing which was the prelude to an idolatrous orgy. Notice, however, in the quotation, how it all began when they sat down to "eat and drink." Eating and drinking can lead to other things, depending on the situation. To deny that is to be in spiritual denial. This is especially true when eating and drinking has both religious and sexual overtones as it did in Corinth.

First Corinthians 10:8

> Neither let us commit fornication as some of them committed fornication, and twenty-three thousand fell in one day!

This refers to the infamous incident in Numbers 25 when the Israelites were defeated by their own desires. Balaam was unable to defeat the Israelites by cursing them, though he tried very hard to do so, because God did not allow it. He was, however, able to defeat them in a stealthy way (Numbers 31:16). Balaam advised the Moabites to invite the Israelites to participate with them in an idolatrous meal. They did this, and the Israelites were pulled into idolatry, thus incurring the wrath of God. Their temptation began with a meal and ended in fornication and idolatry. The discrepancy between 23, 000 who fell in one day here and the 24, 000 who died in Numbers 25:9 did not seem to concern the early church fathers. Some suggest that both numbers were meant to be approximations, one on the high side and one on the low side. Some have suggested that there is a textual variant that explains the issue, but there is no real reason from the manuscript evidence to think that Paul did not write 23, 000. It seems obvious to this writer that 23, 000 and 24, 000 are rounded numbers, not meant to be exact.

1 Corinthians 10:9

> Neither let us tempt Christ, as some of them tempted (him), and were destroyed by the serpents!

The first phrase is problematic to some: "Neither let us tempt Christ." There are three different readings in the manuscript tradition. The oldest and most diverse reading is *christos*. A considerable number of manuscripts have *kurios*. A couple of manuscripts read *theos*. Between the three possibilities of Christ, Lord, and God, Metzger and the United Bible Societies' editors chose Christ. The reasons given by Metzger are that Christ is the most problematic because it was difficult for them to explain how Christ was tempted or tested in the wilderness. Also, he says that "Christ" is contextually justified because of the reference to Christ in verse 4. In addition, it best explains the rise of the other readings as attempts to take away the difficulty of having Christ in the desert with the Israelites (Metzger, p.560).

The reference to destruction by serpents surely recalls the incident of Numbers 21 where the people of God spoke against God, complaining about the food God had provided for them (Numbers 21:5). God sent the poisonous snakes among them, and many died for their rebellious attitudes! We must not lose sight of the fact that this rebellion involved their lust for food.

First Corinthians 10:10

> Neither let us speak rebelliously as some
> of them spoke rebelliously, and were destroyed
> by the destroyer!

One of the key Hebrew words that recurs in the narrative of the rebellion in the wilderness is the word *lun,* which means to grumble, complain, or to speak in a rebellious way (Numbers 14:2, 27, 29, 36; 16:11, 41; 17:5). They did this both before and after Sinai because of their food, their water, and because of the task God set before them in taking the promised land (Exodus 15:24; 16:2, 7, 8; 17:3). One instance that resulted in destruction was the grumbling of Korah and those who rebelled with him. Another instance involved complaining over food and resulted in great destruction. This happened when the people lusted for meat and put God to the test (Numbers 11:33). This is likely the specific instance to which Paul refers because it involves their desire to eat meat and how that desire led them to let their lust take over. The desire to eat meat that has been sacrificed to idols is what Paul probably sees as a parallel between the experience of the Corinthians and the experience of the Israelites. This would be consistent with the previous reference to the fornication that followed the eating and drinking in Numbers 25.

First Corinthians 10:11–12

> And these things happened to them as
> examples, and it was written down for our
> instruction, (for us) to whom the ends of the
> ages have arrived. So, then, let him who thinks
> he is standing be careful that he does not fall!

These examples in the early part of chapter ten are all from the experience of Israel. They are examples of people who were "baptized" and sharing in spiritual "food and drink" (1 Corinthians 10:1–2). Yet these people were led away from God through their complaining, through their lusts, through seemingly innocent meals, and through the idolatry! They thought they were strong. They thought they were "standing" in a relationship with Yahweh, but they fell! The application of these examples is a strong warning not to take these temptations for granted, but to wisely fear the dangers they present to our souls!

First Corinthians 10:13

> Temptation has not overtaken you other than what is (characteristic) of human beings. God is faithful, who will not allow you to be tempted beyond what you are able, but will with the temptation provide the way out, so you will be able to bear up under it.

By the examples from the experience of Israel, Paul is showing the Corinthians that they are not being tempted any differently than others were tempted before them. Those who came out of Egypt were only human as were the Corinthians. They dealt with the same human desires for food, drink, sex, and security. They did not handle their temptations well. They allowed their temptations to lead them into sin and into destruction. The way to "bear up under," *hupophero,* these temptations is to refuse to take the first step carelessly. When people take the first step, the second is easier. By the time they take the second or third step, they are often in so deeply they have difficulty getting out. The way of escape or "the way out" is described clearly in verse 14!

First Corinthians 10:14

> Wherefore, my beloved, flee from idolatry!

Israel, in the examples given above, did not flee from idolatry. They flirted with idolatry. They went to dinner with the idolaters as if they were immune to the temptations that environment would present. Those people who "sat down to eat and drink" around the golden bull calf in Exodus 32 were reverting to the pagan culture with which they were all too familiar! God warned the people in Leviticus 18 that they were not to follow the cultural customs of Egypt from whence they had come nor the cultural customs of Canaan where they were going. They knew the rites and rituals of pagan fertility cults quite well! Yet their lust for food and drink and fornication, all of which often revolved around idolatry, led them to compromise their relationship with God. The way to avoid idolatry was to never go to dinner with the idolaters! Flee means to run the other way! Paul already warned them to "flee from fornication" (1 Corinthians 6:18). Now, in the context of the discussion in chapters 8–10, Paul is warning them to "flee from idolatry" by refusing to participate in meals in which the food has been offered to idols!

First Corinthians 10:15

> I speak as to intelligent people! You judge
> what I am saying!

In view of some Corinthians' claims to be "wise" or "intelligent" people (1 Corinthians 3:18–21; 4:10, 18; 6:5; 8:1), Paul is asking them to use that intelligence. He is asking them to acknowledge that it is very risky to exercise their perceived "right" to eat the meat sacrificed to idols, considering the well-established temptations to themselves and others if they do so.

First Corinthians 10:16–17

> The cup of blessing which we bless, is it not a sharing of the blood of Christ? The loaf which we break, is it not a sharing of the body of Christ? Because we who are many are one loaf, one body, for we are all partakers of the one loaf.

Paul pointed out earlier that the Israelites were "baptized into Moses" and were all partakers of the same spiritual food and drink (1 Corinthians 10:1–2). Yet their participation in the meals of pagans led to their downfall (1 Corinthians 10:3–12). The Corinthians, like Israel before them, were baptized into the congregation of God (1 Corinthians 12:13). They, like Israel before them, were partakers of the same spiritual food and drink in the Lord's Supper. "The cup of blessing which we bless" is the cup in the Lord's Supper (1 Corinthians 11:25). The word *eulogeo* means to bless or thank God for something. This word is used interchangeably with the word *eucharisteo* in the Gospel accounts of the feeding of the five thousand, the feeding of the four thousand, and the institution of the Lord's Supper (Matthew 14:19; 15:36; 26:26; Mark 6:41; 14:22–23; Luke 9:16; 22:17–19; 24:30, 53). To "bless" something means to praise or thank God for something. The section called *Berakoth* or "blessings" in the Mishnah talks about the various prayers of thanksgiving that were said by the congregations of Jews in Jesus's day. Each Lord's day, the Corinthian church and all other churches of Christ shared in these blessings or thanksgivings at the Lord's table.

Paul says the "cup of blessing" is a *koinonia,* a sharing, a participation, or a fellowship in the blood of Christ. The participation in the cup of wine was symbolic of a spiritual participation in the cleansing blood of Christ. There was an understood spiritual undertone to the participation in the cup. This was done by people who were spiritually connected to Christ and to his soul-cleansing blood. The participation in the "bread of affliction" (Deuteronomy 16:3) was also a spiritual thing. Only those who actually were part of the body of Christ and claimed the body of Christ as their sacrifice could participate in the loaf at the Lord's Supper. By participation in this rite, the participant was claiming a personal spiritual connection to Christ and his redemptive work. There was no separating the act and the spiritual connections proclaimed in that act. Paul is trying to show that the same kind of thing was true for those who participated in the sacrificial meat of the pagans (Justin Martyr, Apology I. 65–67). To participate in the Lord's Supper if one does not have that spiritual connection with Christ is a lie. To invite the unbaptized to participate is to compromise the fundamental teaching about salvation. The unbaptized do not participate in the body and blood of Christ. We need to invite people to be baptized into the redemptive death of Christ (Romans 6:3, 5; 1 Corinthians 12:13; Colossians 2:12–13). Then we should invite them to participate in the fellowship of the Lord's Supper. We have a responsibility to teach this clearly and lovingly in the assemblies of the Lord's church!

First Corinthians 10:18–22

> Look at Israel according to the flesh. Are not those who eat the sacrifices sharers from the altar? What, then, shall I say? That what is sacrificed to an idol is anything or that an idol is anything? But on the other hand, the

things they sacrifice, they sacrifice to demons and not to God, and I do not want you to be participants with the demons! You are not able to drink the cup of the Lord and the cup of demons (at the same time) are you? You are not able to have a share at the Lord's table and the table of demons (at the same time) are you? Or shall we cause the Lord to be jealous? Are we stronger than he is?

Paul now compares the practice of Israel with the practice of the pagans. In the Hebrew Scriptures, many of the sacrifices brought by the people involved sacrificial meals. In the first chapter of First Samuel, we find Elkanah and his family going up to the tabernacle at Shiloh to sacrifice to the Lord (1 Samuel 1:3). In doing this, there was a sacrificial meal, and the family members received portions of the sacrifice to eat (1 Samuel 1:4–5). The priests also participated in the sacrifices of the people, and in the time of Elkanah's family, the evil priests Hophni and Phinehas were taking more than their share of the sacrifices from the people (1 Samuel 2:12–14). These sacrificial meals were common (Leviticus 6:26; 7:15, etc.). Those who offered the sacrifices, both people and priests, were participants or sharers in the meat that was offered. Part of the sacrifice was consumed on the altar. That was considered God's part in the "feast." Part of the animal was eaten by the people and the priests. The people saw themselves as eating a fellowship meal with God. The sacrifice was a proclamation of their good relationship with God or a proclamation that they were again accepted into God's fellowship because of their sin offering. The participation in the sacrificial meal was very much connected with the fact that the sacrifice and its benefits were specifically applicable to the participants. They connected or reconnected with God through the sacrifice and through the meal. Only those for whom the sacrifice was brought participated. So it makes no sense for those who cannot claim the sacrifice to participate in the meal!

When the pagans made their sacrifices, they were doing so to connect with the demonic powers that stood behind the pagan cults. They were sacrificing their animals to "the gods," the *Elohim*, the "mighty beings" of darkness. These mighty beings are called demons by Paul. Paul understands the command "You shall have no other gods *before me*" and the warning "the Lord your God is a jealous God" to be applicable to his readers because it is based on a fundamental understanding of God's nature (Exodus 20:1–5). He asks the questions rhetorically. How can we drink the cup of the Lord Jesus and the cup of demons at the same time? The answer is, "We cannot!" We will make God jealous if we believe what he said in Exodus 20. When he asks, "Are we stronger than he is?" the obvious answer is, "Of course not!" We do not want to risk the wrath of God like the Israelites did in the desert! Therefore, 1 Corinthians 10:14, is still the bottom line of the entire discussion in chapters 8–10. "Flee from idolatry!" We must not flirt carelessly with those things we know to be dangerous temptations. We must flee!

First Corinthians 10:23–26

> "All things are lawful," but not all things are beneficial. "All things are lawful," but, not all things build (people) up! Let no one seek his own interest but that of the other (person). Eat whatever is sold at the meat market, asking no questions for the sake of conscience. For, "The earth is the Lord's, and the fullness of it (as well)."

This is reminiscent of 1 Corinthians 6:12ff where the Corinthians were asserting the idea, "All things are lawful for me," but Paul countered with God's commands. While they may have demanded their "right" to eat sacrificial meat, Paul reminds them that exercising their "right" might not really be beneficial for the salvation and spiritual edification of others. He commands the Corinthians not to seek their own interests but to look out for the spiritual interests of others. This is very similar to Paul's admonition in Philippians 2:4ff. It is a repeat of his exhortation in 1 Corinthians 9:19–22 where he stated that he enslaved himself to the needs of others, putting his own preferences on hold so that he might save others. If they choose to eat the meat, let them do so without knowing its origin. All of the living creatures God created are given to man for food (Genesis 9:4ff; 1 Timothy 4:4–5). Meat is just meat, but…

First Corinthians 10:27–28

> If anyone who is an unbeliever invites you and you want to go, eat what is set before you without asking questions for the sake of conscience. But if anyone should say, "This is temple food," do not eat for the sake of the one who made it known and for the sake of conscience. I say this not just about your own conscience but for that of the other, so that my freedom is not condemned by another's conscience.

If an unbeliever who has invited one of the Corinthians reveals that the food on the table is "temple food" that has been offered in pagan worship, Paul commands that the Christian decline to eat. This decision is made for the sake of the unbeliever, so the unbeliever will know that the Christian will not knowingly have fellowship with any other higher being besides the Creator. In addition, the decision to abstain is made for the sake of the believer's conscience, so that the believer does not incur guilt for provoking God to jealousy! Also, while the believer may think he/she has a "right" or the "freedom" to do something (like eating meat anywhere), Paul does not want other people seeing the behavior of Christians and judging that behavior to be against Christian principles.

First Corinthians 10:30–11:1

> If I partake with gratitude, why am I slandered over that for which I give thanks? Therefore, whether you eat or drink or whatever you do, do all things for the glory of God! Do not present any reason for stumbling to Jews or to Greeks or to the church of God! Just as I always in every way seek not to please myself but I seek what is beneficial to the many, so that they might be saved! Be imitators of me as I also am of Christ!

Paul seems to anticipate the argument of those who insisted on their right to eat temple food when he asks the question, "If I partake with thanksgiving (to God), why am I slandered for that over which I have given thanks?" The fact that one thanks God for the food does not remove the fact that the food is closely associated with paganism and pagan rites. Paul has already asked how one can participate in the table of the Lord and the table of demons at the same time. His directive is only to eat if one can do so and bring glory to God. One should not eat if doing so causes God to be jealous and his people to be slandered as idolaters. Paul insists that he chooses his actions, not based on his own desires, but based on what is spiritually beneficial to everyone else "so that they may be saved." It is in this unselfish behavior, looking out for the spiritual good of others, that Paul asks the Corinthians to imitate him as he tries to imitate the unselfish Christ. Though the people who eventually divided the letter into chapters and verses placed the last statement in chapter 11, "Be imitators of me as I am of Christ" is clearly intended to be the conclusion of the discussion in chapters 8–10.

Reflections on Chapter 10

1. Why do you think Paul brings up the eating and drinking of the Israelites in 1 Corinthians 10:1–2 (see 1 Corinthians 9:1–2)?
2. What kind of eating and drinking is in view in 1 Corinthians 10:7?
3. In the context of the discussion in chapters 8–10, what does Paul mean when he says, "Flee from idolatry"?
4. Compare what it would take to "flee from idolatry" with what it would take to "flee from fornication" (1 Corinthians 6:18; 10:14).
5. How is Christian participation in the Lord's Supper similar to the pagan's participation in a pagan meal?
6. How is the Christian's participation in the Lord's Supper similar to Jewish participation in a sacrificial meal?
7. What reason does Paul give for abstaining from temple meat in 1 Corinthians 10:20–22?
8. If the statement "Be imitators of me, as I am of Christ" belongs to the discussion of chapter 10 instead of the discussion in chapter 11, then what is the basic message for us?

11

First Corinthians 11:2

> I praise you because you all remember me,
> and just as I delivered the traditions to you, you
> hold fast (to them).

Paul held a unique position among the Corinthians. He was their spiritual father in the gospel (1 Corinthians 4:15–16). He was the one who first taught them the gospel of Christ and brought them to salvation (1 Corinthians 6:11; 16:15–16; 2 Corinthians 3:1–3). Paul was also an apostle of Christ and demonstrated the power and authority of his apostleship among them (1 Corinthians 2:4–5; 2 Corinthians 12:12). As he told the Thessalonians, he expected all those he taught to hold firmly to the traditions he received from the Lord Jesus and passed on to them (1 Corinthians 11:23; 15:3; 2 Thessalonians 2:15). These were not human traditions, passed down simply from humans to other humans. They were divine traditions, passed down from Christ, to the apostles, and to all believers (see John 13:20; 20:21).

First Corinthians 11:3–5

> And I want you to know that the head of
> every man is Christ, and the man is the head
> of the woman, and God is the head of Christ.

> Every man praying or prophesying having his head covered is shaming his head. Every woman praying or prophesying while her head is uncovered is shaming her head.

The order of creation suggests the headship Paul explains here. God created the man from the dust of the ground (Genesis 2:7). God saw that it was not good for the man to be alone, so he created a "helper to be his counterpart" (Genesis 2:18). Paul refers to this order of headship in 1 Timothy 2:11–13. It seems to be because of this principle of headship that Paul gives the instructions about head coverings for women in the assembly. The difficulty to the reader of Scripture comes in the fact that these requirements are not repeated in Paul's instructions about dress elsewhere, nor are they repeated by any of the other apostles. To be sure, the principle of modesty is repeated in 1 Timothy 2:9 to the Christians at Ephesus, and it is taught by Peter in 1 Peter 3:3–4. It is the specific application of those principles given in Corinth that is not repeated elsewhere.

This causes one to think that there may have been particular cultural or circumstantial reasons why Paul insisted on the veiling of women in Corinth. Perhaps it was the prevalence of cult prostitutes from the temple of Aphrodite or other temples in the city. Is Paul telling the men of Jewish background they need not wear the *tallit*, the prayer shawl that some Jewish men wear over their heads? Is this part of an attempt to counter the practice of many Greek pagan women who participated in pagan cultic activities with heads uncovered (Marlowe, Feb. 2005)? We will comment later on Paul's statement that the covering must be in place "because of the angels" (1 Corinthians 11:10).

In any case, the man who prays with his head covered dishonors or shames "his head" or Christ. The woman who prays with her head uncovered shames or dishonors "her head" or her

COMMENTARY ON FIRST CORINTHIANS

husband. Why is this the case? Is it because of immodesty and moral disgrace? Why does the man dishonor Christ if his head is covered? Is it because this somehow shows lack of leadership on his part? This passage does talk about women praying and prophesying. It is likely that the women were praying aloud with the church in corporate prayers said together in the manner of some synagogue blessings. The man would go before the ark of scrolls and lift up his hands to lead the congregation, and they would repeat aloud certain blessings or prayers from the psalms or from the Torah. The text also mentions women prophesying. They may have been doing this in the assembly, but in 1 Corinthians 14:34–35, Paul tells them to stop it (see comments on 1 Corinthians 14:34ff).

First Corinthians 11:5c–6

> For it is one and the same if she is shaven!
> For if a woman is unveiled, let her also be
> shorn! And if it is disgraceful for a woman to
> be shaven or shorn, let her be veiled!

Isaiah 3:17, 24 pictures Jerusalem as a lovely, haughty woman who is punished and degraded by God with baldness and poverty. Baldness is seen as debasing. Since Paul equates baldness with being unveiled in the sense that it is *aischron,* "shameful," there must have been a moral disgrace of some kind in being unveiled, especially in Corinth. That disgrace was then reflected on the husband to some degree as if the woman was disrespecting her husband by being unveiled.

First Corinthians 11:7–10

> For a man, being the image and glory of God, ought not have his head covered. But the woman is the glory of man. For the man is not from woman but the woman is from the man. For the man was not created because of the woman, but the woman because of the man. For this reason, the woman ought to have (a symbol of) authority on (her) head because of the angels.

This argument returns to the order and purpose of creation. The man was created first, and the woman was created to be a helper for the man (Genesis 2:7, 18). The two certainly complement one another, and one is not complete without the other. But there is an order in creation. Man is primary. The *exousian* or "symbol of authority" seems to be a reference to the head covering worn by the woman. The word is literally just *authority* or *power* but is said to be "upon the head," and the context here is the covering worn by the woman. The reason the woman should have this covering on her head is "because of the angels." This is probably a reference to the pre-flood rebellion of those angels called Watchers who, according to the Jews, took wives from the daughters of men and were largely responsible for the great wickedness before the flood. There was considerable discussion of this in the Jewish literature between the testaments. In Genesis 6, we have the Hebrew expression, *Bene-ha-elohim*, "the sons of God," which is found only there and in the Book of Job. In Job, the expression clearly has reference to the angels (Job 1:6; 2:1; 38:7). Peter gives a successive order of events from Genesis beginning with the "angels that sinned," followed by the flood, then the rescue of Lot and the destruction of Sodom and Gomorrah (2 Peter 2:4ff). So Peter seems to see the "angels that sinned" as something that took place in the narrative of Genesis. Jude recounts the angels who left their proper habitation, then mentions Sodom and Gomorrah who, "*in like manner with these* went after strange flesh" (Jude 6–7). The Jewish book of First Enoch gives a detailed story about how the Watchers lusted after women and took wives from them (1 Enoch 6:1–8:4). The intertestamental *Testaments of the Twelve Patriarchs* gives a description of the same events and makes a clear moral application to the manner in which fornication results from the immodest dress of women (Testament of Reuben 5:1–7).

All of this seems to fit perfectly with the context here in First Corinthians and lends support to why the woman should wear the head covering, showing her modesty and the dedication of her person to her own husband. The second century Latin father, Tertullian, commented on 1 Corinthians 11:10, saying, "For if, on account of the angels, those to wit, whom we read of as having fallen from God and heaven on account of lusting after females, which such angels yearned after" (On the Veiling of Virgins VII). Having said all of that, it seems likely that Paul's phrase, "because of the angels," is meant to be a moral reminder to motivate modesty on the part of women, so they will show that they belong only to their own husbands or are under the protection and care of their own fathers.

First Corinthians 11:11–15

> So neither is the woman without the man,
> nor the man without the woman in the Lord.
> For just as the woman came from the man, so
> also the man comes through the woman. And
> all things come from God! Judge these things
> among yourselves! Is it proper for a woman
> to pray to God uncovered? Does not even

> long-standing custom teach you that if a man
> wears long hair it is a dishonor for him? But if a
> woman wears long hair it is a glory to her! But
> her hair is given to her as a covering.

The fact that there is an order of priority and headship does not mean that women are not vitally important in God's plan. Neither man or woman is complete without the other. "It is not good for the man to be alone" (Genesis 2:18). Both man and woman are vital to God's plan for the family (Genesis 2:24). That being said, there is modesty and propriety to consider. Paul uses two different words to try to communicate this matter of propriety. The first word is *prepon*, which means something that is fitting or proper. This word is also used in Ephesians 5:3 to describe behaviors that are not fitting or proper for people with godly, Christian values. The second word Paul uses is *phusis*, which can mean either that which is established by birth or natural endowment, or something that has been established through long-standing practice. The second alternative is probably the meaning here because men and women will grow long hair if they are left in their base natural state. It was against long-standing practice for men to wear their hair long in the culture to which Paul was writing. It was not seen as proper or normal to do so. On the other hand, it was generally accepted that long hair on a woman was a glory to her and something beautiful. Paul's point is that it goes against accepted practice (especially in the Corinthian culture) for a Christian woman to pray to God unveiled. Again, it is quite remarkable that Paul did not place the same demands on the Ephesians, nor did Peter place the same demands on the women of the Black Sea region (1 Timothy 2:9, 3:2–4; 1 Peter 3:3).

First Corinthians 11:16

> If anyone seems to be contentious, we
> have no such custom, neither the churches of
> God.

Paul must be talking about the custom of casting off social
propriety and modesty because he did not enjoin the wearing of a
head covering on women in other locations, but did demand that
they dress modestly and in a way that did not draw undue attention to themselves. So the churches of God were ordered by the
apostles to maintain proper, modest, culturally appropriate dress
in the assemblies.

First Corinthians 11:17–19

> Now in giving you this command I do
> not praise you, as you are coming together not
> for the better but for the worse. For first of all,
> when you come together in the assembly, I hear
> divisions exist among you, and I partly believe
> it. For there must be factions among you, so
> that the approved ones may become evident
> among you.

These divisions or factions were mentioned in 1 Corinthians
1:10ff, 3:1–2, and 4:12 along with hints of the same in 6:1ff. The
leaders of these factions are "the approved ones," *hoi dokimoi,* of
verse 19. These are the ones who were using the weekly assembly of the church to show how many followers they had. They
were doing this by forming clear and distinct groups within the
assembly, in contradiction to the unity we enjoy in Christ. The
word *ekklesia* in this passage refers to the gathering of Christians

as in Acts 20:7 and Hebrews 10:25. We have the verb, *sunercho-mai*, "come together," in 1 Corinthians 11:17, 18, 20, 33, 34 as well as in 1 Corinthians 14:23, 26. This passage is about what was actually happening and what is supposed to happen when the church comes together in the Lord's Day assembly. This is further supported by the early references to the same assembly in Didache 14:1 and Justin Martyr, Apology 1:65–67.

First Corinthians 11:20–21

> When, therefore, you come together in
> one place, it is not to eat the Lord's Supper. For
> as you eat, each one takes his own supper, while
> this one is hungry and that one gets drunk.

Christ designed the Lord's Supper to be a united fellowship meal for the body of Christ (1 Corinthians 10:16–17). The contrast here is between "the Lord's Supper" and each person's "own supper." This supper is not a selfish, self-indulgent thing. It is an unselfish inclusion of all those who have been baptized into the body of Christ (1 Corinthians 10:17; 12:13). Some were overindulging, and others were being left out. Factions were prominent. Instead of a spiritual sharing, showing the solidarity of the body of Christ, it was a selfish display of division and disunity.

First Corinthians 11:22

> Do you not have houses to eat and drink
> in? Or, do you despise the assembly of God,
> and shame those who have nothing. What shall
> I say to you? Shall I praise you? In this I will
> not praise you!

The selfish meals of individuals and their friends can be eaten at home, but the assembly of the body of Christ is the place for the unity meal, the fellowship meal, the sharing and participation of all baptized believers in the body and blood of Christ. The repetition of the word "come together" in this section of the letter emphasizes the fact that the Lord's Supper is designed to be a "together thing." It is for the assembled church to demonstrate its unity and participation in Christ's redemptive work. Paul is not praising this divisive behavior, but is shaming them for it! This passage has nothing to do with the propriety of eating meals in buildings. This passage is about the kind of meal that is to be eaten in the Lord's Day assembly. The *ekklesia* never refers to a building in the New Testament!

First Corinthians 11:23

> For I received from the Lord, what I also passed on to you, that the Lord Jesus, on the night he was betrayed, took bread, and when he had given thanks, he broke it and said, "This is my body which is for you. Do this in remembrance of me!"

The word for a tradition is *paradosis*, which comes from the same root as *paradidomi*. The verb means to pass something on to someone else. Paul uses the word *paralambano*, "receive from" to indicate the source of what he "passed on" to the churches. Paul received things from Christ and passed them on to others. These were divine traditions, not human traditions. These are the traditions to which we must hold fast (1 Corinthians 15:3; Galatians 1:11–12; 2 Thessalonians 2:15). The rite or ritual of the supper instituted during the last Passover feast before the death of Christ is a rite for the church. Jesus took what Moses called "the bread of affliction" (Deuteronomy 16:3). What once called to mind the affliction or suffering of Israel in slavery now calls to mind the suffering of Christ that satisfied the justice of God (Isaiah 53:10–11). Jesus, referring to the "bread of affliction," said, "This is my body, which is for you!" The word *broken* is not in the early manuscripts. John makes it clear, in spiritual fulfillment of Exodus 12:46, that Jesus was the spiritual paschal lamb, and his bones were not broken (John 19:33–36). The "breaking" of the loaf is not significant in the ritual. Jesus did the same thing when he fed the 5, 000 and the 4, 000 so that he could divide up the loaf and distribute it. The giving of thanks, showing gratitude toward God for his loving sacrifice of his Son is a central feature. In addition, the participation of all baptized believers to show their fellowship in that redemptive work is at the heart of the ritual we perpetuate in the church of Christ. The words, "This is my body," are not magic words designed to work a miracle on the unleavened bread. These words in Latin are *Hoc est corpus meum.* In medieval times, people came to see these words as an incantation by which the bread was changed into the literal flesh of Christ. These words in any language are the words of Christ to remind his people that through his great suffering, we are made righteous in the sight of God. By participating in the bread, we show that his body, his sacrifice, is our sacrifice to God. By that same participation, we show that we are part of his body, the church that was purchased with his own blood. The body of Christ was offered for us once for all time (Hebrews 10:5, 10). Jesus told us to repeat the rite of giving thanks and partaking of the bread in remembrance of him. Like the Passover in Exodus 12–13, our sacred meal is a reminder of who we are as Christians and the price that was paid for our redemption.

First Corinthians 11:25

> Likewise, also the cup after the supper, saying, "This cup is the New Covenant in my blood. Do this, as often as you drink it, in remembrance of me." For as often as you eat this bread and drink this cup, you proclaim the Lord's death until he comes!

The New Covenant is that which was promised in Jeremiah 31:31–34. It is contrasted in that prophecy with "the covenant which I made with your fathers in the day that I took them by the hand to bring them out of the land of Egypt, which covenant they broke, although I was a husband to them, says the Lord" (Jeremiah 31:31–32). A covenant is a pact or an agreement between two or more parties. The agreement or covenant often called The Old Covenant is the agreement made between God and Israel at Mount Sinai. Moses clearly read all of God's stipulations for this agreement to the people of Israel, and they responded by saying, "All that the Lord has spoken, we will do and be obedient" (Exodus 24:7). God offered the pact or the "deal" to Israel, and they accepted it. Then, the deal was made official when Moses splattered the sacrificial blood on the people and poured the other half of the blood on the altar. The agreement was thus signed in blood, the blood of the covenant (Hebrews 9:18). The New Covenant, foretold by God in Jeremiah 31, is an agreement between God and each individual who trusts in Christ's death and resurrection and accepts Jesus Christ as Lord and King. God offers the New Covenant to people in the preaching of the gospel (Luke 24:47; 2 Thessalonians 2:14). Those who obey the gospel by imitating the death, burial, and resurrection of Christ accept God's offer. Their hearts are sprinkled clean by the blood of Christ as their bodies are washed in the pure waters of baptism (Hebrew 10:22). When we participate in the cup at the Lord's

Supper, it is a sharing or participation in the blood of Christ (1 Corinthians 10:16). We are acknowledging our participation in the sacrificial blood of Christ. We are sharing in the symbol, the fruit of the vine, but proclaiming our share in the blood which keeps cleansing our sins every day. At the same time, we are mentally and spiritually renewing and affirming our covenant with God based on the death of Christ. So the Lord's Supper is a sharing, a participation, a fellowship, a *koinonia* with Christ and with all others who share this relationship with Christ. As we do this together week after week, we are proclaiming to the world that we believe in the power of the redemptive death of Christ! We proclaim this faith every Lord's Day "until he comes." As we eat the Lord's Supper, we look forward to the day when Jesus returns and we can "sit down at the table with Abraham, Isaac, and Jacob in the kingdom of God" (Matthew 8:11). In this passage when Paul speaks of eating "this bread" and drinking "this cup," he is making a distinction between this particular eating and drinking and all other eating and drinking. In 1 Corinthians 10:20–21, he made a clear distinction between the "cup of the Lord and the cup of demons." He made a clear distinction between "the table of the Lord and the table of demons." In 1 Corinthians 11:20–22, he makes a clear distinction between "the Lord's supper" and one's "own supper." It is only "this bread" and "this cup" as opposed to all others in which we remember the redemptive work of Christ, have fellowship together in that redemptive work, and proclaim our unending trust in that redemptive work!

First Corinthians 11:27

> So then, whoever might eat the bread or drink the cup of the Lord in an unworthy manner, is guilty of the body and blood of the Lord. So, let a man put himself to the test, and in this way let him eat of the bread and drink of the cup.

Contextually, the "unworthy manner" of taking the Lord's Supper is the divisive, factious, selfish manner in which the Corinthians were doing it. They were making it impossible to take the Lord's Supper as God wanted it to be taken. The Greek word *anaxios*, "unworthily," is an adverb, and modifies the words *eat* and *drink*. It describes the way we go about eating and drinking. It does not describe the soul of the person who is involved. To do it the way the Corinthians were doing it is disrespectful of the purpose and intent with which Jesus instituted it. The Lord's Supper is a fellowship or communion! The Lord's Supper is a remembrance! The Lord's Supper is a communal proclamation of our common faith in the redemptive work of Christ! The way or manner in which we go about it should reflect and respect those things! As the writer of Hebrews expressed to a Jewish audience, they should beware of "trampling underfoot the Son of God," or "counting the blood of the covenant with which you were sanctified as an unholy thing." The Corinthians needed to be careful lest they make this most sacred rite into something the very opposite of what God intended! When it says, "Let a man put himself to the test," Paul is calling for an attitude check. He wants them not to be "puffed up on behalf of one man and against another" (1 Corinthians 4:6). He wants them to be unified in Christ, not divided (1 Corinthians 1:10–14). He wants them to respect the unity of the body of Christ, not destroy it (1 Corinthians 3:16–17). So in examining one's self, Paul wants the person to form an attitude of humility, acceptance of all who are in Christ, and reflection on one's relationship with God and with other Christians!

First Corinthians 11:29

> For he that eats and drinks without considering the body, eats and drinks judgment to himself!

This passage is almost reminiscent of Old Testament wrath. It brings to mind people like Nadab and Abihu, Korah, and others who did not show proper respect for the commands of God. When Paul speaks of not considering or discerning "the body," it is likely that he is talking about the church, the congregation, the body of Christ into which we are all baptized (1 Corinthians 12:13). This is precisely what the Corinthians were doing! They were eating and drinking selfishly, proudly, divisively, and in total disregard of their brothers and sisters in Christ. They were not discerning or considering the body of Christ. To do this was to disrespect the rite of the Lord's Supper and to do it in a totally unworthy manner! Those who keep doing this are not going to escape the judgment of God!

First Corinthians 11:30

> For this reason, many among you are sick, weak, and several have even died! But if we would examine ourselves, we would not be judged! When we are judged by the Lord we are disciplined, so that we might not be condemned with the world!

The phrase "for this reason" goes back to the fact that the Corinthians were eating and drinking judgment upon themselves because they were conducting the Lord's Supper in a totally unworthy or disrespectful manner. Evidently, God was exacting judgment on them in the form of sickness, weakness, and even death in some cases. This is quite consistent with God's behavior in Old Testament times. Paul seems to imply that these things were consequences of the Corinthians' offending behavior in the Lord's Supper. Perhaps 1 Corinthians 3:17 is the most appropriate comment where Paul says, "If anyone destroys the temple of God, him will God destroy, for the temple of God is holy and that is what you are!" However, if the Corinthians could accept God's discipline, correct their abuses during the Lord's Supper, and correct their factious behavior in general, they could rid themselves of these temporal judgments. This brings up the notion of whether God may still bring temporal judgments on people to get them to repent today. Some passages, like Revelation 8–9, seem to suggest that he does so from time to time! In any case, Paul urged them to correct their divisive behavior so they would not end up being condemned with the rest of the ungodly world!

First Corinthians 11:33

> So then, my brothers, when you come together to eat, wait for one another! If anyone is hungry, let him eat at home, so that you might not come together resulting in judgment! And the rest of the things I will set in order when I come!

This admonition is the solution to the problem that began to be presented in 1 Corinthians 11:17. Instead of making the Lord's Supper a display of disunity, division, and factions, they should "wait for one another." If they were wanting a common meal, eaten to satisfy their own physical hunger, they should do that at home, not in the assembly (1 Corinthians 11:22). They should consider everyone in the assembly as equal sharers in the body and blood of Christ and treat one another accordingly in the Lord's Supper. In this way, they would be "discerning the body" or considering the entire church membership as fellow participants in the supper and in the redemptive work of Christ. Paul planned to make a visit to the Corinthians and suggested that he would set in order whatever else might need to be corrected at that time.

Reflections on Chapter 11

1. What is the order of headship Paul describes in the beginning of this discussion about dress in the assembly?
2. When it says that the woman who prays unveiled "dishonors her head," who or what is the "head" she dishonors?
3. Are there any passages in the Old Testament Scriptures that speak of the implications of women being shorn or going bald?
4. What is similar and what is different from Paul's instructions to the Corinthians in the instructions he gives to the women in Ephesus and those Peter gives to the women in the Black Sea region (1 Timothy 2:9–10; 1 Peter 3:1–5).
5. To what situation do the instructions given in 1 Corinthians 11:17–34 apply?
6. What is different when comparing one's own supper to the Lord's Supper?
7. What exactly was the "unworthy manner" in which the Corinthians were eating the Lord's Supper?
8. What are Paul's final instructions regarding the Lord's Supper in 1 Corinthians 11:33–34?

12

First Corinthians 12:1

> Now concerning those things that are from the Spirit, I do not want you to be ignorant. You know that when you were gentiles you were led away, following after idols that do not speak. Wherefore, I make known to you that no one who is speaking by the Spirit of God, says, "Jesus is anathema," and no one can say, "Jesus is Lord," except by the Holy Spirit.

The formula "now concerning," *peri de*, shows that Paul is now moving to yet another matter about which the Corinthians had asked him in their letter (1 Corinthians 7:1, 25; 8:1; 16:1, etc.). Literally, this discussion is about "things of the Spirit." It is probably correct to infer from what follows that he is speaking of those *charismata* or gifts given by the Spirit to empower Christians to carry out various ministries in the church (1 Corinthians 12:4, 7, 11, 18, 28). Paul is contrasting the things given by the Spirit to the church with the spiritual experiences of the pagans in and around Corinth. Pagans also had people they called prophets or oracles who supposedly spoke messages from the gods. Perhaps some of these pagan oracles were saying things like "Jesus is cursed" to turn pagans away from Christ (see Romans 9:3, 1 Corinthians 16:22, and Galatians 1:8 on Paul's use of *anathema*). Those who truly acknowledged Jesus as Lord did so because of the revelation of the Holy Spirit through the apostles and others who brought the gospel of Christ (Acts 2:36; Romans 10:9; 1 Timothy 6:12–15). Paul's topic in the following section of this letter is how the various manifestations of the Holy Spirit are supposed to work in Christ's church.

First Corinthians 12:4

> There are diversities of gifts, but the same Spirit. There are diversities of ministries, but the same Lord. There are diversities of workings, but the same God who works all things in every (individual). To each one is given the manifestation of the Spirit for the common benefit.

As in the rest of this book, the matter of spiritual gifts and how they were being mishandled goes back to the root problem of faction and disunity. Paul describes these spiritual things given to church members in four different ways in this passage. First, he calls them gifts, *charismata*. This is the same term he uses in Romans 12:6 where he says we have "*gifts* differing according to the grace that has been given to us." Paul uses the phrase, "the grace that has been given to me (us)" in reference to divine gifts of some sort, including Paul's own gift of apostleship (e.g. Romans 12:3, 6; Galatians 2:9; Ephesians 3:2, 7, 8; 4:7). So the gifts given by God differ, but the same Spirit gives those gifts. The second word Paul uses is *diakonion*, ministries. This shows the reason why the Spirit bestows these gifts on various Christians. The purpose is to equip the saints for the work of ministry, for the building up of the body of Christ (Ephesians 4:12). The gifts are to be used in carrying out ministries. Still, though the ministries in which these gifts are used differ, it is the same Lord Jesus that is behind the different ministries. Thirdly, Paul describes these spiritual things as "workings," *energemata*. This word is often used by Paul to talk about how God uses his power to work through human beings. The same word is used for how God worked through Peter and Paul as apostles (Galatians 2:8–9). The word is also used with reference to the working of God when he raised Christ from the dead (Ephesians 1:19–20). A spiritual gift is one way that God works through individuals to accomplish some ministry in the church. Finally, Paul calls these spiritual things "manifestations of the Spirit" (1 Corinthians 12:7). The Holy Spirit manifests himself in different ways through different people, but always for the common good of the body of Christ. Paul's point is that God creates the diversity in the body in order to cover the scope of ministries that need to be carried out, just as the human body has many parts with many functions, but they all work together for the common good of the body (1 Corinthians 12:7, 11, 18). The parts of the body do not compete with one another, but cooperate with one another.

First Corinthians 12:8–11

> For to one is given through the Spirit a message of wisdom, and to another a message of knowledge by the same Spirit. To another, faith, by the same Spirit, to another gifts of healing by the same Spirit, to another the working of mighty deeds, to another prophecy, to another the discerning of Spirits, to another (various) kinds of tongues, to another translation of tongues. In all these things one and the same Spirit is working, distributing to each one as he wills.

Notice how many times Paul repeats the mantra "by the same Spirit," just as in 1 Corinthians 12:4–6, he speaks of the same Spirit, the same Lord, and the same God. There is not a different power working in the various gifts, but the same power, no matter the gift. There is unity in this God-ordained diversity. The body illustration is used in this chapter as it is in Romans 12 and Ephesians 4. The different functions of the body parts are compared to members of the church with different gifts. In each case, the different functions all work for the common good of the body. It is difficult to determine the exact nature of some of these gifts. What was the gift of faith and how did it differ from the faith we all have in Christ? What was the gift of *dunameis,* "mighty deeds" or "miracles"? What did all this entail? What is the difference between a message of wisdom, a message of knowledge, and the gift of divine revelation through prophecy? This is unclear. When we look at Acts 2:6, 8, 11, it seems clear that these tongues were known languages, languages actually spoken natively by groups of people. They were languages that were previously unknown to the speakers. The gift of *hermeneia,* or "translation," was the ability to translate the message delivered by the one speaking in the foreign language. John describes the "discerning of spirits" in 1 John 4:1 where he speaks of testing the spirits to determine whether they are from God or they are demonic spirits speaking through a false prophet. While we may not be able to precisely define each of these gifts listed by Paul, the point is clear that the Spirit of God distributes the gifts for the mutual benefit of the body of Christ (1 Corinthians 12:11, 18). The sampling of gifts listed in 1 Corinthians 12:8–11 is only a partial list. Several others are listed in 1 Corinthians 12:28ff as well as in Romans 12:6ff and Ephesians 4:11. Paul makes no distinction between those gifts that some today categorize as "miraculous" as opposed to those that we often categorize as "non-miraculous." All of them were simply abilities given by God to individual Christians.

First Corinthians 12:12–13

> For just as there is one body and it has
> many members, and all the members of the
> body being many, are still one body, in the
> same way is Christ. For in one Spirit we were all
> baptized into one body, whether Jew or Greek,
> whether slave or free, and we were all given the
> one Spirit to drink.

In context, this is Paul's explanation for how Christians gain access to the gifts of the Spirit. All of us who are members of the body of Christ, the church, were baptized into the body when we were baptized into Christ (Romans 6:3–4, 17–18; Galatians 3:27; Colossians 2:12–13). Paul uses terminology differently than Luke. For Paul, baptism in water is also baptism in the Spirit. All who are baptized into Christ are granted access to "drink from the one Spirit." As we do that, by allowing the influence of God's Spirit to permeate our lives, God distributes gifts of one kind or another to us. In Ephesians, Paul emphasizes again that every single Christian is given spiritual gifts to use in the ministry of the church. "To each one is this grace given, according to the measure of the gift of Christ" (Ephesians 4:7). "He ascended on high and led captivity captive and he gave gifts to men" (Ephesians 4:8). "He gave some apostles, some prophets, some evangelists, some shepherds and teachers to equip the saints for the work of ministry" (Ephesians 4:11–12). In 1 Corinthians 12, Romans 12, and Ephesians 4, the gifts are the divinely aided functions ordained by God for the various members of the body of Christ.

Having made these general statements, it does appear that there were some gifts given only by the laying on of the hands of the apostles, unless there was a direct divine intervention like in Acts 2 and Acts 10. Paul mentions giving Timothy a gift, "Which is in you by the laying on of my hands" (2 Timothy 1:6). Though Luke does not use the terminology of "spiritual gifts," he seems to have reference to certain gifts of the Spirit when he says, "When Simon saw that it was through the laying on of the apostles' hands the Holy Spirit was given, he offered them money" (Acts 8:18). Luke does not specify what gifts were under consideration in Acts 8, but in Acts 19:6, he specifically mentions tongues and prophecy as gifts given by the laying on of Paul's hands. This is even more interesting when one realizes that Paul mentions three gifts specifically that were only meant to be temporary, namely, tongues, knowledge, and prophecy (1 Corinthians 13:8–10). Two of these are the very ones given by the laying on of Paul's hands. To then conclude that all spiritual gifts were temporary is much more than Scripture says or implies. It does seem that some gifts were given specifically for the confirmation of the word as it was first preached by the apostles (Mark 16:20; Hebrews 2:3–4). One might infer that those gifts given for that purpose have also faded away because that purpose has been accomplished. The theology of Paul, however, remains. That is, that Christ has given gifts to every Christian by virtue of their baptism into Christ.

First Corinthians 12:14–18

> For the body is not one member, but many. If the foot should say, "Because I am not a hand, I am not of the body," it does not for this reason cease to be a part of the body. And if the ear should say, "Because I am not an eye, I am not of the body," it does not for this reason cease to be part of the body! If the whole body were an eye, where would the hearing be? If the whole body was about hearing, where would

the sense of smell be? But now God has placed
the members in the body, just as he wills!

God did not design human bodies nor did he design the church body with only one member, one function. A body is many parts, many functions, working in concert toward common ends. The body needs hands and feet, eyes and ears. All the members are parts of the same body, fed and cleansed by the same blood, but their individual functions are different! God, according to verse 18, is the one who determines the different gifts, the different ministry functions of the individual members of the body of Christ (1 Corinthians 12:7, 11, 18). One of the worst mistakes we make today in the church is trying to convince people that all of us have the same responsibilities in the work of the Lord. Not all people are evangelists or elders or teachers. Some are showers of mercy, managers, helpers, and givers. We have different gifts, but when we put them all together and work toward a common goal, we become as God would have us to be. The body of Christ will always need people with different gifts to carry out God's work!

First Corinthians 12:19–21

If all were one member, where would the
body be? But now, there are many members,
yet one body. The eye cannot say to the hand,
"I have no need of you," and again, the head
cannot say to the feet, "I have no need of you."

Each of us, regardless of our gifts, have need of the others in the body to function as God intended. We need people who have the gift of mercy to fill a vital niche in ministry. We need those who have the gift of organization and management to keep all of the ministries of the church going smoothly. We need those with the gift of giving to help us finance the many works of the Lord. We need those with the gifts of teaching to keep us filled with God's word! We need evangelists to teach the gospel to all who come under our influence. We need shepherds to watch after our souls and care for people spiritually. This list could go on ad infinitum. The bottom line is that the members of the body, regardless of their gifts, need one another and should appreciate one another. They should not be "puffed up on behalf of the one and against another" as they were in Corinth (1 Corinthians 4:6).

First Corinthians 12:22–24

> But much more those members of the body considered to be weaker are necessary, and those (members) of the body considered to be dishonorable, to them are given more abundant honor, and our unseemly parts are treated with greater modesty, while our more presentable parts have no need for this. But God has mixed the body together, so that to those parts of lower status, more abundant honor is given.

Though this part of Paul's argument is a bit hard to follow, it seems that he is talking about the need to pay honor and esteem to even the lowliest members of the body. By showing esteem to those members whose ministries are less public, less known, and less seen by others, we promote unity in the body. God's desire is that all members of the body have encouragement and appreciation from all other members. God wants the "little people" to know they are important, and that their contributions to the ministries of the church are important. This minimizes jealousy and pours cool waters on the fires of competition. Paul explains this in the next phrase.

First Corinthians 12:25–26

> So that there might not be any division
> in the body, but the members might show
> the same degree of care for one another! And
> whenever one member suffers, all the members
> suffer with it! When one member is glorified,
> all the members rejoice with it.

Paul returns to the beginning petition of the book where
he begged the Corinthians to pursue unity of mind and action
(1 Corinthians 1:10). To avoid division and maintain unity, all
members of the body of Christ need attention. All the members
would suffer if neglected. When one member suffers and we rally
to the support of that member, then that member is affirmed and
encouraged because he/she feels appreciated and important in the
eyes of the others. When one member is glorified because of some
success or accomplishment, all the members rejoice with that
member! When others rejoice with us, we also feel affirmed and
appreciated. This kind of atmosphere quells division and competition and encourages cooperation and unity!

First Corinthians 12:27

> You are the body of Christ and individu-
> ally you are members of it! And God has placed
> in the church first apostles, second prophets,
> third teachers, then mighty (deeds), then gifts
> of healing, helpfulness, administration, differ-
> ent kinds of languages.

The previous comments indicate that though one has been
given the gift of apostleship like Paul, and another has only the

gift of helpfulness, every gift and its ministry is important, and all the members should encourage each other and praise the contributions of each one. There does seem to be an order of sorts presented here, with apostles, prophets, and teachers at the top, and the ability to speak in other languages at the bottom. This may be due to the Corinthians' exaltation and preference of the showy gift of tongues when, in actuality, the gifts by which the entire body could be edified were much more important to the growth of the church (1 Corinthians 14:1–5). Again, it seems worth pointing out that Paul makes no distinction between those gifts we call miraculous and those gifts we would classify as non-miraculous. They are all part of the same list, all given by the same God for the building up of the body. As we mentioned earlier, he does later say that some of these gifts were meant by God to be temporary, but he never splits them into categories (1 Corinthians 13:8–10). Then Paul asks some rhetorical questions to show that God wants this diversity of gifts to be present.

First Corinthians 12:29

> All are not apostles, are they? All are not prophets, are they? All are not teachers, are they? All do not have the gift of mighty deeds, do they? All do not have the gifts of healing, do they? All do not speak in different languages, do they? All do not translate, do they? But be zealous for the greater gifts! Still, I show you a more excellent way!

The answer to all of these questions is "No!" We do not all have these gifts. We each have different gifts! God wants it that way (1 Corinthians 12:7, 11, 18, 28). Having said all of this, Paul urges the Corinthians to desire the greater gifts by which others can be edified. He makes it clear that prophecy is much more important for the whole church than tongues because it has the power to instruct, comfort, encourage, and convict the whole church (1 Corinthians 14:1–5, 19, 23). The more excellent way is the way of love, using our gifts unselfishly for the good of all! He makes this identical point in Ephesians 4:16 where he explains that when each member of the body is doing its part, using the unique gifts given to each one, the body builds itself up in love!

Reflections on Chapter Twelve

1. In 1 Corinthians 12:4–6, Paul says there are different
   _____, _____, and _____.
2. In 1 Corinthians 12:4–6, Paul says all of the things mentioned in question 1 are the work of the same _____,
   the same _____, and the same _____.
3. In 1 Corinthians 12:7, the things described in 1 Corinthians
   12:4–6 are called _____ of the Spirit.
4. For what purpose are these things mentioned in 1 Corinthians
   12:4–7 given to the church according to 1 Corinthians 12:7?
5. Who causes the diverse functions of the members of the body
   according to 1 Corinthians 12:11? According to 1 Corinthians
   12:18? According to 1 Corinthians 12:28?
6. According to 1 Corinthians 12:13, how do the members of
   the body gain access to the reservoir of the Spirit?
7. The various members of the body show appreciation for one
   another because if one member suffers, all the rest _____
   with it, and if one member is glorified, all the rest _____
   with it (1 Corinthians 12:26).
8. Which gifts does Paul encourage the people to seek and desire
   (1 Corinthians 12:31)?

13

First Corinthians 13:1–2

> If I speak in the languages of men and angels, but do not have love, I have become a sounding brass or a clanging symbol. And if I have (the gift of) prophecy, and I know all mysteries and all knowledge, and if I have all faith so that mountains are moved, and I do not have love, I am nothing.

Here Paul enumerates several of the gifts mentioned in 1 Corinthians 12:8–10. When he mentions languages of men and angels, this may be a case of hyperbole to show that no matter how amazing and obscure the language one is able to speak, if the ability to speak it is not used unselfishly, it is only noise. Prophecy, *propheteia*, is the ability to receive revelations directly from God and convey those messages to people. The words "the gift of" are supplied by translators. The gift of knowledge is similar to the gift of prophecy and is also listed in 1 Corinthians 12:8–10 as is the gift of faith. This must have been an enhanced, extraordinary ability to trust in the working of God. Without love, this and all other gifts are meaningless. Surely, Solomon had an extreme measure of the gifts of wisdom and knowledge from God (1 Kings 2:29–34).

First Corinthians 13:3

> And if I give away all of my possessions
> and if I hand over my body to be burned, and I
> do not have love, it profits me nothing.

It may be that Paul is here speaking about the gift of giving, which he mentions in Romans 12:8. If God has given one the gift of generosity, and that person does not give out of love, it does the individual no good in the sight of God. Jesus spoke of those who give alms or do acts of benevolence so that they can be seen by other people and says they have no reward from their father in heaven (Matthew 6:1ff). On the other hand, deeds done in love profit both the doer and others!

First Corinthians 13:4

> Love is longsuffering. Love is kind. It is
> not jealous, it is not boastful, it is not puffed
> up. It does not act indecently. It does not seek
> its own (*interests, gratification?*), it does not
> keep a record of evil.

This list tells us what love does in respect to other people. Love is "longsuffering, putting up with one another in love" (Ephesians 4:3). Love does not give up on other people easily, and it keeps giving them chances to change and grow. Love acts kindly as God has been kind to each of us (Ephesians 4:32–5:1). Love is not jealous of the other members of the body, but rejoices with those who rejoice (1 Corinthians 12:26). Love is not boastful and is not puffed up. The verb *phusiao,* meaning puffed up or arrogant, is used in 1 Corinthians 4:6, 18, 19, and 5:2. It is repeated in 1 Corinthians 8:1 where it says that knowledge puffs people up but love builds people up. This word, along with other words for boasting or bragging, describes an attitude problem among some at Corinth. It was a self-centered and self-seeking attitude that made unity all but impossible. Love does not display this attitude. Love does not act indecently. It does not try to take advantage of others sexually. It does not act inappropriately toward others. It does not seek its own interests or its own gratification without regard to others. Love does not keep a record of past wrongs and bring them up to others periodically. Love forgives people and moves on as God has forgiven each of us (Ephesians 4:32).

First Corinthians 13:6–7

> It does not rejoice in unrighteousness, but it rejoices together with the truth. It bears everything, believes everything, hopes everything, endures everything.

Real *agape* never rejoices in unrighteousness or supports unrighteousness. Love rejoices with God's truth and loves what is right (Psalm 15:4). Love is willing to bear all things. It can put up with much hurt, disappointment, and failure. Love tries to believe in others and their potential. Love hopes for the best in others and endures through all circumstances. All of these statements show that love is a commitment to keep on seeking what is in the best interests of others no matter what. This is what Jesus did for us (Philippians 2:4–9).

First Corinthians 13:8

> Love never fails. But if there are (gifts of) prophecy, they shall become useless. If there are (gifts of) languages, they shall cease. If there is

the (gift of) knowledge, it shall become useless. For we know partially and we prophesy partially, but whenever the complete comes, the partial shall become useless.

Prophecy, tongues, and the gift of divinely given knowledge were all gifts listed in 1 Corinthians 12:8–10. These gifts, says Paul, would become useless and cease. The reason for this is explained in the following sentence. At the time Paul wrote First Corinthians, the gifts of prophecy and knowledge gave people the ability to give small revelations from God on various occasions. They were pieces or portions of divine revelation. These small portions of divine revelation did not give people the entire picture of divine revelation. They were *ek merous,* "partial" or "in part." The word *teleion*, "complete," is the opposite of "partial." It is all of whatever the partial is part of. Since these things like prophecy, knowledge, and languages were all partial means of revelation, it seems to this writer that the final revelation of God's will for man would be the "complete." When the apostles and prophets of the first century had received all that God was going to reveal, and when God inspired them to write it down, then the complete had come and the gifts of divine revelation became redundant or superfluous (Ephesians 3:3–5). As mentioned earlier, tongues and prophecy were two gifts that were explicitly said to have been given by the laying on of apostolic hands (Acts 19:6).

This passage teaches that love will continue indefinitely, while the gifts of tongues, knowledge, and prophecy would cease. These three gifts would cease when the "complete" came. Paul gives us some illustrations to clarify what he had just said.

First Corinthians 13:11

> When I was a child, I spoke like a child, I
> thought like a child, and I reasoned like a child.
> When I became a man, I put away the childish
> things.

In this illustration, childhood and childish things are the temporary period of tongues, prophecy, and knowledge. The coming to maturity or manhood is the time when the "complete" comes and the partial is done away.

> *We now see in a mirror dimly, but then (we*
> *will see) face to face.*

The *now* is like the period of childhood when we only see indistinctly or dimly in the mirror. The time reference to the future *then* parallels the time which the child becomes an adult. Then, when revelation is complete, we will be able to see clearly, or face to face.

> Now I know in part, but then I
> will know just as I am known.

This clearly connects us back to 1 Corinthians 13:8–10. The time when we know *ek merous,* or in part, is the time before the complete comes. It is the time of childhood before we put away the childish things involving tongues, knowledge, and prophecy. It is the time when we only see dimly in the mirror. But *then* is the time we will see clearly, the time when we will know fully, the time when we have the complete revelation of God. Paul wants the Corinthians to know that some of the gifts that were so sought after by the Corinthians when he wrote the letter were only temporary in God's great plan.

> But now faith, hope, and love, these three,
> remain. But the greatest of these is love.

The word, *menei*, "remains," is contrasted with those things that will be done away with, those childish things we put away, and the time of seeing dimly. When the complete comes and the partial is done away, these three things will still remain. Faith will last until Jesus comes and we see for ourselves (2 Corinthians 5:7). Hope will last only until our reward is realized (Romans 8:24–25). Love is eternal. It will never go away. God is love. If we do all that we do in love, this is a principle that will stand us in good stead with God from now through eternity. We know what love is through the example of Jesus Christ (1 John 3:16).

Reflections on Chapter Thirteen

1. What three spiritual gifts are mentioned in 1 Corinthians 13:1–3 and in 1 Corinthians 12:8–10?

2. The use of any of these gifts without _____ is useless and vain.

3. What is it that love does not do in 1 Corinthians 13:4–6?

4. What does love do in 1 Corinthians 13:4–6?

5. What three spiritual gifts does Paul clearly say will be done away with in 1 Corinthians 13:8–10?

6. Which two of these gifts do we know for certain were given by the laying on of apostles' hands (Acts 19:6)?

7. The time of tongues, prophecy, and knowledge is compared to the time of _____ in 1 Corinthians 13:11.

8. The time of tongues, prophecy, and knowledge is compared to seeing in a mirror _____ in 1 Corinthians 13:12.

9. The time of tongues, prophecy, and knowledge is a time of knowing _____ in 1 Corinthians 13:12.

10. The time when tongues, prophecy, and knowledge cease is compared to the time a child becomes a _____, to seeing in the mirror _____, and to knowing _____.

11. What remains when tongues, prophecy, and knowledge are done away (1 Corinthians 13:13)?

14

First Corinthians 14:1–2

> Pursue love! Be zealous for spiritual gifts, but rather that you may prophesy! For the one who speaks in a language (unknown to others) is not speaking to men but to God, for no one understands, and he speaks mysteries by the Spirit.

The entire point of chapter 13 is reduced to the command, "Pursue love!" Love is the more excellent way of conducting oneself as a Christian. When he says, "Be zealous for spiritual gifts," he returns the reader to 1 Corinthians 12:31 where he said, "Be zealous for the greater gifts." Prophecy is one of those greater gifts that can be readily understood and can edify everyone. To speak in a language unknown to others around us does not help anyone spiritually. In 1 Corinthians 14:28 Paul instructs such people to refrain from using this gift in the assembly unless there is a translator.

First Corinthians 14:3–4

> But he who prophesies speaks to people edification, and encouragement, and comfort! He who speaks in an (unknown) language edi-

fies himself. But the one who prophesies edifies the assembly.

Paul is talking about selfish versus unselfish behavior in the assembly. Loving behavior is to do what is best for all assembled. Without a translator, it is best for the assembly if the tongue speaker stays silent. In contrast, the clearly understood message of the prophet could build everyone up, encourage them to do God's will, and bring them comfort. Because edification, encouragement, and comfort are clearly desired outcomes of the church gathering, everyone in the assembly should be able to clearly understand what is said, prayed, sung, or read.

First Corinthians 14:5

> I wish you all to speak in (other) languages, but rather that you should prophesy. And greater is the one who prophesies than the one who speaks in tongues, unless he can translate so that the assembly might receive edification.

The word *oikodomeo* means to build up. Paul is talking about spiritual edification or building people up in their faith and in their walk with God. The assembly is not built up if they do not understand. This should give us pause if we are doing public Scripture readings out of antiquated versions of the Bible, which few can understand, or if we are singing songs in the assembly that use antiquated language like "night with ebon pinion brooded 'oer the vale" or "in vain in high and holy lays my soul her grateful voice would raise." Most people today would gain nothing from these words. Perhaps we do these things because we are selfish in our traditions and not because of love for others.

First Corinthians 14:6–7

> But now, brothers, if I come to you speaking in tongues, what shall I profit you unless I speak to you in a revelation or with some knowledge, or with a prophecy, or with a teaching. Even so, if someone gives a lifeless sound, whether on flute or harp, and gives no (clear) distinction among the tones, how will it be known what is being played on the flute or on the harp?

The tongue speaker is here compared to someone making indiscriminate noise on a flute or harp without any clear tune or sequence of tones. There is no way, in such a case, to identify the tune, to know what is being played. So, when one speaks in a language unknown to the people in the assembly, there is no way to understand what is being said. Without understanding there can be no edification, encouragement, or comfort given. A "lifeless sound" is one that has no clear meaning or intent.

First Corinthians 14:8–12

> And if the trumpet gives a sound that is unclear, who shall prepare for battle? So also you, unless you through the tongue give a clear message, how shall what is spoken be understood? For you will be speaking to the air! As it happens there are many kinds of sounds in the world, and none is without meaning. If I do not understand the power (meaning) of the voice, I shall be to the one speaking as a barbarian, and the one speaking shall be a barbarian to me.

> So also you, since you are zealous for spiritual gifts, be zealous that you might abound toward the building up of the church!

Paul gives illustrations from the world of sounds to make his point. A trumpet must give a clear sequence of tones, one meaning to attack, one meaning to retreat, and others with specific meanings if the message is to be understood by the army. Similarly, one who speaks to others must covey a clear message to all who hear or that person is just speaking to the air. Speaker and listener will be like two people of different cultures and languages who cannot communicate with one another. They will be as "barbarians" to one another, people who cannot communicate in the common tongue like the rest of society.

First Corinthians 14:13–15

> Wherefore, let him that speaks in a (different) language, pray that he might translate. For if I pray in a (different) language, my spirit prays, but my mind is unfruitful. What is it, then? I will pray with the Spirit, but I will also pray with the mind. I will sing with the Spirit, but I will also sing with the mind.

The mind or understanding of individuals is crucial to accomplishing God's intentions for the assembly. In context, to sing or pray with the Spirit is to sing or pray in a foreign tongue or language which is not understandable to the assembly. Today we do not "sing with the Spirit" in the same sense as those in Corinth did. In Paul's day, the Spirit gave one the gift of tongues, but that gift did not necessarily provide the speaker or the hearers with understanding. Paul urges the person with the gift of tongues to

pray for another spiritual gift, the gift of interpretation or translation (see 1 Corinthians 12:10). Verse 13 does indicate that prayer
was connected to the reception of spiritual gifts. One could pray
for different gifts, and God could grant those prayers. In this particular context, one is granted access to spiritual gifts through baptism into the body of Christ (1 Corinthians 12:13). As one drinks
from the reservoir of the Spirit, one can then pray for specific spiritual gifts, and God might choose to grant the one who prays that
gift (1 Corinthians 14:13). Perhaps Luke 11:13 is a helpful comment here, where Jesus said the Father will give the Holy Spirit
to those who ask him. In any case, singing or praying in a tongue
does not encourage, comfort, edify, or instruct anyone else in the
assembly without an interpreter. Surely, a modern-day application
is that everything we say or sing in the assembly should be readily
understandable to all!

First Corinthians 14:16

> So then, if you bless with the Spirit, how
> will the one who fills the place of the unlearned
> say the Amen at your thanksgiving? You give
> thanks well enough, but the other (person) is
> not edified.

This is probably a reference to the prayers at the Lord's
Supper. Paul spoke earlier of the "cup of blessing which we bless"
(1 Corinthians 10:16). He spoke of how Jesus "gave thanks" as he
instituted the Lord's Supper (1 Corinthians 11:24). The Gospel
accounts of the feeding of the 5000, the feeding of the 4000, and
the institution of the Lord's Supper seem to use *eulogeo*, "bless,"
and *eucharisteo*, "give thanks," interchangeably (Matthew 14:19;
15:36; 26:26f, etc.). Ancient Christians sometimes referred to
the Lord's Supper as the Eucharist because it was all about giving

thanks and praise to God for what he has done for us in Christ. But if the assembly is English speaking, and the prayers of thanksgiving are said in Russian, the assembly will not be able to voice their assent by saying "Amen," because they do not understand. By the way, this shows that the "Amen" was more a function of the listeners than it was for the speakers. Does your congregation say the "Amen" at the giving of thanks?

First Corinthians 14:18–19

> I thank God that I speak in tongues more than all of you! But, in the assembly I would rather speak five words with my understanding, that ten thousand words in a tongue!

Understanding leads to participation and edification for all. The word *nous*, "mind or understanding," is in verses 14, 15, and 19. It is a key component in the assembly. Understanding is necessary so that all of the songs, prayers, and lessons communicate easily, and the sentiments are easily shared by the community assembled!

First Corinthians 14:20

> Brothers, do not be children in (your) thinking, but in wickedness be babes. And in (your) thinking be mature.

Paul is asking the church to be mature in their thinking about what to do in the assembly. He wants them to be mature enough to see what is edifying and helpful to all, as opposed to what is only self-seeking and does not help the group. He expects them to be "mature" and accept the divine wisdom given by Paul the apostle (1 Corinthians 2:6).

First Corinthians 14:21

> In the law it is written, "In other languages and with strange lips, I will speak to this people, and even in this manner they will not obey me!"

The apostle cites Isaiah 28:11–12 regarding how the people of Israel refused to listen to God, regardless of the language in which the message was spoken to them. The result was their destruction. According to 1 Corinthians 2:6, it is the mature who respect divine revelation and obey it. As opposed to being mature (1 Corinthians 2:6) or spiritual (1 Corinthians 2:13, 15), some of the Corinthians were immature and carnal (1 Corinthians 2:14; 3:1). The wisdom from God regarding the gift of tongues was that it did not have much of a place in the Christian assembly. Would the Corinthians listen to that wisdom?

First Corinthians 14:22

> So, then, tongues are for a sign, not to believers, but to unbelievers, but prophecy is not for unbelievers, but for believers.

The Sunday assemblies of the church were primarily for baptized believers in the time of Paul. The gospel of salvation was primarily preached elsewhere when God's people were trying to win the lost. Pentecost was mostly a gathering of unbelievers (Acts 2:5ff). The gospel was shared with the Eunuch, Cornelius, Lydia, the jailer, and with the Corinthians outside of the assemblies of the church (Acts 2, 8, 10, 16, 18). The assembly of the church was not primarily a place of evangelism, but a place of worship, edification, and instruction for the church. Tongues, as on the day of Pentecost, were used as a proof or sign to convince unbelievers of the presence and power of the risen Christ (Acts 2:33). When unbelievers did come and visit the assemblies of the church, it was important that they, as well as the believers, were able to understand what was being said in the prayers, songs, and teachings.

First Corinthians 14:23

> If, then, the whole church comes together in one place, and all speak in (different) tongues, and some unlearned or unbelievers come in, will they not think that you are out of your mind? But if all prophesy, and one who is an unbeliever or unlearned comes in, he is convicted by all, he is called to account by all, the secrets of his heart are made known, and in this way, falling on his face he will worship God, proclaiming, "Truly, God is among you!'"

Though tongues were meant to be a sign to unbelievers when the gospel of the death and resurrection of Christ was proclaimed, an unbeliever who visited a Christian assembly would not be helped at all by listening to people speak foreign languages. He would think everyone had lost their minds. But if the unbeliever could hear clear prophecy, clear teaching expressed in his own tongue, several good things could result. The unbeliever could be convicted of the truth because of a clear explanation. The unbeliever could be examined or called to account if the truth he learned contradicted his own belief or practice. The word of God could expose the secret sins of his/her life. The result would be a person who is so convicted that he/she is caused to turn to God. Again, the basic application is that everything done in the assembly should help God speak clearly to the hearts of everyone there, believers and unbelievers alike.

First Corinthians 14:26

> What is it, then, brothers? Whenever you
> come together, each one has a psalm, or has a
> teaching, or has a revelation, or has a tongue,
> or has a translation. Let everything be done for
> building (people) up!

Different individuals had different gifts and different ways of contributing to the assembly. There was singing in the assembly (1 Corinthians 14:14–15, 26). The manner of this singing varied, depending on the psalm or song that was sung. The early church was taught to speak to one another in song (Ephesians 5:19). They were taught to "teach and instruct one another with songs" so that the message of Christ might live in them richly (Colossians 3:16). They were taught to sing praise to the Lord (Romans 15:8–11). The governor, Pliny the Younger of Bithynia, said that the Christians "chanted verses alternately among themselves in honor of Christ, as if to a god" (Letters, X. xcvi. 7). Nothing is said about any particular person being a song leader in the ancient church. This text says, "Each one has a psalm," which seems to indicate that various people would either sing or start a song for the assembly. Philo's description of singing in private Jewish gatherings is probably somewhat similar to the singing that went on in ancient Christian assemblies (*The Contemplative Life*, 80). The main emphasis here is the need for the song to edify the people present at the assembly. The same is true of any other participant, whether prophet or teacher or one who led prayers. "Let all things be done for edification" is the line which summarizes the teaching of the chapter because love demands that everyone is considered in what is done during the assembly.

First Corinthians 14:27

> If anyone speaks in a (foreign) language,
> let it be just two, or at most three, and they in
> turn, and one should translate. If there is no
> translator, let him be silent in the assembly, and
> let him speak to himself and to God.

Now he gets specific about how those with the gift of tongues should behave in the assembly. In 1 Corinthians 14:2, 4, Paul says the one who speaks in tongues is speaking to himself and to God but not to the assembly, unless someone conveys the message to all through translation. In this passage, Paul clearly limits the tongue speakers' involvement in the assembly, even if there is a translator, but commands that without a translator, they should be silent. The command *sigato*, be silent, means that they should not speak out.

First Corinthians 14:29

> And let two or three prophets speak, and
> let others discern.

As Paul limits the number of tongue speakers, he also limits the number of prophets. This may have been simple practicality due to limits in time. In any case, he says, "and let others discern." The gift of discerning spirits was listed in 1 Corinthians 12:10 after the gift of prophecy. This seems to have involved the ability to distinguish true prophets, those speaking by the Spirit of God, from false prophets who were speaking from lying, seductive spirits. John later wrote to the Asian Christians that they should "test the spirits to see whether they are from God." His reason for this directive was "for many false prophets have gone out into the world" (1 John 4:1). Paul said that people would often listen to "seducing spirits and doctrines of demons" (1 Timothy 4:1f). Similarly, in his admonitions to the Thessalonians, he urged the leaders there not to despise prophecy or quench the Spirit but to "test everything and hold on to what is good" (1 Thessalonians 5:19–21). Later on, elders or qualified teachers were appointed to both "exhort in the healthy teaching and convict those who speak against it" (Titus 1:9). Perhaps, during the period when the apostolic revelations were still being given and collected, this Spirit-given gift provided extra confirmation to people that the message spoken was either the word of God or not.

First Corinthians 14:30

> But if a revelation is given to one who is seated, let the first (prophet) be silent. For you are all able to prophecy one at a time, so that all may learn and all may be encouraged. And the spirits of the prophets are subject to the prophets. For God is not a God of disorder, but of peace!

As Paul limited and ordered the tongue speakers, so he limits and organizes the prophets. These instructions ensure that one does not dominate the speaking to the exclusion of others and that only one person is speaking at a time. Speakers are not competing for attention, but are yielding to others and guaranteeing that all legitimate speakers will have the attention of the assembly. Crucial to this passage is the goal stated by the apostle, "So that all may learn and all may be encouraged!" Paul has now used the command, *sigato*, "let him keep silent," twice. Tongue speakers should keep silent if there is no translator, and prophets should be silent if a revelation is given to another.

First Corinthians 14:34

> As in all the assemblies of the saints, let
> the women keep silent in the assemblies, for
> it is not permitted for them to speak, but let
> them be in subjection as the law also says.

Some may argue here that women were praying and prophesying because Paul talks about that earlier in 1 Corinthians 11:5. In chapter 11, Paul did not stop to discuss this because he was talking about the proper dress for women in the assembly. In contrast, in this passage, whether women were, in fact, prophesying in Corinth or not, Paul directed that they stop doing it in the assembly. This harmonizes with his directives to Timothy for the Ephesian church where he does not allow the women to teach or exercise authority over the men, but to be in subjection (1 Timothy 2:11–12). That directive is also about the assembly because Paul mentions the men praying while they lifted up holy hands (1 Timothy 2:8). In the Mishnah, the Pharisees speak at length about who may "go before the ark and lift up the hands" to lead the synagogue congregation in prayer (Berakoth 5:4; Megilla 4:3–7). This was reserved for the men. Women did participate in the corporate prayers when prayers were recited from the psalms or traditional Jewish blessings were said, but they did not lead the prayers in front of the synagogue before the ark. The Torah says that the man would "rule over" the woman (Genesis 3:16). Paul seems to see that as a principle that governs their behavior in the assembly as well as elsewhere. This seems not to have just been a directive for one local church because Paul begins by saying, "As in all the assemblies of the saints."

First Corinthians 14:35

> If they would learn anything, let them ask
> their own husbands at home. For it is a shame
> for a woman to speak out in the assembly. Has
> the word of God gone out from you? Or has it
> only come to you?

Clearly, the apostle prohibits the women speaking out as teachers in the assembly. Nor were they allowed to engage in scriptural debate, giving point and counterpoint with the teachers in the assembly. They were commanded to reserve such discussions for private settings in the home. Now, since we live in a different time, and we not only gather in the Sunday assembly but in other smaller groups at different times during the week, it is difficult for us to determine how far we should apply this teaching. On the one hand, there is the privacy of one's home. At the other end of the spectrum is the public Sunday gathering of the church when "the whole church comes together in one place" (1 Corinthians 14:23, 26). What should women do in Bible classes or in small group studies or in devotional settings? Can women ask questions and bring up passages for discussion? Did Priscilla do this when she and her husband took Apollos aside and taught him the word of God more perfectly in Acts 18? So we must use some judgment when applying these texts to situations outside of the Sunday assembly and be careful not to bind where God has not bound. Still, we need to respect the spirit of what God teaches us about male and female roles. When Paul asks the rhetorical question, "Has it (the word of God) come to you only?" he wants the Corinthians to acknowledge that God's word has been revealed to Paul and the other apostles first of all (1 Corinthians 2:6–15). Paul is speaking and writing to the Corinthians by divine revelation.

First Corinthians 14:37

> If any man thinks he is a prophet or spiritual, let him recognize that the things I am writing to you are the Lord's command.

Paul makes similar statements in other places (1 Corinthians 2:10–13; Galatians 1:11; Ephesians 3:3–5; 2 Thessalonians 2:15). Paul wrote these letters by divine inspiration and with the authority of Christ (2 Corinthians 5:20–21). To deny that the Spirit was speaking through the apostles was to acknowledge one's self as a false prophet (1 John 4:6).

First Corinthians 14:38

> If anyone does not understand this, let him/her continue to be ignorant. Be zealous to prophesy, but do not forbid to speak in (foreign) tongues. But let all things be done appropriately and in an orderly manner.

The apostle does not give in to those who will not acknowledge his authority. Earlier, he calls these "natural" or "carnal" people (1 Corinthians 2:14; 3:1f). He reiterates his appeal to exalt prophecy over tongues, but does not prohibit speaking in tongues if it is done as prescribed in 1 Corinthians 14:27–28. The main instruction for the assembly was that everything done should be for the building up of the whole body, and it should be done in a pleasant, appropriate, and orderly fashion. The attention of the epistle in chapters 11 through 14 is focused on how to dress and behave during the gathering of the whole church.

Reflections on Chapter 14

1. What is the principle that governs the use of all spiritual gifts?
2. What lofty goals are accomplished by the one who prophesies according to 1 Corinthians 14:3?
3. Who does the one who speaks in tongues edify or build up according to 1 Corinthians 14:4?
4. Why is the one who utters a prophecy greater than the one who speaks in tongues in the assembly (1 Corinthians 14:5)?
5. How are the calls of the trumpet compared to tongues and prophecy (1 Corinthians 14:8)?
6. What is the goal of the things done in the assembly according to 1 Corinthians 14:12?
7. What verse suggests that prayer plays a role in receiving spiritual gifts?
8. In the context of 1 Corinthians 14:13–16, what does it actually mean to pray with the Spirit or to sing with the Spirit?
9. What should the church receive from what is said in the assembly according to 1 Corinthians 14:19?
10. Tongues are for a sign to _____, but prophecy is for _____.
11. Under what circumstances are the following people to keep silent in the assembly? A. Tongue speakers? B. Prophets? C. Women?

15

First Corinthians 15:1

> I make known to you brothers, the gospel which was preached to you, which also you received, in which also you stand, through which you are saved, if you hold on to the message which was preached to you, unless you believed in vain!

The gospel preached by Paul did not come from man but through revelation from the risen Christ (Galatians 1:12). The term *gospel*, as far as we can determine, originated in Isaiah 52:7 where the prophet talks about the good news of peace and salvation, the good news of the benevolent reign of God. This good news is also the "message" of Isaiah 53:1ff, the message of the suffering servant who "was wounded for our transgressions," etc. Paul brings these ancient passages together in Romans 10:13–17. The gospel message of Isaiah 52–53 is the gospel preached by Phillip to the Eunuch (Acts 8:35). This message is all about the redemptive death, burial, and resurrection of Jesus and how we become united with that great redemptive work of God (1 Corinthians 15:3–4f). This gospel is all about "the grace of Christ" (Galatians 1:6). It is that good news that invites man into the fellowship of God (1 Corinthians 1:9; 2 Thessalonians 2:14). The foundational proof of the redemptive work of God is the resurrection of Christ. This was the primary focus of the Pentecost sermon (Acts 2:23–36). He was "delivered up for our trespasses and raised for our justification" (Romans 4:25). If we become Christians and take our stand on the gospel, and it turns out there is no resurrection, then our faith is empty, useless, and vain (1 Corinthians 15:16–17).

In 1 Corinthians 15:1, Paul says "you received" the gospel. This word, *paralambano*, means that we have received something that was passed down from someone else. In Paul's writing, it is connected to the word *paradosis*, which is something "passed down" or a "tradition." But unlike things that were passed down only by human beings to other human beings, the traditions Paul has in view were passed down by the risen Christ to the apostles and to the church. Paul uses these terms in Galatians 1:8–12 and makes the point very clearly that he received the gospel by revelation from Jesus Christ. He uses this same language in 1 Corinthians 11:23 and 15:3. The gospel, the good news of Jesus Christ, was received from Christ himself and passed on by the apostles to the world.

First Corinthians 15:3

> For I passed on to you of first importance,
> that which also I received, that Christ died for
> our sins according to the Scriptures, and that
> he was buried, and that he was raised the third
> day according to the Scriptures.

Since Paul said these things which he passed down to the church were "according to the Scriptures," we conclude they were foretold in the Hebrew Scriptures. Paul himself references Isaiah 52:7; 53:1 in Romans 10:15ff when talking about the gospel of Christ. The risen Jesus said, "Thus it is written, that the Christ should suffer, and rise from the dead the third day" (Luke 24:46).

The atoning death of Christ is certainly portrayed in Isaiah 53. The resurrection and exaltation of Christ seem to be portrayed in Isaiah 52:13. According to the writer of Hebrews, the enthronement of Christ is pictured in Psalm 2:7, Psalm 8:5, and Psalm 110:1 (Hebrews 1:5; 2:6ff; 8:1; 10:5–10). On Pentecost, Peter spoke of the resurrection of Christ from Psalm 16:10 (Acts 2:27). Paul told Timothy that these Old Testament Scriptures were able to make one wise unto salvation "through faith in Christ Jesus" (2 Timothy 3:15).

First Corinthians 15:5

> And that he appeared to Cephas, then to the twelve, then, he appeared to over 500 brothers at one time, of whom most remain (alive) until now, but some have fallen asleep. Then he appeared to James, then to all of the apostles. And last of all, as to a child born too early, he appeared to me also.

Paul's preaching to the Corinthians and others included the proof of many post-resurrection appearances by the risen Lord. This list of post-resurrection appearances is impressive. Perhaps the appearance to Peter is the appearance to Simon mentioned by Luke (Luke 24:34). He appeared to "the twelve" minus Judas and Thomas, then to the twelve, minus Judas, in John 20:19–29. We have no other record of this appearance to the 500, but Paul knew enough of them to confidently state that most of them were still alive. When he says, "Some have fallen asleep," he was referring to their deaths. He uses the same terminology for death in 1 Thessalonians 4:13ff and in 1 Corinthians 15:50ff. The appearance to James is almost certainly an appearance to Jesus's brother (Matthew 13:55). Jesus's brothers did not believe on him until after the resurrection (John 7:5). After the resurrection, they were present, along with his mother, awaiting the Spirit's coming on Pentecost (Acts 1:14). Jesus's brother James was considered to be an apostle by Paul (Galatians 1:19). He later became the de facto leader of the Jerusalem church (Acts 15) and the author of the Epistle of James (James 1:1). After appearing to James, Jesus appeared to "all of the apostles." It is not clear to what occasion this has reference. Finally, he appeared to Saul of Tarsus on the Damascus road. Paul says this appearance was similar to "a child untimely born." Perhaps he means it was not expected. It was a surprise and a shock. It certainly changed the trajectory of Paul's life abruptly and completely! Paul is basically saying what Peter said in Acts 2:32, "This Jesus did God raise up whereof we are all witnesses."

First Corinthians 15:9

> For I am the least of the apostles; I who am
> not sufficient to be called an apostle, because I
> persecuted the church of God! But thank God I
> am what I am, and his grace toward me did not
> turn out to be vain, but I have labored more
> abundantly than all of them, yet not I but the
> grace of God which is with me!

Paul often felt inadequate for the task before him. He states this clearly in 2 Corinthians 2:16, then goes on to say that his "adequacy" does not come from himself, but from God (2 Corinthians 3:5–6). One of the reasons he sometimes felt inadequacy was his past as a persecutor of God's church (Acts 8:1–4). He grieved over this, but rejoiced that God had poured mercy out upon him as an example to other sinners (1 Timothy 1:13–16). While he sometimes felt inadequate, he insisted that he was equal in the eyes of

Christ to all of the apostles, and had been accepted as such by the leading apostles, Peter, James, and John (Galatians 2:6–10). The divine gift of apostleship was working just as strongly in Paul as it was in all of the other apostles!

First Corinthians 15:11

> Wherefore, whether it is I or they, so we preach and so you believed.

Specifically, Paul is talking about his preaching and the preaching of the other apostles regarding the death, burial, and particularly, the resurrection of Jesus!

First Corinthians 15:12

> And since Christ is preached that he is raised from the dead, how say some among you that there is no resurrection of the dead. And if there is no resurrection of the dead, then neither has Christ been raised. And if Christ has not been raised, then our preaching is vain, and your faith is vain.

The resurrection is the foundation of Christian faith. It validates the redemptive work of Christ and validates all of Jesus's claims about his identity. Jesus said "the gates of Hades" would not prevail against his church. He broke open those gates when he came forth from the grave. He was dead and is alive again and has the keys of death and of Hades (Revelation 1:17–18). But without the resurrection, there is no gospel, and the trust we place in Jesus is empty and useless!

First Corinthians 15:15–17

> And we are found false witnesses for God
> because we testified according to God, that he
> raised Christ, whom he did not raise if the dead
> are not raised. But if the dead are not raised,
> neither has Christ been raised, and if Christ has
> not been raised, then your faith is empty and
> you are still in your sins!

There is no question that Jesus was crucified by Pontius Pilate. That is a well-attested historical fact. But whether that death was different from other deaths is the point at issue. Was that death a divinely planned satisfaction of the justice of God for the sins of all mankind? Was Jesus really delivered up to death "by the determinate counsel and foreknowledge of God" (Acts 2:22–23)? Only the resurrection validates that claim! Without the resurrection, the death of Christ was just one more death among countless millions of deaths.

First Corinthians 15:18–19

> Furthermore, those who have fallen asleep
> in Christ have perished, and if we have put our
> hope in Christ in this life alone, we are of all
> men most pathetic!

Life after death is a strongly awaited hope for those who believe in the resurrection. We wait for the redemption of our bodies on the day of redemption (Romans 8:23; Ephesians 4:30). If our hope in Christ ends at the grave, then we are a people to be pitied, deluded by an empty promise of resurrection and eternal life! Some mock the faith by saying, "Where is the promise of his coming? For since the day that the fathers fell asleep, all things continue as they were since the beginning of creation" (2 Peter 2:4). But the Lord is not slack concerning his promise to return and judge the world (2 Peter 3:9).

First Corinthians 15:20

> But now Christ is raised from the dead, the first fruits of those who are asleep. For since through man came death, also through a man came resurrection from the dead. For just as in Adam all died, so also in Christ all shall be made alive. Each in his own order. Christ, the first fruit, then those who belong to Christ at his coming!

Deuteronomy 26:1–11 commanded the children of Israel to bring the first of their produce in a basket as an offering to the Lord. It was a show of gratitude with eager anticipation of the rest of the harvest. If Christ is the first fruits, then there is anticipation of others to be raised after him. Adam brought physical death into the world because decay began as a result of his sin. The tree of life was removed from man in Genesis 3, and human beings began to die. After Adam died, then others died. After Christ was raised, others will be raised. Christ has the keys of death and Hades (Revelation 1:17–18). For that reason, we trust his word when he says, "The hour is coming when all that are in the tombs shall hear his voice and shall come forth. They that have done good unto the resurrection of life, and they that have done evil to the resurrection of condemnation" (John 5:28–29). Paul says those who belong to Christ will be raised at his *Parousia*, his coming. The return of Christ is promised in Acts 1:11; 3:21, 1 Thessalonians 4:13–18, 2 Thessalonians 1:7–9, 2 Peter 3:9, Jude 14, and in other places.

First Corinthians 15:24–27

> Then comes the end, when he delivers the kingdom to God the Father, when he shall have destroyed all principality and all dominion and power. For he must reign until he has put all the enemies under his feet. Death is the last enemy to be destroyed. For he placed all things in subjection under his feet.

The end comes at the return of Christ; that is, the end of this world as we know it. At that point, the unique reign of the Messiah is concluded. Part of finishing that reign is the destruction of demonic powers that serve the cause of darkness. The *archai, exousiai,* and *dunamai* are often mentioned in Paul's writings. They are the powers against which we all struggle (Ephesians 6:12). Satan is the ruler of the *exousiai* of the air (Ephesians 2:2). Christ was exalted above all of these demonic beings after his resurrection (Ephesians 1:19–21). He is the head over all of these beings who oppose him and his people (Colossians 2:10). Though they may try, they cannot separate us from God's love in Christ without our consent (Romans 8:35–38). Christ is the Creator of these beings and will eventually destroy them for their rebellion (Colossians 1:16). The Hebrew Scriptures say that he, the Messiah, must reign until he has put all of his enemies under his feet. Paul alludes to two passages here. Psalm 8:6 says God would put all things in subjection under his feet. Psalm 110:1 says that God is placing the Messiah on his throne until God makes his enemies his footstool. Both of these texts played a great role in the formation of Christian thinking (Acts 2:34–35; Ephesians 1:22; Hebrews 1:3; 2:8–10; 8:1, etc.). The last enemy to be finally defeated by the Messiah is death. This will happen when all of the dead are raised, and death itself is destroyed (John 5:28–29). This will happen when all appear before the tribunal of Christ, and death and Hades are cast into the lake of fire forever (Revelation 20:13–14).

First Corinthians 15:27b

> But when he says all things are subjected to him, it is evident that he is excepted who subjected all things to him, so that God might be all things in all.

When the ancient text says that all things will be made subject to the Messiah (Psalm 8:6), it obviously does not include God giving up his eternal reign. There was never any ultimate difference or competition between the reign of God and the reign of the Messiah. They are the same for all practical purposes. It seems that the Godhead will once again be together in the same way as before the Son became a human being with a separate will. This is a mystery which will never be completely understood by mere mortals.

First Corinthians 15:29

> Then what about those who are being baptized for the dead? If, in fact, the dead are not raised, then why are they baptized for them?

Paul speaks of those who are baptized for the dead in the third person. These are to be identified with those who are saying there is no resurrection of the dead in 1 Corinthians 15:12. They are inconsistent, says Paul, because if the dead are not raised, and there is no life beyond death, then why would people be baptized for them? We don't have any more information on this group or what their intent was in being baptized for the dead, but it certainly showed some kind of concern for the dead and some kind of belief that the actions of the living can affect the dead in some way. It was not Paul or the faithful Corinthians who were baptizing for the dead, but "some among you" who say there is no resurrection (1 Corinthians 15:12).

First Corinthians 15:30–32

> And why do we place ourselves in danger every hour? I die every day! Indeed, you, brothers, are my boasting, which I have in Christ Jesus our Lord! If just in the manner of men I fought with the beasts in Ephesus, what profit is that to me? If the dead are not raised, "Let us eat and drink, for tomorrow we die!"

Paul first showed the inconsistency in the ones who were maintaining their disbelief in the resurrection by questioning their weird practice of baptism for the dead. Next, Paul argued from his own behavior. Why was he willing to place himself in constant danger for the sake of the gospel? Why was he willing to face the wild animals in Ephesus (see also 2 Corinthians 1:8–9)? What good would this have done Paul if he had no hope after the grave? His philosophy would have been very different if he did not trust in the resurrection of Christ and the resurrection of all of the dead! He would have said, like the ungodly in Isaiah, "Let us eat and drink, for tomorrow we die" (Isaiah 22:13).

First Corinthians 15:33

> Do not be deceived! "Evil companions corrupt good morals!" Come to your senses in a righteous manner and stop sinning, for some

have no knowledge of God! I speak so you may
be ashamed!

When Paul says, "Do not be deceived," he is appealing to
the Corinthians not to allow themselves to be deceived by those
among them who were denying the resurrection! The quotation
is probably from the Greek playwright, Menander. Jerome, in his
letter to Magnus, an orator from Rome, was explaining why he
sometimes referenced pagan writers in his religious works, and he
points to Paul as an example. "In another epistle, Paul quotes a
line of Menander, 'Evil communications corrupt good manners'"
(Jerome, Letters, LXX). The evil associations or companions Paul
has in mind are those who deny the resurrection and corrupt
the minds of the Corinthians. He has a similar thought in mind
regarding teachers who were bad influences in his second letter
when he tells them not to be "yoked together with unbelievers" (2
Corinthians 6:14). The sinning he tells the Corinthians to stop is
the sin of tolerating people who are undermining the very foundation of the Christian faith.

First Corinthians 15:35

But someone may say, "How are the dead
raised? And with what kind of body do they
come (forth)."

The strong adversative conjunction, *alla*, which begins this
section of text, suggests a possible counter to Paul's arguments
regarding the resurrection. Since human bodies decay and are
often totally destroyed, what kind of body is supposed to come
from the grave? What body will be raised if there is no more body
to be raised or if there remains only a very decayed corpse? To this
hypothetical objection, Paul now gives an answer.

First Corinthians 15:36–37

> Foolish person! What you sow does not
> come to life unless it dies! And as for what you
> sow, you do not sow the body which shall be,
> but a naked kernel, whether it turns out to be
> wheat or some other kind!

While the hypothetical questioner seems to assume it is ridiculous to think of a decayed or decomposed corpse rising from the dead, Paul explains that the body that is put into the ground is a mere seed of the body that will come forth. The dead body placed in the ground is like a kernel of grain. The resurrection body is like the plant which springs forth from the seed. The plant is much different and much more glorious than the seed.

First Corinthians 15:38

> But God gives to it a body as he has willed,
> and to each seed a body of its own.

There is a one-to-one relationship between the individual seed and the plant that springs forth from it. This means that individual identity is preserved in the resurrection. If it is my body that is planted in the ground, it will be my body, and mine alone, that comes forth in the resurrection. Paul says we are waiting for "the redemption of our bodies" in the same way that the creation waits for its own redemption (Romans 8:20–23).

First Corinthians 15:39–41

> Not all flesh is the same flesh, but there is one
> (kind for humans), another for animals, another

for birds, and another for fish. There are also heavenly bodies, and earthly bodies. And there is one glory for the heavenly (body) and another for the earthly (body). There is one glory for the sun, another for the moon, and another for the stars. For one star differs from another in glory.

While it is a bit difficult to follow Paul's reasoning here, he seems to be saying that human beings will still be human beings in the resurrection, but human beings in a much more glorious state. When he mentions the different glory of the celestial bodies and says, "one star differs from another in glory," he may be saying that even in the resurrection, different people may have different degrees of glory. He seems to be going back to the previous declaration that God gives "to each seed a body of its own." Each person maintains his/her own individuality in the resurrection, and just as bodies differ among people now, so they will differ according to the individual when they are raised.

First Corinthians 15:42–44

The resurrection of the dead is the same way. It is sown in corruption. It is raised in incorruption. It is sown in dishonor. It is raised in glory. It is sown in weakness. It is raised in power! It is sown a natural body. It is raised a spiritual body. If there is a natural body, there is also a spiritual one.

The apostle returns to his analogy of the seed. As he stated before, the body we have now is like the seed, and the body we will have then is like the plant. The natural body, the "seed" that is sown in the ground, is characterized by corruption, dishonor, and weakness. The spiritual body of the resurrection is characterized by incorruption, glory, and power! Paul seems to see it as logical that if there is a natural body, there must be a spiritual body. The redemption of our bodies in the resurrection will take place on the day of redemption (Romans 8:23; Ephesians 4:30). Our bondage to corruption began with the sin of Adam and Eve when sickness and death entered the world (Romans 8:19–20). Adam and Eve would have lived indefinitely if they had not lost access to the tree of life. They had physical bodies, but those bodies were designed to be eternal. Perhaps this will be the nature of the resurrection body.

First Corinthians 15:45–49

> Similarly, it is also written, "The first man Adam became a living being. The last Adam (became) a life-giving spirit." But, the spiritual (man) was not the first, but the natural, then (came) the spiritual. The first man was from the earth, made of earth. The second man was from heaven. As was the (man) made of earth so are those made from earth. As was the heavenly (man) so also are those who are heavenly. And just as we have carried the image of the earthly (man), we will carry the image of the heavenly (man).

In this passage, *heavenly* and *spiritual* seem to be synonyms. These words describe a basic nature that is not subject to weakness and corruption. The man God created from the dust of the ground (Genesis 2:7) brought death into God's world. God called the man *Adam* because he was made from the *adamah*, the ground. Jesus, the man who came from heaven, brought resurrection and life. Just as earthly Adam was first and the heavenly Christ was second, so each of us lives in an earthly body first, and later, we receive the heavenly one that is incorruptible. After the resurrection, we will be like Jesus in his heavenly state (1 John 3:2). Elsewhere, Paul calls our heavenly body "a house not made with hands, eternal in the heavens" (2 Corinthians 5:1).

First Corinthians 15:50–52

> This I say, brothers, that flesh and blood cannot inherit (the) kingdom of God, neither can corruption inherit incorruption. Behold, I tell you a mystery. We will not all sleep, but we will all be changed, in a moment, in the blink of an eye, at the last trumpet! For the trumpet will sound and the dead will be raised incorruptible, and we will be changed!

When Paul talks about inheriting the kingdom of God, he is talking about the eternal kingdom after the judgment. He uses this same terminology in 1 Corinthians 6:10 and in Galatians 5:21. Jesus spoke in similar terms (Matthew 8:11; 13:43; 25:34). The perfected kingdom of God will be incorruptible, and it is no place for the corruptible flesh and blood of the present, fallen world. Those who are still living at the time of the resurrection will be changed in the blink of an eye from mortal to immortal, from corruptible to incorruptible. Those who have died will be raised with a new, incorruptible body at the same time. This description of the resurrection is perfectly in line with what Paul describes in 1 Thessalonians 4:13–18.

First Corinthians 15:53–55

> For this corruptible (body) must put on incorruption, and this mortal (body) must put

on immortality. And whenever this corruptible (body) shall have put on incorruption, and this mortal (body) shall have put on immortality, then shall come about the saying that is written, "Death is swallowed up resulting in victory! Where, O Death, is your victory? Where, O Death, is your sting?"

The word *body* is understood from the verses above because we are talking about the resurrection of the body which was planted in the ground. When this change from corruptible to incorruptible and from mortal to immortal takes place, then the words of these prophetic passages come true. The first part of the citation may be a paraphrase or allusion to Isaiah 25:8, "He will swallow up death forever." The second part is from Hosea 13:14, where the Septuagint reads, "Where is your just punishment, O Death? Where is your sting, O Hades?" (translation mine). While the wording may be a little confusing due to some textual issues between the Hebrew Text and the Septuagint, the meaning is still clear. The fear and horror of death is only there for those who have not dealt with their sin and its guilt. For those in Christ, there is no punishment or sting in death. For those in Christ, death does not overcome us because Jesus has the keys of Death and Hades (Revelation 1:17–18).

First Corinthians 15:56

The sting of death is sin, and the power of sin is the law. But thanks be to God who gives us the victory through our Lord Jesus Christ.

Sin separates people from God (Isaiah 59:2). The wages of sin is spiritual death (Romans 6:23). We are "dead in trespasses and sin" until we are reconciled to God (Ephesians 2:1, 5). In that state, we are "separate from Christ, alienated from citizenship in Israel, strangers from the covenants of promise, without hope, and without God in the world" (Ephesians 2:12). It is God's law that convicts us of our sin (Romans 3:20; 7:7, 9). When we die to law as a system of justification (Romans 7:6) and we come under a system of justification by grace (Romans 6:14), then sin no longer has power over us. Those in Christ Jesus have no need to fear death. "Blessed are the dead, who die in the Lord from now on" (Revelation 14:13). Those who fall asleep in Jesus need not fear (1 Thessalonians 4:13f). We do not fear death but eagerly await the resurrection and the "redemption of our bodies" (Romans 8:23).

First Corinthians 15:58

> So, then, my beloved brothers, be stead-
> fast, unmovable, always abounding in the work
> of the Lord, knowing that your labor is not in
> vain in the Lord!

Earlier, the apostle talked about how the Corinthians had received the gospel and taken their stand in the gospel, and then he reflected their doubts saying, "Unless you believed in vain" (1 Corinthians 15:2). If there is no resurrection, said Paul, the apostolic preaching is vain, and the faith of those who accepted it is vain, and those who have died in Christ have perished (1 Corinthians 15:15–18). Here, having argued passionately for the coming resurrection, Paul urges his readers to be diligent in the Lord's work, "knowing that your labor is not in vain in the Lord." This can only be the confidence of one who knows that Christ is coming again, knows that the dead will be raised, knows that our bodies will be transformed, and knows that we will spend eternity with Christ! He wants them to be unmoved from their faith in the resurrection of Jesus, and in their own eventual resurrection from the dead.

Reflections on Chapter Fifteen

1. In 1 Corinthians 15:1–2, Paul describes four different ways in which the Corinthians interacted with the gospel. List them.
2. What is the essence of the gospel message according to 1 Corinthians 15:3–4?
3. Who was the last one Paul listed to whom the risen Christ appeared?
4. According to 1 Corinthians 15:12, some among the Corinthians were saying that there is no_____?
5. If there is no resurrection, then _____ has not been raised, the apostolic preaching is _____, the Corinthians were still in their _____, and those who had fallen asleep in Christ had _____ (1 Corinthians 15:13–18).
6. What is the last enemy that will be destroyed (1 Corinthians 15:26)?
7. What is Paul actually trying to say, in context, when he says, "Evil companions corrupt good morals" (1 Corinthians 15:33)?
8. Why does Paul use the illustration of the seed and the plant in his discussion of the resurrected body?
9. The sting of death is _____, and the power of sin is the _____.
10. When Paul says "Our labor is *not in vain* in the Lord," with what earlier passages in 1 Corinthians 15 does that statement connect?

16

First Corinthians 16:1

> Now concerning the collection for the
> saints, just as I commanded the churches of
> Galatia, you also do likewise. On the first day
> of the week, let each of you set something
> aside, placing in the treasury whatever he has
> profited, so that when I come there will be no
> collections.

This collection for the poor Judean saints is mentioned here, in Romans 15:30ff, and in 2 Corinthians 8–9. Paul had ordered or commanded the Galatian churches (Antioch of Pisidia, Lystra, Derbe, and Iconium) to do precisely the same thing as he ordered the Corinthians to do. He ordered them to take a collection, *kata mian sabbatou*, every first day of the week. The preposition *kata* indicates that this was a regular thing. The first day of the week, or literally, "the first of the seven" was the day of Christ's resurrection (Matthew 28:1ff; Mark 16:1ff; Luke 24:1ff; John 20:1). It was called "the Lord's Day" because it was resurrection day (Revelation 1:10; Didache 14:1). There seems to be no other logical reason for commanding them to set aside this collection on the first day of the week, besides the fact that it was the day of the Christian assembly when the whole church came together (Acts 20:7). It is true that the specific collection Paul has in mind was a special collection designed for a temporary purpose, but it is also true that contributing to a common fund administered by church leaders had been a practice since the beginning of the church (Acts 4:35, 37; 5:1). This practice was clearly carried on in the churches of the second century as well (Justin Martyr, Apology I. 65–67). We certainly have here a command to a number of churches and an example that seems to have been carried on by churches in successive generations because it was established by the apostles. Why would we not continue to follow this apostolic practice?

First Corinthians 16:3–4

> And whenever I do come, I will send whomever you approve along with letters, to carry your gift to Jerusalem. And whomever you consider worthy to go, he shall go with me.

Paul later sent Titus to Corinth to encourage the completion of this special gift. He also spoke of some brothers who were well-respected among the churches across the empire who would accompany the contribution to Jerusalem and ensure that the money was handled properly in the sight of all of the churches (2 Corinthians 8:16–22). Paul later explained why he did not end up coming to the Corinthians when he had planned to come, but sent Titus instead to accompany the contribution (2 Corinthians 2:1–4; 8:16–22).

First Corinthians 16:5–7

> I will come to you whenever I pass through Macedonia. For I am passing through Macedonia, and I will remain with you, if possible, and spend the winter, so that you can

COMMENTARY ON FIRST CORINTHIANS

> send me forth wherever I go. For I do not want
> to see you now just in passing, for I hope to
> remain with you for some time if the Lord
> permits.

Later on, some of the Corinthians accused Paul of being care-
less in telling the church he would visit soon because he ended up
not coming. He explained that he had truly intended to come,
but the Lord always has the final say in our plans (2 Corinthians
1:15–18). He did not come to them for one thing because a door
of ministry was opened for him by the Lord (2 Corinthians 2:12).
He also did not come to them when he first planned because he
did not want to come to them with a rebuke and wanted to give
them more time to make corrections and absorb what was said in
the first letter (2 Corinthians 2:1–4).

First Corinthians 16:8–11

> But I will remain in Ephesus until
> Pentecost. For a great and powerful door was
> opened for me, and many are opposed to it! If
> Timothy comes to you, take heed so that he
> can come to you without fear. For he does the
> work of the Lord just as I do! Therefore, let no
> one despise him! But send him forth in peace
> that he may come back to me! For I am waiting
> for him along with the brothers.

Paul told the Corinthians he was sending Timothy to them
to remind them of Paul's ways and Paul's teaching (1 Corinthians
4:17). Since some in Corinth were puffed up and pitting one person against another (1 Corinthians 4:6), Paul wanted to make
sure they respected and listened to Timothy, his representative.

187

Timothy was not an apostle, but he was a faithful evangelist, sharing apostolic teaching with those whom he encountered (2 Timothy 4:5). His orders not to despise Timothy recall his own words to Timothy himself (1 Timothy 4:12).

1 Corinthians 16:12

> Now concerning Apollos the brother, I have encouraged him often to come to you with the brothers. And it has not yet been his desire to come. He will come whenever he has a convenient time.

The introduction *peri de*, or "now concerning," indicates that the matter of a visit from Apollos was something about which the Corinthians had written Paul (1 Corinthians 7:1, etc.). The Corinthians were in need of good, solid, unifying influences. Apollos would have been very good for them, and for this reason, Paul had encouraged him to go and compliment the influence of Timothy, but Apollos had not yet felt that circumstances favored a visit. It seems likely that Apollos did finally go, and ended up accompanying the contribution to Jerusalem (2 Corinthians 8:16–22).

First Corinthians 16:13–14

> Be vigilant! Stand fast in the faith! Act like men! Hold Fast! Let all that you do be done in love!

Considering those Corinthians who were exalting human erudition over divine wisdom, those dividing into factions, those encouraging eating meat in the environs of the pagan temples, those making a mockery of the assembly, and those who were denying the resurrection of the dead, it is no wonder that Paul gives these terse commands. They needed to be awake and aware of things that were undermining the faith and unity of the church. They needed to unite on divinely revealed apostolic teaching and all speak the same thing. They needed to stand fast in the gospel of Christ, unmoved by pagan philosophies. They needed to be courageous in their Christian commitment. They needed to follow the admonitions of 1 Corinthians 13 and act in love toward one another.

First Corinthians 16:15–18

> I urge you, brothers, (you know the house of Stephanus, that they are the first fruits of Achaia, and they have committed themselves to the ministry to the saints), that you submit yourselves to such people and to all who are working together and laboring. And I rejoice at the coming of Stephanus, and Fortunatus, and Achacius because they have filled up what was lacking from you. For they refreshed my spirit and yours! Therefore, get to know such people!

There are three formal petitions in First Corinthians. The first is in 1 Corinthians 1:10 where Paul urges the people to shun divisions, speak the same thing, and be united in thinking and judgment. The second, similarly focused, is in 1 Corinthians 4:16, where the apostle urges the Corinthians to imitate him, his teachings, and his ways because he is the recipient of divine revelation. He urged a single apostolic standard of faith and practice and sent Timothy to reinforce this (1 Corinthians 4:17; 16:10). Finally, in 1 Corinthians 16:15, Paul appeals to the Corinthians to follow the leadership of those who were living out their faith in the right way. The family of Stephanus was comprised of such people. They had dedicated themselves to minister to the saints. They were busy doing the Lord's work for the good of the body of Christ. Stephanus, Fortunatus, and Achacius were the kinds of examples the Corinthians would do well to follow. Submitting to their loving, spiritual leadership would go a long way toward building the unity about which Paul was so concerned. They had refreshed the spirits of both Paul and the other Christians. This admonition is remarkably similar to the one Paul gives the Thessalonians (1 Thessalonians 5:12–13).

First Corinthians 16:19

> The churches of Asia greet you. Aquila
> and Prisca send many greetings in the Lord,
> along with the church that is in their house.

When Paul first came to Corinth, he met Aquila and Priscilla and worked with them making tents. Prisca is the familiar or informal way to say Priscilla's name. They, along with other Jews, had been expelled from Rome by the edict of Claudius (Acts 18:1ff). Later, when Paul wrote to the Romans, this Christian couple was back in Rome, hosting the church in their house (Romans 16:3–5). Paul had seen this couple before he wrote this letter, and sent their warmest greetings to the Corinthian church.

First Corinthians 16:20–24

> All the brothers send greetings to you.
> Greet one another with a holy kiss! The greet-
> ing of Paul with my own hand. If anyone does
> not love the Lord, let him be anathema. *Marana*

Tha. The grace of the Lord Jesus be with you.
My love be with all of you in Christ Jesus!

This passage is more than just a polite goodbye. Paul's admonition for them to greet one another is a plea for unity. It is similar to his plea in Romans 16:16. It is an outward act of acceptance toward one another! Paul often authenticated his letters with a short sentence or two written in very large letters in his own hand. Paul's limitations with his eyes caused him to write with very large letters (Galatians 6:11; 2 Thessalonians 3:17). One cannot love the Lord Jesus without keeping his commands (1 John 5:1–4). According to Kuhn's research, *Maran-Atha,* is a Hebrew/Aramaic expression, which most probably means either "the Lord is present" or "may our Lord come" (Kuhn, K. G., *Theological Dictionary of the New Testament* IV. 466–472). It is used in connection with the Lord's Supper in Didache 10.6, where it accompanies an admonition to repentance. This reminds us of 1 Corinthians 11:26 where Paul says we "proclaim the Lord's death until he comes." The curse upon those who do not love the Lord Jesus and do not show that love in their conduct, is given in expectation of the *parousia* or coming of the Lord in judgment. Perhaps in the context of this letter, the invocation hearkens back to 1 Corinthians 3:17 where Paul warns, "If anyone destroys the temple of God, him will God destroy, for the temple of God is holy, and that is what you are." Paul closed by saying that he loved all of them, certainly implying that he wanted the divided Corinthians to love one another (see chapter 13).

A TEACHER'S COMMENTARY ON SECOND CORINTHIANS

By Dan R. Owen, Ph.D.

INTRODUCTION

The second letter of Paul to the Corinthians is perhaps the most emotional letter in the New Testament library. The letter certainly reflects the ups and downs, the joys, and the sorrows of being a minister of the gospel of Christ. Paul calls his ministry a ministry of the New Covenant (2 Corinthians 3:6), the ministry of the Spirit (2 Corinthians 3:8), and the ministry of righteousness (2 Corinthians 3:9). He calls it the ministry of reconciliation (2 Corinthians 5:18), which involves the proclamation of "the message of reconciliation" (2 Corinthians 5:19). There is no more vital ministry on earth, and with this in mind, Paul insists that "we do not give up" (2 Corinthians 4:1, 16).

Paul's relationship with the Christian converts in Corinth was certainly an up and down relationship, and because he cared about them so deeply, it was an emotional roller coaster for Paul himself. He often felt like he loved them more openly and freely than they loved him in return (2 Corinthians 6:11–13; 7:1–3). Surely, all who minister faithfully for any length of time will experience the same things! The ministry of the gospel is all about building relationships with people while trying to teach them God's truth. This is always challenging!

Paul certainly wrote 2 Corinthians not long after having written 1 Corinthians. He was still involved in the collection of the contribution for the saints in Judea, which he spoke about in his first letter (1 Corinthians 16:1–2; 2 Corinthians 8–9). He commended the church for following the instructions of the first letter with regard to the man who was living with his father's wife (1 Corinthians 5; 2 Corinthians 7:8–13). He had planned to come to Corinth soon, but was deterred from doing so by another great door of opportunity the Lord placed in front of him (2 Corinthians 1:15–2:1). Since Paul indicates that the Corinthians committed to the contribution for the Jewish saints a year earlier, it cannot have been much more than eighteen to twenty-four months after writing First Corinthians that he wrote Second Corinthians (2 Corinthians 8:10; 9:2).

Some have suggested that the letter called Second Corinthians is actually two or three Pauline letters combined. While I understand the feelings that led them to this conclusion, I believe it is unnecessary. To some, chapters 8–9 regarding the contribution seem somewhat disconnected from the previous part of the letter, and chapters 10–13, which are so vehement in their attacks on the false teachers, seem also to reflect a different spirit than do the earlier parts of the letter. The more one reads the epistle, however, the less necessary these conclusions seem to be.

As early as chapter 3, Paul is talking about some people who were presenting letters of introduction and recommendation to the Corinthians, while perhaps implying that Paul carried no such letters (2 Corinthians 3:1–2). In that same chapter, Paul emphasized that he and his companions were ministers of the New Covenant and could see Christ in the pages of the Hebrew Scriptures, whereas others could not because of a veil lying over their hearts (2 Corinthians 3:15–16). He seems to call these people "unbelievers" for whom the gospel is veiled because Satan has "blinded their minds" (2 Corinthians 4:3–4). He later calls the Corinthians not to be "yoked together" with such unbelievers, but to "come out from among them" (2 Corinthians 6:14–7:1). Later on in the book, he openly compares himself with these people and shows that his credentials are spiritual, observable, and directly from God (2 Corinthians 11:16–12:10). So it seems that the more cryptic references to his antagonists in the earlier part of the book connect very well with the more open attacks on these Judaizing teachers in chapters 10–13.

In chapter 7, Paul commends the Corinthians for their sincerity and diligence in resolving the matter of the man living with his father's wife (2 Corinthians 7:11–13). He also urges them toward sincerity and diligence in the matter of the positive work of giving to the poor saints in Judea. While the false teachers were disparaging Paul for not keeping his promise to come to Corinth, for not having letters of recommendation, and for other things, and while they were confusing the minds of the people over basic Christian doctrine and practice, Paul sees this work of helping the Judean saints as a way to unify and focus the church toward something good and positive.

New Testament manuscripts provide no evidence that Second Corinthians was ever anything but one unified letter. So it seems that we should seek to ascertain the thematic elements that unite the entire epistle. That is what we will do in what follows.

In short, it seems that the more one studies the epistle, the more all of its parts really do seem to fit into a cohesive whole. Paul was trying to help these people and encourage them at the same time as others were trying to drive a wedge between Paul and his converts. There were many emotions involved on both sides, but Paul was trying to solidify these Christians in the midst of a difficult and volatile situation!

The Translation Used Here

In this commentary, as in my commentary on First Corinthians, the translation is my own translation of the United Bible Societies' Greek New Testament and *Nestle-Aland's 28*[th] *Edition Greek New Testament*. The critical text in these is virtually identical.

1

Greetings!

Second Corinthians 1:1–2

> Paul an apostle of Christ Jesus through the
> will of God and Timothy the brother, to the
> church of God which is in Corinth, along with
> all the saints who are in the whole of Achaia.
> Grace to you and peace from God our Father
> and the Lord Jesus Christ.

As in the book of Galatians, Paul emphasizes the fact that
his apostleship is a result of God's own will and choice (Galatians
1:15ff). The letter is written to the church in Corinth, but also
includes those Christians in the rest of Achaia, a larger audience
than that which he addressed in his first epistle. This would certainly include people like Phoebe and the church in Cenchrea
(Romans 16:1). This likely indicates that many of the issues plagu-
ing the Corinthians were also troubling the other congregations in
the southern part of Greece. The greetings from the Father and
the Lord Jesus show that the admonitions in the letter are not just
from Paul but from God himself.

Suffering and Comfort

Second Corinthians 1:3

> Blessed be the God and Father of our Lord
> Jesus Christ, the Father of tender mercies, and
> the God of all comfort, who comforts us in all
> our afflictions, so that we can comfort those in
> any affliction, through the comfort with which
> we ourselves are comforted by God.

The word *thlipsis*, translated affliction or tribulation or suffering, is a word which describes all kinds of pain and hardship. Paul's life, like everyone's life, was a series of ups and downs. He suffered much but had much joy as well. Paul had been the recipient of much suffering (2 Corinthians 6:4–10; 11:16–29). He had also been the recipient of much joy and encouragement (2 Corinthians 1:10–11; 7:13). He knows his readers are no different, except in their degree of suffering. Most of Paul's suffering was in direct connection with his ministry as an apostle and preacher to the Gentiles. When we endure suffering faithfully, and we experience the comfort of God in those times, we can comfort others who experience similar suffering.

Second Corinthians 1:5

> Because just as the sufferings of Christ
> abound toward us, so also through Christ our
> comfort also abounds.

As in other passages, Paul sees the suffering of Christians who are part of the body of Christ as an extension of the sufferings of Christ himself. Paul said, "I bear in my body the wounds of Jesus"

(Galatians 6:17), and "I fill up what is lacking in the afflictions of Christ" (Colossians 1:24). According to Paul, knowing Christ and the power of his resurrection also means knowing "the fellowship of his sufferings, being conformed unto his death" (Philippians 3:10). When the body of Christ, the church, suffers, Christ is suffering. Christians who suffer are suffering "with Him" in expectation that they will also be glorified "with Him" (Romans 8:17). But just as Christ suffered and was comforted by his Father and the angels who were sent to minister to Him, so we also receive the comfort of God when we suffer faithfully!

Second Corinthians 1:6

> And whether we are afflicted, it is for your comfort and salvation, and whether we are comforted, it is for your comfort, which works by the steadfastness of these sufferings which we suffer. And our hope for you is firm, knowing that just as you are partakers of the sufferings, so you are also partakers of the comfort.

Paul was suffering for the salvation of souls and to accomplish the work of the Lord. When he suffered bravely and remained faithful, it gave hope and courage to the people of God. As stated earlier, when he was comforted by God in his sufferings, he was able to comfort others who suffered. Paul believed and taught that we must suffer with Christ before we can be glorified with him (Romans 8:17–18). Based on his own experience in Asia and in other places, he assured the Corinthians that though they may share in suffering, they will also share in God's comfort. Paul had a story to tell them, a story of great struggle and great deliverance.

Paul's Suffering and Deliverance in Asia

Second Corinthians 1:8–10

> For we do not want you to be ignorant,
> brothers, about the affliction which befell us
> in Asia, so that we were exceedingly burdened
> beyond our power, so that we were in doubt
> even of life, but we had within ourselves the
> sentence of death so that we were not trusting
> in ourselves, but in God who raises the dead,
> who also delivered us from so great a death and
> will deliver us, in whom we have placed our
> hope that he will yet again deliver us!

In his first letter to the Corinthians, when discussing the resurrection of the dead, Paul briefly mentioned his suffering in Asia. For the sake of those who were denying the resurrection, he said, "If only in the manner of men I fought with the wild beasts in Ephesus, what profit is that to me? For if the dead are not raised, 'Let us eat and drink, for tomorrow we die'" (1 Corinthians 15:32). Paul did not choose to undergo suffering like what he had undergone in Ephesus for worldly reasons. He was forced to suffer because of his Christianity and because of his proclamation of Christ and the true God! He was willing to suffer because he believed in the resurrection and eternal life with Christ! He called the Ephesians to turn from idolatry to the true God and Savior, and as a result, he threatened the livelihood of those who depended on idolatry to make their money (Acts 19:17–27). Paul was delivered from death by a faithful Creator, and he trusted that as long as God needed him to further his great purpose, God would continue to deliver him (Philippians 1:23–25). Paul had experienced this divine deliverance many times as recounted in 2 Corinthians 11:16–29.

Second Corinthians 1:11

> As you work together with us through your prayers, so that thanks may be given by many people for the grace that was shown to us, through many prayers.

Paul believed that prayer was powerful in the outcomes of circumstances. He credited the prayers of many people, including the Corinthians, for the deliverance given to him by God. He wanted the Corinthians to know how important their prayers were in his life and work. He wanted to feel a partnership with them in everything and wanted them to feel it as well. Paul's struggle in this book was the feeling that the Corinthians did not always reciprocate his feelings for them (2 Corinthians 6:11–13; 7:2).

Second Corinthians 1:12–14

> For our boasting to you is this, the testimony of our conscience that with godly sincerity and pure motives, not with fleshly wisdom, but in the grace of God we conducted ourselves in the world, and even more so toward you. And we are not writing to you anything but what you read and understand, and I hope that you will understand until the end. Just as you have known us in part, that we will be the object of your boasting just as you will be the object of our boasting in the day of the Lord Jesus.

Paul is already on the defensive with his readers. His motives have been questioned by others and his defense is that the Corinthians know he was transparent and sincere in everything he did among them. Later, he says that he was not, "like many" peddling the word of God (2 Corinthians 2:17). He was not like those who depend on "letters of recommendation" (2 Corinthians 3:1). He insists later that he never treated any of them unjustly or sought to exploit them for financial gain or behaved in any corrupt way, nor did he cause anyone there to sin (2 Corinthians 6:3; 7:2). Paul's desire is that the Corinthians could boast or brag about Paul as much as he would brag about them on the day of judgment. It is obvious, though, as the apostle writes this letter, that he does not believe the Corinthians are as positive about Paul as Paul is about them.

Why Paul Changed his Plans to Visit Corinth Again

Second Corinthians 1:15

> And in this confidence I had wanted to come to you at first, so that you might have a second benefit, and by you, to pass through to Macedonia and again, from Macedonia to come to you, and from you be sent forth to Judea.

This seems to be the same plan of travel that was partially enunciated in 1 Corinthians 16:5–9. However, we all know that circumstances often dictate that we must change our plans. Paul was an instrument of God's will. He could plan, but was always open to change those plans if God wanted him elsewhere.

Second Corinthians 1:17

> When planning this, I did not do so insincerely, did I? Or the things that I decide, do I decide in a fleshly manner, so that the "Yes! Yes!" or the "No! No!" might rest with me?

Clearly, the Corinthians seem to have been upset that Paul had not come to them as he told them he planned to do. The text seems to imply that others, probably the Judaizing teachers among the Corinthians, were accusing Paul of not being trustworthy. Paul did not purposefully try to mislead the Corinthians about his plans. Paul is frustrated in this letter because he is sincerely trying to help the Corinthians spiritually, working for their salvation, while another group of people was working to drive a wedge between him and those he converted to Christ. Unfortunately, ministers of the gospel often find this to be the case in present experience for a variety of reasons.

Second Corinthians 1:18

> God is faithful because our word to you was not "Yes and No." For the Son of God, Jesus Christ, who was preached among you by us, by me and Silvanus and Timothy, is not "Yes and No" but in him is the "Yes."

God is trustworthy. He is not fickle or insincere or indecisive. But with God rests the final say in everyone's plans. The will of God is paramount. Christ has the final "Yes," the final say in anyone's plans if they live for him. Paul is telling the Corinthians that he does not make plans independently of the will of Christ. When he plans, he does so, saying, "If it is God's will," I would like to do this or that, knowing that God has the final say.

Second Corinthians 1:20

> For as many as are the promises of God, with him is the 'Yes.' Wherefore, also, through him is the Amen through us to the glory of God.

The promises of God are sure and dependable. He cannot lie (Hebrews 6:18). His promises represent his unbreakable will, the predestined plan of God. All of us work inside of that will. As we try to do God's will, he uses all the events of our lives, both pleasant and unpleasant, for the good of his purpose (Romans 8:28). It is in the stated promises of God, the unchangeable purposes of God, that we find the stability and the solid foundation of life. We do not find our stability in the plans of finite men and women because our plans often change when circumstances dictate that they must. When this happens, we adjust and try to glorify God in the process. This is what Paul had done.

Second Corinthians 1:21–22

> It is God, who establishes us with you because of Christ, and has anointed us, and has sealed us and given us the down payment of the Spirit in our hearts.

These statements deal with the unfailing promises of God. God promised a special anointing of the Holy Spirit to his apostles. Paul was a recipient of this special anointing. God has, for the sake of Christ, made us his people, his elect. This is based on the promise, "In your seed all the nations of the earth shall be blessed" (Genesis 22:18; Galatians 3:16). The blessings of God are in Christ where those who have accepted the gospel by being baptized into Christ now find themselves (Genesis 22:18; Ephesians 1:3). God has given us all of the spiritual gifts we need to do his work (1 Corinthians 1:4–7; 12:8–10, 28ff). He has also given every Christian the seal of the Spirit, the indwelling presence of the Spirit, as a down payment on our eternal inheritance (Romans 5:6; 1 Corinthians 12:13; Ephesians 1:13–14). These are things that do not change with the circumstances of life. Our plans may be uncertain, but these things are not.

Second Corinthians 1:23

> And I call upon God as a witness for my soul, that it was to spare you that I did not come to Corinth. Not that we lord it over your faith, but we are fellow workers for your joy, for you stand by faith.

There were actually two reasons that Paul decided it was not God's will that he come to Corinth at the time he had originally planned. One reason, as expressed here, is that he did not want to come again to Corinth in a very heavy-handed manner, having to confront them to the degree he had done in the first letter (2 Corinthians 2:4). Paul says repeatedly in this letter that God gave him authority as an apostle and preacher of the gospel for building people up and not for tearing them down (2 Corinthians 10:8; 13:10). He wanted to come to them when things were less tense so he could have a more lasting, positive influence on them. This certainly speaks to the methods of ministers as we patiently and lovingly correct people, yet encourage them, so they will not become discouraged. When to correct and how much to correct is a constant decision evangelists and elders must make. While correction needs to be done, much correction can be done privately and on an individual basis in the context of a loving, supportive relationship (Galatians 6:2). Paul's prayerful judgment was that his visit to Corinth needed to be delayed in order to cultivate a better, long-term relationship. Instead of coming to Corinth himself, he sent his young protégé, Titus (2 Corinthians 7:13–16). The second reason Paul was convicted that he didn't need to go to Corinth when he had first planned, was that a great door of opportunity was opened to him in the Lord (2 Corinthians 2:12). While that door resulted in the "smell of Christ" being spread to other places, it kept Paul from coming to Corinth when he had planned to come. Paul saw all of this as God's providential will.

Reflections on Chapter 1

1. What are some of the great benefits of suffering to Christians according to 2 Corinthians 1:3–6?
2. What particular sufferings were fresh on Paul's mind, and where else can we read about these sufferings?
3. Why were the Corinthians a bit upset with Paul according to 2 Corinthians 1:15ff?
4. Compare the way Paul viewed his plans with the way we view our plans and discuss.
5. Why did Paul delay his trip to Corinth according to 2 Corinthians 1:23? According to 2 Corinthians 2:12f?
6. Does the delay of Paul's trip to Corinth have anything to say to preachers about whether we should delay preaching on certain topics at times and save them for a better time? Discuss.

2

S econd Corinthians 2:1

> I decided this in myself, that I would not
> come to you again with sorrow! For if I cause
> you sorrow, who is it that makes me happy but
> the one who is made sorrowful by me? And I
> have written this same thing to you, so that
> when I come, I might not have sorrow from
> those who ought to give me joy, being confident
> in all of you that my joy is the joy of you all!

Paul is speaking about his own feelings and the relationship he has with the Corinthians. He immensely dislikes making people sad when those same people bring him so much joy as they try to serve God. He did not want his next visit to Corinth to be confrontational and stressful, but joyous. Helping people grow spiritually is about not only teaching them the truth, but building positive, encouraging relationships with them. Paul is confident that the very same things that bring him joy, seeing people trust Christ and serve Christ, are the very things that would bring real joy to his readers.

Second Corinthians 2:4

> For out of much affliction and anguish of
> heart I wrote to you with many tears, not so

that I might make you sorrowful, but so that
you may know the love which I have so abun-
dantly for you!

In Paul's first letter to the Corinthians, he rebuked them for
tolerating the man living with his father's wife, rebuked them for
solving their problems in pagan courts instead of among God's
people, corrected them for flirting with idolatry, rebuked them
for the divisive way they were celebrating the Lord's Supper, and
rebuked them for the selfish manner in which some of them were
using their spiritual gifts. He had to correct these things, but he
did not enjoy causing them distress in the process. He would not
have risked telling them God's truth about these matters if he had
not loved them deeply and if he was not seeking their salvation.
Also, Paul had earned the right to say anything to the Corinthians
because he had built a relationship with them and had lived with
integrity in front of them (2 Corinthians 6:11–13; 7:2–4).

How to Treat the Penitent Man

Second Corinthians 2:5–6

For if anyone has caused sorrow, he has
not caused me sorrow, but in part, so that I
might not press too hard, he has caused sorrow
for all of you. Sufficient to such a person is the
correction carried out by the many.

In 1 Corinthians 5, Paul instructed the Corinthian church
to excommunicate the impenitent man during the assembly of
Christians. They were not to extend the fellowship of the church
to this man any longer. The Corinthian church obeyed Paul's
instructions in this matter (2 Corinthians 2:5; 7:10–12). "The

many," the whole church, had withdrawn fellowship from this man. Now, evidently, the offender had repented, and the church needed to welcome him back into their fellowship and welcome him to the Lord's table again, and they seem to have been reluctant to do so. The word *sufficient* indicates that there had been enough corporate censure. Now there needed to be corporate forgiveness and acceptance.

Second Corinthians 2:7

> So that you should all the more forgive him and comfort him, lest this one be drowned in too much sorrow. Wherefore, I appeal to you, confirm your love to him!

The purpose of good church discipline is "for the destruction of the flesh, so that the spirit may be saved in the day of the Lord Jesus" (1 Corinthians 5:5). If the church rejects a person, even when that person has repented, they risk breaking the spirit of the individual and driving them away from God forever. This was never the objective of Paul's instructions! We should not make it difficult for penitent people to be welcomed back into the good graces of the church. Sometimes we add extra requirements like walking down the aisle and making a public confession before we are willing to accept a person back. There is no biblical basis for this. Though there is nothing wrong with a person making a public admission of wrong, the biblical objective is simply that the person turns away from the sin in which he/she was involved and begins doing what is right again. The church leaders may wish to welcome the penitent person back publicly and inform the church that the person is now trying to live faithfully, but there is no biblical precedent for making a person "walk the aisle." First John 1:9 is talking about confessing one's sins to God, and James 5:16

is talking about individuals who have sinned against one another, acknowledging their sins to one another and praying for one another. When Peter was telling Simon the Sorcerer how to get right with God, he simply instructed him to "repent, therefore of your wickedness, and pray to the Lord that the thought of your heart may be forgiven you" (Acts 8:22). We should never require more of people than God requires! We should readily confirm our love and support to penitent people!

Second Corinthians 2:9

> For this reason I wrote to you, so that I might know the proof of you, whether you are obedient in all things.

The tearstained letter written out of much affliction and anguish of heart (2 Corinthians 2:4) is the same letter written to see if the people would be obedient (2 Corinthians 2:9). Given the discussion of the man who was excommunicated, this is certainly the letter we call First Corinthians. Obedience in small things is easy, but to obey in things which involve the entire church and the personal feelings of individuals is often difficult. The Corinthian church had shown themselves to be compliant with God's instructions through the apostle Paul.

Second Corinthians 2:10

> And to whomever you forgive anything, I also forgive. For whoever I forgive, if I forgive anything, it is for your sakes in the presence of Christ, so that we may not be taken advantage of by Satan, for we are not ignorant of his way of thinking!

The man who had openly lived in sin with his father's wife had not directly sinned against Paul. Paul readily forgave him when the man repented, removed himself from unlawful congress, and began to conduct himself properly again. Paul communicated his forgiveness or acceptance of the man to encourage the Corinthian church to follow suit and accept him as well. Paul, like all of us who are truly leading spiritually, influenced others by his example as much as by his teaching! Satan always finds more than one way to destroy the souls of men and women. If he did not succeed in destroying the man through sin, he thought he might succeed by influencing the church not to forgive the man and accept him back. Only those who think about God's will for all parties and from every angle can avoid being outsmarted by the father of lies!

2 Corinthians 2:12

> But when I came to Troas for the gospel of Christ and a door was opened for me in the Lord, I had no rest for my spirit because I did not find Titus, my brother, but bidding farewell to them I went forth into Macedonia.

The two Corinthian epistles and Romans were written before Paul was arrested in Jerusalem in Acts 21. In 2 Corinthians, as in Romans and 1 Corinthians, there is no hint of the arrest and confinement that took Paul from Jerusalem to Rome. We know that Paul came to Troas after a three-month stay in Greece (Acts 20:3–7). Both 1 Corinthians 16 and Romans 15:30ff talk about the contribution Paul was intending to take to the poor saints in Jerusalem. So, if we imply from 1 Corinthians 16 and 2 Corinthians 8–9 that the gathering of the contribution from the people at Corinth had been going on for at least a year, then it is likely that within the space of eighteen months to two years, both First and Second

Corinthians had been written by Paul. The plans Paul describes in Romans 15 and both First and Second Corinthians are not the way things turned out in the Book of Acts. It is likely that after both of the Corinthian letters were written, Paul wrote Romans during his three-month stay in Greece recorded in Acts 20:3. In Romans, the contribution seems to be completely ready to go to Jerusalem (Romans 15:25–31; *The Life and Epistles of Saint Paul*, Conybeare and Howson, pp. 496–497).

When Paul came to Troas, he was anxiously looking for Titus because, among other things, Titus had been sent to Corinth in the place of Paul to see how the Corinthians were doing and to report on whether they had complied with the things written by Paul in First Corinthians. Paul was anxious about the situation in Corinth and about his relationship with them, and found no relief for that anxiety when he went to Troas (2 Corinthians 2:12–13). That being said, there was "a door opened" for Paul, some kind of great opportunity to do God's work. So Paul moved on to do God's work without any report on the situation in Corinth. The reason Second Corinthians was written seems to have been that Paul later did find Titus who reported to him everything that was going on in Corinth (2 Corinthians 7:5–7).

The Challenge of Being a Minister of Christ

Second Corinthians 2:14–16

> But thanks be to God who always leads us in a triumphal procession in Christ, and through us manifests the smell of the knowl-edge of him in every place. For we are a sweet smell of Christ for God among those who are saved and among those who are perishing. To the one group, a smell of death resulting in

death, and to the other group a smell of life resulting in life. And who is sufficient for these things?

Both Gerhart Delling (*Theological Dictionary of the New Testament* III: 160) and Conybeare and Howson (p. 444, note 5) agree that the verb *thriambeuo* used here means to lead people in a Roman triumph parade. The victorious Roman commander would lead the prisoners along with his victorious troops in a parade through Rome to the Capitol. Incense was offered, filling the air with its sweet smell. The parade ended with the death of the prisoners and the accolades heaped upon the victors. For this reason, for the prisoners, the smell was the smell of death, but for the victors, it was the smell of life and reward. Paul carried the smell of Christ wherever he went! Though he was filled with anxiety when he left Troas, God still used Paul, even with all of his fears and anxieties, to spread the smell of Christ to new places. For those who accepted and obeyed the gospel, it was the smell of life, but to those who rejected Christ and his wonderful gospel, it was the smell of death and punishment. No matter what was happening in Paul's personal life or what circumstances surrounded him, God always managed to use him to spread the "smell of Christ." Surely, every evangelist, every elder, every teacher, and every Christian wants the same thing to be true of him/her.

At the end of 2 Corinthians 2:16, Paul asks a very reflective question when he says, "And who is adequate (or sufficient or competent) for these things?" What flawed human being, whether apostle or prophet or evangelist or teacher, is adequate to represent Christ everywhere, all the time, in every circumstance of life? To be God's man, God's ambassador, is a great and difficult responsibility (2 Corinthians 5:18–20). Paul felt very inadequate for such a daunting task, but he came to realize that God could and did use him in every circumstance to reveal the message and the character of Christ to others. His adequacy was not in himself but in the powerful working of God (2 Corinthians 3:5–6). As ministers today, we must remember that we can't, but God can! God can do more through our feeble efforts than we ever imagined.

Second Corinthians 2:17

> For we are not (like many) peddling the word of God, rather, as of sincerity, as of God in the presence of God, we are speaking in Christ.

Paul was a true seeker of souls. Paul truly sought to share the word of God without addition or subtraction. Paul believed what he taught and was sincerely trying to share the blessings of Christ with others. He desperately wanted the Corinthians to trust in that fact based on what they had actually experienced in the eighteen months Paul had worked with them (Acts 18:11). There is a great principle here. All of us who teach and preach the word must earn the respect of the people we serve. The people will make their judgments about our sincerity and dedication by observing us and associating with us over time. If we prove ourselves to be diligent, trustworthy, sincere, and consistent in telling God's truth, people will respect us and be much more willing to follow our spiritual leadership. When Paul says that he is not "like many" peddling the word of God, he is referring to a group of anonymous teachers who were trying to drive a wedge between him and the Corinthians. The "like many" of 2 Corinthians 2:17 and the "like some" of 2 Corinthians 3:1 describe the same group of interlopers. These are likely the same ones who were unable to see Christ in the Hebrew scriptures because they had a veil over their hearts (2 Corinthians 3:14–15). They are the ones for whom the gospel is veiled, the unbelievers whose minds have been blinded by the god of this world (2 Corinthians 4:3–4). Paul mentions this same group repeatedly in 2 Corinthians 10:2, 7, 11, 12; 11:4, 12–13.

Sincerity and transparency were obvious in Paul's day-to-day interactions with people. His teaching and his conduct were consistent. Paul knew that the Corinthians could see this sincerity and consistency. It was this that gave him his spiritual credibility, and he was depending on them to see this.

Reflections on Chapter 2

1. How is Paul's personal relationship with the Corinthians getting tangled up with his responsibility to preach the truth to them in 2 Corinthians 2:1–3? Talk about how this can create difficulties for preachers or elders.

2. Having heard from Titus about how the Corinthians responded to Paul's tearstained letter, how does he advise the Corinthians to treat the man who had been living with his father's wife (2 Corinthians 2:5–10; cf. 1 Corinthians 5)?

3. Explore what it means to the minister of Christ to be "the smell of Christ in every place."

4. What do you think was in Paul's mind when he wrote "And who is sufficient for these things" in 2 Corinthians 2:16? Discuss your feelings about self-sufficiency and competence to be a representative of Christ.

5. Discuss the two kinds of teachers/preachers that are mentioned in 2 Corinthians 2:17 and how we see those in the church today.

3

Second Corinthians 3:1

> Are we beginning to commend ourselves
> again? We don't need, do we, as do some, letters
> of commendation to you or from you?

This refers to his statement in 2 Corinthians 2:17 about some who were peddling the word of God and were less than sincere. Paul had never needed to "commend himself" nor prove himself to the Corinthians except through his teaching, his consistent example, and the signs of an apostle which he had performed before them (1 Corinthians 2:4–5; 2 Corinthians 12:12). Paul was being forced into a situation where he was being compared with other teachers who were trying to gain the allegiance of the Corinthians. Paul wanted the people to follow Christ alone as he did (1 Corinthians 4:16; 11:1). He believed that comparing people and competition between people was a fruitless and unprofitable endeavor that only led to division and strife (2 Corinthians 10:12). Therefore, to prove his credibility, he reverted back to what the Corinthians had seen and heard from Paul in the year and a half that he had spent with them.

DAN R. OWEN

Living Letters!

Second Corinthians 3:2–3

> You are our letter, written in our hearts,
> known and read by all men. Making it plain
> that you are a letter from Christ, ministered by
> us, written not with ink, but by the Spirit of
> the living God, not on tablets of stone, but on
> tablets that are human hearts!

The Corinthian converts were a living letter to all who observed them or heard about them. The Corinthians' lives and actions communicated the changes that had been made in them through Paul's ministry and through the power of Christ. Their lives also told of ways in which they had not yet allowed God to change them. Paul and his companions often told others about the good things they had seen in the lives of their converts, and probably, about some of their concerns. The lives of the Corinthians, like Paul's life and our lives, are open letters read by all people about what God is doing (or not doing) in us. Paul wanted his own living letter, his own conduct, to stand as his only letter of recommendation to all who would bother to "read" it.

The Corinthian Christians were a letter from Christ to the world "ministered by us." It was through Paul's ministry of reconciliation and through him sharing the message of reconciliation that the Corinthians came to know Christ and be changed by Christ (2 Corinthians 5:18–20). Inasmuch as Christ had changed the thinking and the behavior of the Corinthians, this living letter had been written "by the Spirit of the living God." The fruits of the Spirit had been manifested in them (Galatians 5:22–23). The Spirit writes his letters in human hearts and minds, changing people from the inside out (Ephesians 4:22–24).

Second Corinthians 3:4–5

> And we have this kind of confidence
> toward God through Christ, not that we are
> sufficient in ourselves to consider anything
> as from ourselves, but our sufficiency is from
> God.

When Paul asked the rhetorical question in 2 Corinthians 2:16, "And who is sufficient for these things," he anticipated that no man by himself would be adequate as a vehicle to spread the knowledge of Christ everywhere he went and to everyone he met. But God works through weak human beings. We are truly clay jars, cracked and easily broken, but God has entrusted us with the treasure of the "message of reconciliation" (2 Corinthians 4:7; 5:18–19). God works through those who try to serve him in spite of our weaknesses and imperfections. Our confidence is in God and not in ourselves (2 Corinthians 1:9)!

Ministers of the New Covenant

Second Corinthians 3:6

> He has made us sufficient as ministers of
> the New Covenant, not of the letter, but of the
> spirit, for the letter kills, but the spirit gives life.

Like Paul and his coworkers, evangelists today are ministers of the New Covenant. God foretold the coming of this New Covenant through Jeremiah (Jeremiah 31:31–34). We who preach today, like Paul, are not trying to persuade people to walk with God according to the covenant or agreement that God made with Israel at Sinai (Exodus 19:5–6). We are trying to preach the gospel of Christ, the "message of reconciliation" in which God offers the New Covenant to all who will accept it. The Sinai covenant was an agreement between God and the nation of Israel (Exodus 19:5–6; 20:1). The New Covenant is an agreement between God and each individual who hears and obeys the gospel. The New Covenant is offered through the preaching of the gospel and is accepted through obedience to the gospel on the part of each individual. We are trying to "persuade men" to accept this covenant because we know that they will all face God in judgment (2 Corinthians 5:10–11). Paul says he is not a minister of the letter, but of the spirit. The "letter" is the literal contextual meaning of the Hebrew Scriptures. The "spirit" is the spiritual meaning of the Hebrew Scriptures as it applies to Christ. The letter is the literal paschal lamb slaughtered and eaten on the fourteenth day of Abib. The spirit is Christ the Lamb of God who takes away the sin of the world. The letter is physical circumcision. The spirit is the circumcision of the mind and heart (Romans 2:28–29). The letter is the Levitical high priest who went into the physical holy of holies on Yom Kippur with sacrificial blood. The spirit is Christ, our High Priest, who enters heaven itself with his own sinless blood to atone for the sins of those who accept his covenant. The risen Christ explained the spiritual meaning of the Hebrew Bible to his apostles prior to his ascension when he explained the passages in the Law, the prophets, and the Psalms that applied to Christ (Luke 24:44–47). Some of Paul's opponents in the Galatian churches and in Corinth were ministers of the letter, trying to push Judaism on the people, but Paul wanted it to be crystal clear that he and those like him were ministers of the New Covenant. There is no answer for sin in Judaism. There is no adequate atonement (Hebrews 10:4). Only Christ, our perfect priest and our perfect sacrifice, is the answer.

Second Corinthians 3:7–9

> And if the ministry of death, written and
> engraved in stone came with glory, so that the
> sons of Israel were not able to look at Moses'
> face because of the glory of his face which was
> passing away, then how much more shall the
> ministry of the spirit be accompanied with
> glory? For if the ministry of condemnation was
> glorious, how much more shall the ministry of
> righteousness abound with glory!

The comparison begun in 2 Corinthians 3:6 is carried forward and expanded in 2 Corinthians 3:7–9. The ministry of the
New Covenant (2 Corinthians 3:6) is the same as the ministry of
the spirit (2 Corinthians 3:8) and the ministry of righteousness (2
Corinthians 3:9). The ministry of the letter (2 Corinthians 3:6)
is the same as the ministry of death (2 Corinthians 3:7) and the
ministry of condemnation (2 Corinthians 3:9). There is also the
comparison between the glory of the "letter" and the glory of the
"spirit." The glory of the first one was remarkable, but fading away
(2 Corinthians 3:7, 11, 13). The glory of the second ministry is
more glorious than the first and is not fading away but "remains"
(2 Corinthians 3:11).

Second Corinthians 3:10–13

> For what came with glory is made less glo-
> rious, in part because of that which so greatly
> surpasses it in glory. For if that which is passing
> away came with glory, how much more rather
> will that which remains be glorious. Having this
> hope, then, we have a great deal of confidence.

The word *katargoumenos*, "passing away or fading away," is in 2 Corinthians 3:7, 10, 13 and always describes the letter, the ministry of death, and the ministry of condemnation. Again, the "letter" is the literal Jewish way of looking at the Hebrew Bible without seeing Christ in it. Clearly, by repeating the term "passing away," Paul is emphasizing the temporary nature of the ministry of the letter as he did in other places (Galatians 3:23–25; Ephesians 2:14–15). When he says, "Therefore, having this hope, we have great confidence," he is talking about the hope of the New Covenant, the spirit as opposed to the letter, the ministry of the Spirit, or the ministry of righteousness. Later on, Paul calls it "the ministry of reconciliation" (2 Corinthians 5:18). Paul is confident that in being ministers of the New Covenant, we are acting in the best way possible in concert with God's eternal plan for man's salvation.

Second Corinthians 3:13b

> And we are not like Moses, who put a veil over his face, so that the sons of Israel might not gaze upon the end of what was passing away, but their minds were hardened.

When we read the verses that follow, we realize that Paul is setting up sort of an allegorical contrast. As ministers of the New Covenant, we are not like Moses. We are not like Moses in one respect. Moses put a veil over his face (Exodus 34:33, 35). We who are ministers of the New Covenant *do not* put a veil over our faces. The reason Moses put the veil over his face was so that the Israelites could not see the end of that old ministry which "was passing away." This is figurative, of course. Moses did not want them to have to look at the brilliance and glory of his face, which gradually faded away the longer he was outside of God's presence.

The fact that they could not see the gradual fading of that glory, in some figurative way, describes their failure to see the ministry of Judaism as a temporary thing. This seems to be what Paul means when he says "their minds were hardened" (2 Corinthians 3:14a). He refers to this situation again in 2 Corinthians 4:4 where he says the "god of this world has blinded the minds of the unbelieving" so that they cannot see the glory of Christ. Specifically, the minds of many of the Israelites were hardened or blinded from seeing the glory of Christ in the pages of the Hebrew Scriptures!

Second Corinthians 3:14

> But their minds were hardened, for until this very day the veil remains whenever the old covenant is read, it not being revealed to them that in Christ it is done away! But until this day, every time Moses is read, the veil lies upon their heart.

Unlike us, who do not have a veil over our faces, those people to whom Paul is referring have a veil over their "hearts" or minds (2 Corinthians 3:15). This causes their minds to be "blinded" or "hardened" and, therefore, prevents them from accepting what the Hebrew Scriptures say about Christ. They can see the paschal lamb in Exodus 12, but not the "Lamb of God who takes away the sin of the world" (John 1:29). They can see the manna sent by God in Exodus, but not the "living bread which came down out of heaven and gives life to the world" (John 6:35, 51). They can see the priests of the Aaronic order offering sacrifices according to the instructions of Leviticus, but they cannot see the one who was made "a priest forever after the order of Melchizedek" (Psalm 110:4; Hebrews 6:20). They can lament the suffering of God's servant Israel in Isaiah 53, but cannot begin at that Scripture, like

DAN R. OWEN

Phillip did, and preach Jesus (Acts 8:35). Such examples could be multiplied.

Second Corinthians 3:16

> But whenever anyone turns to the Lord,
> the veil is removed.

The Lord in this verse is the Lord Jesus. When one accepts Jesus as God incarnate, the promised Messiah, the revealer of the spiritual meaning of Scripture and the eternal plan of God, then one can see Christ in many places in the Hebrew Scriptures. It was the risen Jesus himself who explained all of this to the apostles (Luke 24:44–45).

Second Corinthians 3:17

> The Lord is the spirit, and where the spirit
> of the Lord is, there is freedom.

Contextually, the Lord Jesus is the *spirit* as opposed to the *letter* (2 Corinthians 3:6). He is the spiritual or full meaning of the Hebrew Bible as opposed to the letter or literal contextual meaning. It is in Christ that the Scriptures are fulfilled. When people accept the "spirit" or spiritual meaning of the Hebrew Bible as it is realized in Christ, they are set free from the letter or Judaism, which was always meant to be "passing away" or "fading away."

Second Corinthians 3:18

> And all of us with unveiled face are
> beholding as in a mirror the glory of the Lord.

When we read the "old covenant" (2 Corinthians 3:14) or when we read "Moses" (2 Corinthians 3:15), we see the glory of the Lord Jesus. We see Christ the Lamb, Christ the priest, Christ the sacrifice, and Christ the builder of God's new Temple. We see Christ lifted up like the serpent in the wilderness (John 3:14–15). We see Christ as the true ladder between heaven and earth (John 1:51). We see Christ as the true manna or bread from heaven (John 6:29–35). We see Christ as Jacob's well, the source of living water (John 4:14). This list could go on, but we see beyond the letter or literal reading of the Hebrew Bible to the spiritual shadows that point to Jesus and his glory.

> And we are transformed into the same image from one glory to another as from the Lord, the spirit.

When we read the Hebrew Bible without blinders on, we see Christ and are transformed into the image of Christ. In other words, we are made into followers of Christ, or Christians, not made into Jews. In being transformed into the image of Christ, we are changed from that passing fading glory of the old covenant into that surpassing, superior glory of the New Covenant that is offered to people in the gospel of Christ (2 Corinthians 3:10, 13; 4:4). Some have tried to use "the Lord is the spirit" in 2 Corinthians 3:17 to teach the divinity of the Holy Spirit. Paul is not talking about the Holy Spirit in 2 Corinthians 3:17–18. This understanding completely ignores the context and the contrast between the letter on the one hand, and the spirit on the other hand (2 Corinthians 3:6). Paul uses the terms *letter* and *spirit* in the same way in Romans 2:28–29. Ministers of the New Covenant use the Hebrew Bible to preach Christ! Ministers of the old covenant or the letter do not preach Christ from the Hebrew Bible. Paul made Timothy into a minister of the New Covenant. Paul spoke of the Hebrew Scriptures when he told Timothy, "From childhood you have known the Holy Scriptures, which are able to make you wise unto salvation, *through faith in Christ Jesus*" (2 Timothy 3:15; emphasis mine). The entire book of Hebrews is a great example of preaching Christ from Scriptures like Psalm 8:4–6, Psalm 95:7–11, Psalm 110:1–4, Jeremiah 31:31–34, and Habakkuk 2:3–4. The point of 2 Corinthians 3:18 is that when Christians look into the Hebrew Scriptures, they see Christ and are transformed into the image of Christ, an image which far surpasses the glory of the old covenant! Paul and his companions, unlike his subversive opponents in Corinth, were ministers of the New Covenant.

Reflections on Chapter 3

1. How were the Christians in Corinth letters of commendation from Paul?
2. How were the Christians in Corinth letters from Christ?
3. What does Paul mean when he says his "sufficiency" or competence does not come from himself but from God? See 2 Corinthians 3:5–6.
4. Discuss what it means to be a minister of the New Covenant.
5. In your own words, what is the New Covenant?
6. What does Paul mean by the terms *letter* and *spirit* in this context (2 Corinthians 3:6ff)?
7. According to 2 Corinthians 3:14–15, exactly *when* did the people to whom Paul refers have a veil over their faces?
8. Where can you find a reference to this veil in chapter 4?
9. In verse 16–17, *who* exactly is "the Lord"?
10. In what way is the Lord the spirit? (2 Corinthians 3:6, 17).

4

As God's Ministers, We Never Give Up!

Second Corinthians 4:1

> For this reason, since we have this minis-
> try, just as we were granted mercy, we do not
> give up!

"For this reason" goes back to the fact that through Christ we are able to see the "glory of the Lord" Jesus in the Hebrew Bible. It goes back to the fact that we preach Christ from these Scriptures, not Judaism. "This ministry" in 2 Corinthians 4:1 is the "ministry of the New Covenant" (2 Corinthians 3:6), "the ministry of the spirit" (2 Corinthians 3:8), and the "ministry of righteousness" (2 Corinthians 3:9). It is the "ministry of reconciliation" (2 Corinthians 5:18). We do not give up because this ministry is the most important ministry in the world! Christ told people to go and share the gospel with other people (Matthew 28:19–20; Mark 16:15–16; Luke 24:47; John 20:21). Paul said, "How shall they hear without a preacher, and how shall they preach unless they are sent" (Romans 10:14–15)? If we do not carry the message of reconciliation to the world, who will? If we do not extend God's offer of this wonderful New Covenant to lost mankind, who will? "Knowing the fear of the Lord, we persuade men" (2 Corinthians 5:11)! We do this in view of judgment! It is because we have this vital ministry that we do not, and we must not give up (2 Corinthians 4:1, 16)! The work of preaching the gospel is the most vital work in all of the world!

Second Corinthians 4:2

> Instead, we have renounced the secret things of shame, not walking in craftiness, nor perverting the word of God, but openly and truthfully commending ourselves to every man's conscience in the sight of God.

The word *alla* suggests a very sharp contrast. This phrase is meant to be a sharp contrast to the affirmation "we do not give up" in 2 Corinthians 4:1. Instead of giving up, we have committed ourselves to a ministry that is more important than anything else. To make this commitment, we have renounced the hidden things of shame, those sinful activities that would discredit us and show us to be less than sincere in our preaching and living of the gospel. We don't want to cause anyone to stumble and divert them from Jesus (2 Corinthians 6:3). We do not dilute or change or pervert the gospel, even if certain parties who might have influence over many people want us to do so. Paul insists that ministers of the New Covenant be open and transparent and sincere in their efforts to bring people to salvation (2 Corinthians 1:12–13; 6:3–10). People can see open and transparent sincerity in true Christian preachers. This is our open letter of commendation by which we gain the trust and respect of the people we seek to reach with the saving message (2 Corinthians 3:1–2).

Second Corinthians 4:3

> For even if our gospel is veiled, it is veiled
> among those who are perishing. Among them,
> the god of this age has blinded the minds of
> the unbelievers, so that the light of the glori-
> ous gospel of Christ, who is the image of God,
> might not shine upon them.

Paul is still explaining his comments in 2 Corinthians
3:14–18. The veil is over the eyes of these "unbelievers" when the
Hebrew Scriptures are read (2 Corinthians 3:14–15). Only those
who turn to Christ have this veil removed (2 Corinthians 3:16).
Earlier, he said "their minds where hardened" (2 Corinthians
3:14). The word for "minds" is *noemata* in both 2 Corinthians
3:14 and 4:4. In 2 Corinthians 4:4, the "god of this age" has
blinded their minds. The phrase "the god of this age" is likely a
reference to Satan. In Ephesians 2:2, Paul refers to Satan as "the
god of this world." The word for "god" is a different word in
Ephesians, *aiona,* but is a word often used in ancient literature
to speak of spirit beings from the spiritual realm. In both places,
Paul is referring to Satan. Satan is hardening or blinding the
minds of those who refuse to believe by keeping them tied to the
"letter" or literal understanding of the Law so that they cannot
see Jesus. As a result, they cannot see the light or the "glory" of
Jesus Christ. The word *doxa* in both noun and verb forms is used
fourteen times between 2 Corinthians 3:7 and 2 Corinthians
4:6. The glory of the New Covenant is the glory of God seen in
Christ. Only those who are willing to see Christ can see that glory
and be transformed into its image.

Second Corinthians 4:5

> For we do not preach ourselves, but the
> Lord Jesus Christ, and ourselves as your slaves
> because of Jesus.

This is similar to Paul's statement in 1 Corinthians 9:19 where he said, "For though I am free from all men, I have made myself a slave to all, so that I may gain more of them." Paul was preaching Christ and making himself a servant of the needs of others so that he could win them for Christ. When he says, "We do not preach ourselves," it almost sounds as if the other people who had their letters of recommendation and were peddling the gospel were preaching themselves to some degree and trying to get people to trust in them or in their credentials. We are not the message. Christ is the message. We are, however, representatives of Christ, and our lives and our teaching are what gains or loses credibility in the eyes of those who hear us.

Second Corinthians 4:6

> Because it is God who says, "A light will
> shine out of darkness, who has shone in our
> hearts to illuminate the knowledge of the glory
> of God in the face of Jesus Christ."

Because we have unveiled faces (2 Corinthians 3:18), we look into the mirror of the Hebrew Scriptures and see the face of Jesus, the true glory of God. Because this glorious light has shone upon us, we seek to share it with others by preaching the Lord Jesus. This is what Phillip did when he opened his mouth, and beginning at Isaiah 53, "he preached unto him Jesus" (Acts 8:35).

Second Corinthians 4:7

> And we have this treasure in clay vessels, so
> that the surpassing magnitude of power might
> be from God and not from ourselves.

When Paul reflected earlier on the responsibility of being a representative of Christ all the time, he asked, "Who is sufficient for such things" (2 Corinthians 2:16)? Then he said plainly that he felt no sufficiency or adequacy on his own, but his adequacy to be a minister of the New Covenant came only through God's power and presence (2 Corinthians 3:5–6; 12:8–10). Paul saw himself as a fragile clay vessel. We are also fragile, weak, and easily broken but we hold the greatest of treasures within ourselves, the gospel of Jesus Christ. We are nothing, but the gospel is everything, the power of God to save the souls of men and women (Romans 1:16; 10:16–17).

Second Corinthians 4:8–9

> In everything we are afflicted, but not
> crushed, uncertain, but not in despair, perse-
> cuted, but not forsaken, cast down, but not
> destroyed.

Paul's physical and emotional suffering was real and some-times very difficult to bear. But the fact that he says he was not crushed, did not despair, was not forsaken, and was not destroyed shows the unbreakable determination he had based on the faithfulness of God. He believed that God was with him no matter how much he suffered and that God was using him even in the midst of his suffering. The treasure of the gospel of the glory of Christ was powerful and effective, even if it was carried around in old clay jars like Paul. His statements in verses 8–9 are a restatement of what he affirmed earlier in 2 Corinthians 4:1 when he said, "We do not lose heart." This is vital for every preacher of the gospel who wants to continue in the ministry. We must do whatever is necessary to keep our thinking right so that we do not lose heart and give up! Like Paul, we must not see our preaching of the message of reconciliation as a job, but as a sacred mission which we must fulfill!

Second Corinthians 4:10–12

> Always carrying around the death of Jesus in the body, so that the life of Jesus might be made known in our body. For we who live are always being delivered over to death for Jesus's sake, so that the life of Jesus might be made known in our mortal flesh, so that death works in us, but life works in you.

Paul understood that there was a divine purpose being worked out in his suffering. He was not only preaching about Christ and his suffering, but as part of the body of Christ, he was demonstrating the suffering of Christ to the people around him (Galatians 6:17; Philippians 3:10; Colossians 1:24). Christ suffered in order to redeem others. Likewise, Paul was willing to suffer so that the gospel might be preached and souls might be saved. Jesus's life was about denying self and suffering on behalf of others. Paul manifested that part of Jesus's unselfish character in his own conduct. When God's ministers suffer and do what is right in spite of their suffering, they have a powerful effect on those who see them. They actually live out the unselfish love of Jesus. They live out a lesson of faithfulness to all who see them. In these times of personal suffering, when they faithfully do God's will, they show the people what they have been telling the people, and it is twice as powerful. Paul's faithful suffering was a big part of his living letter of recommendation (2 Corinthians 4:8–10; 6:4–10; 11:23–29). He was both preaching and obviously living as a representative of Jesus. He suffered so that others could live spiritually.

2 Corinthians 4:13

> Having the same spirit of faith according to what is written, "I have believed, therefore, I have spoken," we also believe, therefore we speak! Knowing that the one who raised up the Lord Jesus will also raise us along with Jesus and present us along with you.

The Psalm cited by Paul is a song about a person who trusts in the Lord and trusts enough to speak out and call upon the Lord in times of need. The Psalmist has seen God's deliverance in the past, and because he trusts that God is there and is watching over his people, he speaks out again in times of need and calls upon the Lord. This is the context of Psalm 116:10. Like the Psalmist, Paul is a recipient of God's deliverance! He has been delivered from sin and death by Christ and has been delivered from evil in real life by the same Lord Jesus (2 Corinthians 1:9–10). He trusts in the power of Christ to save us. For that reason, he speaks and will continue speaking about the redemptive power of Jesus in the lives of men and women! Paul speaks out, knowing that no matter what happens to him, Christ will raise him up and present him to God in the judgment! This is the firm hope and faith of all who trust in the risen Lord!

Second Corinthians 4:15

> For everything *we do* is for your sake, so that the grace which has overflowed causing

the gratitude of many people, might result in
the glory of God!

Everything Paul did was for the sake of the salvation of people like the Corinthians. He had made himself a slave to the welfare of others (1 Corinthians 9:20–22). His greatest aim was the salvation of souls. Through the faithful ministry of Paul, Timothy, and other proclaimers of the gospel, the grace of God covered the souls of all who would accept the New Covenant in Christ. The ministry of reconciliation proclaimed the message of reconciliation, and because of these efforts, many were saved. In the process of carrying on this ministry of righteousness, those who preached were often required to suffer. Through this suffering, they only demonstrated the selfless, soul-seeking Christ who was willing to suffer to save the souls of the lost. The result of all of this was saved people giving glory to God for his goodness! This should be the result of our ministry as well!

Second Corinthians 4:16

> Therefore, we do not give up, but even if
> our outward man is decaying, yet our inward
> man is made new every day, for our light and
> momentary affliction works for us more and
> more abundantly an eternal weight of glory.

Throughout the book, Paul reviews his suffering, and does so obviously with a great deal of emotion (2 Corinthians 1:9, 6:3–10; 11:16–29). He described his own afflictions as "light" because compared to the glory of an eternity with God they were truly light. This is the way a committed Christian thinks about present suffering. Paul says, "The suffering of this present time is not worthy to be compared to the glory that will be revealed to us"

(Romans 8:18). Paul admits that he is outwardly decaying. He is scarred and bruised, both physically and emotionally. Yet, he also realizes that God is using him mightily in spite of his weakness and brokenness. The word *affliction* or *thlipsis* is used numerous times in the book to describe a side of life and ministry that is very unpleasant and depressing and frightening. But our God works even in affliction, and he is also a God who comforts our struggling souls (2 Corinthians 1:3–8; Romans 8:28). Paul does not minimize our sufferings here, but assures us that through the burden of this suffering, we are building up a much greater "weight" or "burden" of glory in eternity.

Second Corinthians 4:18

> While we do not look at the things that are seen but the things that are not seen, for the things that are seen are temporary, and the things that are not seen are eternal.

Suffering and external circumstances are things we can see and feel immediately. The powerful work of God in the lives of ourselves and others is more difficult to see. We cannot see the changes that occur in the hearts of people when the word of God works to change their thinking. We cannot see the thousands of thoughts and deeds that are different because of the working of God. We cannot see the work of the angels as they work out the answers to our prayers on divine orders (Hebrews 1:14). The perspective of a person who is able to take suffering in stride is based on that person's trust in God's ability to use his/her suffering as well as the other experiences of life for the good of his purpose. We have an eternal perspective that looks beyond death to judgment and eternity. We also know that God can be with us and work powerfully in us, even in the midst of suffering (Romans 8:29–32;

COMMENTARY ON SECOND CORINTHIANS

Hebrews 12:3–9). Ministers of the New Covenant who do not give up must maintain this perspective on the events of their own lives!

Reflections on Chapter 4

1. What ministry is Paul talking about in 2 Corinthians 4:1 and what earlier passage tells us?
2. Discuss in detail the character of a good minister of Christ according to 2 Corinthians 4:2.
3. What verses in chapter 3 will help us understand 2 Corinthians 4:3?
4. What are some ways in which churches today may market themselves and their services instead of marketing the benefits of a relationship with Christ (2 Corinthians 4:5)?
5. How is the life of Jesus made known to the world when ministers of the gospel suffer (2 Corinthians 4:10–12)?
6. Why does Paul say, "We do not give up"? (See 2 Corinthians 4:1, 16).
7. Discuss the potential benefits and the potential drawbacks of personal suffering in the life of a minister.
8. Are there any practical things a good minister can do so that his inward man can be renewed daily or does this renewal happen automatically?

5

Ministry in View of Judgment and Eternity

Second Corinthians 5:1

> "For we know that if our temporary earthly house is destroyed, we have a building from God, a house not made with hands eternal in the heavens.

The phrase "for we know" is tied to 2 Corinthians 4:18 where we are focused on the things that are not seen. We are focused on the promises of God. We trust in things "not seen" (Hebrews 11:1, 5–6, 8). We are seeking that city with foundations whose builder and maker is God (Hebrews 11:10, 16). We believe, as Paul explained, in the resurrection of the body and the new, incorruptible body that will live forever, unburdened by corruption and decay (1 Corinthians 15:20, 50–58). Paul already said that our outward man is decaying (2 Corinthians 4:16). He was surely marred and scarred by this time in his career, physically waning but spiritually strong. Scripture teaches that we will not just spend eternity as disembodied souls but with bodies, whole and equipped to enjoy life in the new heavens, the new earth, and the new Jerusalem (Hebrews 13:14; 2 Peter 3:13; Revelation 21:1ff).

Second Corinthians 5:2

> For even in this house we groan, as we
> long to be clothed with our house from heaven,
> so that even if we should be unclothed, we shall
> not be found naked.

The word *stenazo*, "groan," is also in 2 Corinthians 5:4. This discussion reminds us of Paul's discussion in Romans 8:18–39 regarding the "sufferings of this present time" versus the "glory that shall be revealed unto us." In that discussion, Paul talks about the fallen creation in bondage to decay. First, he says "the whole creation is groaning" (Romans 8:22). Then, speaking of the Christians, he says, "And not only so, but we ourselves who have the firstfruits of the Spirit, groan within ourselves, as we wait for the adoption, the redemption of our bodies" (Romans 8:23). Later, when he discusses those times of suffering when we don't even know what to pray for, he says the Spirit "intercedes for us with groanings that cannot be uttered" (Romans 8:26). The pain and suffering of the fallen creation surrounds mortal flesh with misery of various kinds. Even those who do not suffer for their faith in Christ have their share of sadness, pain, suffering, and disease. In those times of suffering, we who "look at the things that are not seen" long for the redemption of our bodies and the glory that awaits us after death and resurrection! We groan in our temporary bodies because we are suffering!

Second Corinthians 5:4

> For truly we who are in this temporary
> dwelling groan, being burdened, for which

reason we do not wish to be unclothed, but clothed, so that what is mortal may be swallowed up by life.

We are groaning, says Paul, because we are "burdened," *baroumenoi*. Earlier, Paul described his present struggles as "light and momentary." He also says these temporary afflictions are producing an "eternal weight of glory." The word translated "weight" in 2 Corinthians 4:17 is the same root word as that which is translated "burdened" in 2 Corinthians 5:4. What Paul is saying is that the glory far outweighs the suffering of the present. All Christians should expect a certain amount of suffering in their lives. Jesus told his apostles, "In this world, you will have tribulation, but be of good courage! I have overcome the world" (John 16:33).

Second Corinthians 5:5

And God is the one who made us for this very thing, who gave us the guarantee of the Spirit.

The *arrabon*—"down payment" or "earnest" or "guarantee"—of the Spirit was mentioned earlier in 2 Corinthians 1:22. There, Paul also says we have been "sealed" with the Spirit as he explains in Ephesians 1:13. When we are baptized into Christ, we are sealed or marked with the Holy Spirit. The presence of the Spirit in the Christian is the down payment or guarantee that God will redeem us on the "day of redemption" (Ephesians 4:30). It is a guarantee of our inheritance (Ephesians 1:14). It provides assurance that our hope will not be disappointed, and we will receive the reward that God has promised his faithful people (Romans 5:5). Though we may not possess the miraculous gifts like healing and prophecy, we have the intercessory help of the Spirit (Romans

8:26–27). We are strengthened with power by the Spirit in our inner being (Ephesians 3:16). We have the Spirit working in us to produce the fruits of a beautiful character (Galatians 5:22–23). Paul's point is that God made us to redeem us, and he has given us assurance. God wants to release us from suffering. God wants us to be with him in eternal joy. This is his plan and purpose, not to see us destroyed. As Paul so powerfully affirmed to the Thessalonians, "For God has not destined us for wrath, but for obtaining salvation through our Lord Jesus Christ" (1 Thessalonians 5:9).

2 Corinthians 5:6

> Therefore, being always of good courage, and knowing that while we are at home in the body, we are away from the Lord, for we live by faith and not by sight.

Being of good courage is the opposite mentality from despairing or fainting or giving up (2 Corinthians 4:1, 16). We do not give up because we have the spiritual perspective outlined in 2 Corinthians 4:16–18. We trust in the living Lord Jesus, the resurrection of the dead, the putting on of an eternal new body, and a blissful future with God. We are living or "walking" by faith in God's promises which are not yet seen in their fruition by human eyes (Hebrews 11:1, 5, 7, 8).

Second Corinthians 5:8

> We have good courage and we would be pleased rather to be absent from the body and at home with the Lord.

Paul expressed the same sentiment in Philippians 1:23–24 where he said he would rather depart this world and be with the Lord, but it was better for others that he remained in the flesh and did his work of preaching the gospel of Christ. Paul kept the goal of eternal glory always in mind as he continued to suffer and preach the gospel in this world. He was indeed looking for a better country, a heavenly country, and for that city which has foundations, whose builder and maker is God (Hebrews 11:10, 16).

Second Corinthians 5:9

> Therefore, we make it our ambition, whether at home or absent, to be pleasing to him!

This is the mentality of a genuine, dedicated minister of Christ. His whole aim and purpose is to please Christ, to carry out his will in every way possible. Part of God's will is to proclaim the gospel to everyone possible and to teach and encourage those who obey the gospel, building them up in the faith. The reason ministers try to please Christ and the reason they try to persuade others to follow Christ is stated next.

Second Corinthians 5:10

> For we must all appear before the tribunal of Christ, so that each one might receive a payment for the deeds he has done in the body, according to what he has done, whether good or evil.

The bema or tribunal or bench from which a sentence is passed down is the place from which Pontius Pilate conveyed the death sentence upon Jesus (John 19:13–16). Christ will determine our fate based on what we have done, and whether we have been "pleasing to him" in what we have done. Pleasing God is based on our decision about whether we accept Christ as Lord, as well as our decisions about doing his will on a daily basis. Christ will be our Judge (Romans 2:16; 2 Timothy 4:1–2).

Second Corinthians 5:11

> Therefore, knowing the fear of the Lord, we persuade men, and we are *completely* open before God! And I hope this is evident to you also!

It is because death and judgment are coming that we persuade men. Paul appealed to his converts to accept the purity of his motives based on their personal experience with him. Could they not look back to their time with him and conclude that he was sincerely trying to persuade men to follow Christ in view of the coming judgment? To persuade is to convince and convict and bring people to make decisions. We do not preach so that people can remain the same. We preach so that people will change. We trust that God's word can change their minds (Ephesians 4:22–24). We trust that they will be "transformed" in their decisions and their lifestyles due to this "renewing of their minds" so that they pursue God's good, acceptable, and perfect will (Romans 12:1–2). To persuade, we must present facts, show evidence to support those facts, convey the truth about God's will, and work to show people why they need to obey that will. King Agrippa asked Paul, "Do you think that in such a short time you can persuade me to be a Christian?" (Acts 26:28). Paul went on to say that he not only wanted to persuade Agrippa, but everyone in the audience who was listening as well. That is what we do! We try to persuade people to accept Christ and be saved. Like Peter exhorted and testified with many other words to the Pentecost crowd, urging them to "save yourselves from this crooked generation," we beg and plead with people to accept the grace of God by submitting to his Son, Jesus!

Second Corinthians 5:12

> We are not again commending ourselves, but giving you an opportunity to boast on our behalf, so that you might have something to say to those who boast in appearances and not in heart.

Paul's claims of sincerity and purity of motive in his ministry were not attempts to brag on himself. He was simply appealing to what the Corinthians actually experienced in his time with them. He was appealing to what they had observed firsthand. He was not doing as these manipulative teachers did, "peddling the word of God" or submitting "letters of recommendation" or preaching himself or boasting in outward appearance (2 Corinthians 2:17; 3:1; 4:5; 5:12). Paul wanted the Corinthian Christians to stick up for him in front of his detractors! Unfortunately, many people will not stick up for their preacher when he is criticized. This is very discouraging as it often was to Paul, but what a blessing when people actually do brag on us and stick up for us!

Second Corinthians 5:13

> If we are losing our minds it is for God's sake, and if we are exercising self-control it is for your sake.

When sincere preachers try their best to teach people the truth and influence them for what is right, it is extremely frustrating to have other parties come into the mix and begin detracting from our efforts through unjust criticism. This is one of the ways in which Satan works to neutralize the ministry of good evangelists. This kind of interference drives preachers crazy. But the wise preacher must maintain self-control and continue to say and do what God calls him to say and do. Even when confrontation is necessary, he must be sure that he is behaving in a loving, truthful, Christlike manner.

Second Corinthians 5:14–15

> For the love of Christ occupies our minds, as we think this way: Since one died for all, therefore, all died! And one died for all so that those who live might no longer live for themselves, but for the one who died and rose again for their sakes!

This passage reflects the mindset of the preacher who will not give up because of the gravity of his ministry (2 Corinthians 4:1, 16). Because we are looking at things through spiritual eyes (2 Corinthians 4:18), we are dedicated to the ministry that is of utmost importance in the world. Our persistence and sincerity are motivated by the wonderful love of Christ! We know that he gave himself up for us. We are redeemed by his amazing grace, and this motivates us to be unselfish as he was. We do not live for ourselves as he did not live for himself. We live for him to serve his great unselfish purpose: the salvation of lost mankind! The unselfish example of Christ is compelling as are the examples of others who follow in the footsteps of his unselfish commitment to the good of others.

Second Corinthians 5:16

> So then, from now on we no longer know anyone from a fleshly perspective. And if we have known Christ in a fleshly way, we now no longer know him (in that way), so that if anyone is in Christ, he is a new creation! The old things have gone away? Behold, new things have come!

Paul's repeated use of the word *nun*, "now," indicates a new situation. This is the situation created by dying to ourselves and our sinful nature, and pledging our unselfish service to God. As he said in 2 Corinthians 5:15, we no longer live for ourselves "but for him" who died and rose again for our sake. This is the change in perspective resulting from one's "death to sin" as described in Romans 6:1–6. As a result of this radical change in thinking because of God's word, we consider ourselves to be dead as far as sin is concerned and alive to serve God in Christ Jesus (Romans 6:11–13). Because of this radical change of thinking, we are truly a new creation, transformed in our thinking by the word of God (Ephesians 4:22–24; Romans 12:2). We do not view other people as we once did. Paul could not see the Corinthians or the false teachers encroaching on them from a worldly perspective. He now saw everything through the lens of the Son of Man who came to seek and to save the lost (Luke 19:10). He did not see a battle for popularity or notoriety but a battle for the souls of men and women.

Second Corinthians 5:18

> All things are from God, who reconciled us to himself through Christ, and gave to us the ministry of reconciliation.

If we take the phrase "all things are from God" to be a continuance of verse 17, "all things have become new," this means that now we see everything from a God perspective. As stated in verse 16, we no longer view other people from a fleshly point of view. Our own lives are no longer seen as our own. We live "for Him who died and rose again" (2 Corinthians 5:15). Because we have this spiritual perspective, we view our goals and responsibilities in terms of our own reconciliation and the ministry we have been given. We ourselves are not important in the sense that our selfish desires and preferences are relatively meaningless. What is important is the reconciliation of lost people to God. We have been given the ministry of the New Covenant in which we offer that covenant to people through the gospel (2 Corinthians 3:6). We have been given the glorious "ministry of the spirit" as opposed to the ministry of the letter (2 Corinthians 3:6, 8). We have been given "the ministry of righteousness" in which the righteousness of God is imputed to us because of the sacrifice of Christ (2 Corinthians 3:9).

It is because we have this vital ministry that we will never give up (2 Corinthians 4:1, 16). It is the ministry of persuading men and women to accept the gospel and all of its blessings (2 Corinthians 5:11). It is the ministry of reconciliation because its goal is to bring those who have been separated from God by their sins back into the grace and fellowship of their Creator (2 Corinthians 5:18; Ephesians 2:16). It is under this great ministry that God's enemies are "reconciled to God by the death of his Son" (Romans 5:10).

Second Corinthians 5:19

> Forasmuch as God was in Christ reconciling the world to himself, not counting their trespasses against them, but having given to us the message of reconciliation.

There is so much basic doctrine in this verse! God was in Christ! God came to earth in the person of Jesus Christ (John 1:14; Romans 9:5). God's work in Christ during the incarnation was the reconciliation of the world to himself. The world was lost in sin (John 1:10; 3:16; 12:31). He sent his Son to save the world, not to condemn the world (John 3:17). Because of the death of Christ, God was able to refrain from counting the sins of sinful mankind against them. As Paul explained, "Blessed is the man whose lawless deeds are forgiven and whose sins are covered! Blessed is the man to whom the Lord does not credit sin!" (Psalm 32:1–2; Romans 4:7–8). Not only does God erase past sins when one accepts the gospel of Christ, but he does not credit present and future sins to our account as long as we are trusting Christ and penitently trying to live for him! This is the nature of grace! It is to God's church, and more specifically, to gospel preachers, that God has entrusted the "message of reconciliation!"

Second Corinthians 5:20

> Therefore, we are ambassadors of Christ,
> as though God were exhorting you through us.
> We beg you on behalf of Christ, be reconciled
> to God!

The word *therefore* is based on the fact that we have received the ministry of reconciliation and the message of reconciliation. We have been entrusted with both the responsibility and the means of serving in this ministry as ambassadors of Jesus Christ. As we preach the message of reconciliation, we are speaking for Jesus. Jesus is calling people through the gospel into the fellowship of God (1 Corinthians 1:9; 2 Thessalonians 2:14). Preachers do not just make talks and stir emotions. They speak in order to convince, persuade, and lead people to choose God. The call

251

to "Repent and be baptized," to "Repent and turn again," and "Believe on the Lord Jesus Christ" are God's call to humanity to hear and accept the heavenly invitation to feast upon the love and grace of God (Acts 2:38; 3:19; 16:31).

Second Corinthians 5:21

> God made the one who knew no sin to be sin on our behalf, so that we might become the righteousness of God in him!

Christ had no sin (John 18:38; 19:4, 6; Hebrews 4:15; 1 Peter 1:18). God made him to be sin in the sense that he "laid upon him the sin of us all" (Isaiah 53:6). Christ suffered for us "the righteous for the unrighteous" (1 Peter 3:18). He was treated by God as though he was guilty of the sins of all mankind. In this way, he was made to be sin. His death was a propitiation or an appeasement or a satisfaction offering for our sins (Romans 3:25). This enabled God to be just in punishing sin, and at the same time, to be the "justifier" of those who trust in the redemptive work of Christ (Romans 3:26). We are given the righteousness of God as a gracious gift when we obey the gospel of Christ (Romans 1:17; 3:24; 5:17).

Reflections on Chapter 5

1. Why do ministers of the New Covenant who are getting weary in their present "house" cling to great hope?

2. Why are we "groaning" in our present house (see 2 Corinthians 4:16–17; Romans 8:22–23)?

3. What is our major aim according to 2 Corinthians 5:9?

4. Why is that our major aim according to 2 Corinthians 5:10?

5. Discuss the implications of ministers trying to "persuade" people through the gospel.

6. Who do you think Paul is talking about when he mentions people who boast in appearance and not in heart?

7. What is our motivation to continue serving according to 2 Corinthians 5:14–15?

8. We have not only been given the _____ of reconciliation but the _____ of reconciliation (2 Corinthians 5:18–19).

6

Second Corinthians 6:1–2

> And as we work together with him, we also urge you not to receive the grace of God in vain, for he says, "I have heard you in an acceptable time, and in a day of salvation have helped you." Behold, now is the acceptable time, behold now is the day of salvation!

Paul has established that he has received the ministry of reconciliation and has been entrusted as an ambassador for Christ with the message of reconciliation. He is working together with God for the reconciliation of lost mankind. As he works together with Christ to accomplish the mission of Christ, he appeals to the Corinthians, "Do not receive the grace of God in vain." Paul cites Isaiah 49:8 where God declares that this is a time of his favor, a day in which he wants to come to the aid of his people. God's grace and favor is given to people in Jesus Christ through the gospel! Paul wants his readers to know that God's amazing grace is only found in Jesus, and they should not negate that grace by trusting in the law. For Paul to work so hard for the salvation of people like the Corinthians, and for them to endanger that salvation by putting up with teachers that could derail their faith was very upsetting. We who preach the gospel often work to lead people to salvation, only to see others turn them away from the truth. In his first letter, Paul cautioned those who had accepted the gospel, lest they had "believed in vain" (1 Corinthians 15:2). In that letter, Paul was concerned that they might abandon their faith in the resurrection of Christ and their own resurrection from the dead (1 Corinthians 15:12ff). The threat may not have been exactly the same, but it was certainly some kind of Judaizing threat coming from a group of teachers who had come to the Corinthians with letters of recommendation and were attempting to turn them away from Paul and the things he had taught them. They were called "unbelievers" by the apostle and were described as having a veil over their hearts when the Old Covenant was being read (2 Corinthians 3:1, 14–15; 4:4–6; 6:14; 11:2–3). It was God's grace (2 Corinthians 6:1) that the Corinthians had received, based only on the redemptive work of Christ. God had provided help to them. God's grace in Christ was their only salvation. Paul did not want them abandoning the "grace of Christ" for a "different gospel" (2 Corinthians 11:3ff; Galatians 1:6–9). God has "helped us" through the redemptive work of Christ. We must not turn our backs on the work of God.

Second Corinthians 6:3–4

> We give no opportunity for stumbling to anyone, so that the ministry will not be blamed. But as God's ministers, we commend ourselves in everything.

Paul is trying to discuss a spiritual matter with the Corinthians, but it is mixed up in a personal matter as well. The false teachers among them were trying to turn the Corinthians against Paul and impugn his sincerity and his trustworthiness. This was frustrating and hurtful to Paul. As is the case for all sincere ministers of the gospel, it is very difficult to separate our personal feelings from our ministry. Paul had not only shared the gospel with the Corinthians but his very heart! He had very dear and proprietary feelings toward them, and he was hurt when they did not seem to reciprocate his feelings (2 Corinthians 6:11–13). Paul insists that he personally had not done anything to cause any of them to turn away from Christ. He was appealing to their own experience with him (2 Corinthians 3:1–2). Paul felt that the Corinthians should defend him and refuse to be turned away from him. We who serve as preachers often marvel at the ease with which our brothers and sisters will turn against us in some circumstances. Like Paul, we must struggle to put our own feelings aside and pray that God will help us to be consistent and show Christian grace and behavior, even when we are the object of slander and injustice. In this way, we truly glorify God! Paul is saying that he has tried to conduct himself as a true minister of God in every circumstance. Including…

Second Corinthians 6:4b–8a

> In much endurance, in affliction, in necessities, in hard times, in sickness, in imprisonments, in distress, in labors, in sleepless nights, in fasting, in purity, in knowledge, in longsuffering, in kindness, in the Holy Spirit, in sincere love, in the message of truth, in the power of God with the weapons of righteousness on the right and on the left, through glory and dishonor, through bad reports and good reports.

This is an extension of the thought in 2 Corinthians 6:4 where Paul says "we commend ourselves in everything" or "in every situation." Paul's commendation of himself to the Corinthians is their own observation of him in every circumstance. It is in these widely

COMMENTARY ON SECOND CORINTHIANS

varying circumstances that people see our true colors. Paul had endured many hardships and afflictions and had been a faithful minister in those hardships. He had been a faithful minister "in necessities and in hard times." He had even been a faithful minister in imprisonments, whether in Philippi when he converted the jailer or in Caesarea when he preached to those who held him or later in Rome as depicted in Acts 28. He had been faithful in distress and in hard labor, working hard to provide his own needs (1 Corinthians 9:13–16). He had gone without sleep in doing God's work, had gone without food, and still remained faithful. These life experiences were his bona fides to those people who knew him. He had endured all of these things "in purity," taking no sexual advantage of anyone. He had endured with the knowledge of his duty and God's protection. He had shown longsuffering toward difficult people and kindness toward all, including his enemies. When Paul says "in the Holy Spirit," it is difficult to know his meaning. Perhaps he refers to the "signs of an apostle" which he worked among the people (1 Corinthians 2:4–5; 2 Corinthians 12:12). He ministered to people with "sincere love" and was confident that they felt it. He taught them "the word of truth." He trusted in "the power of God" to work through him, using "the weapons of righteousness" with both hands. These weapons are for the capturing of the hearts and minds of men through the word of God (2 Corinthians 10:3–5). Paul faithfully preached the word when people defamed him and when they praised him. These behaviors in all of these circumstances were his recommendation as a minister and his defense to those who cast dispersion upon him.

Second Corinthians 6:8b–10

> As deceivers, yet true. As ignorant, yet knowing. As dying, yet behold, we live! As disci-

plined, but not dying. As sorrowing, yet always
rejoicing! As often poor, yet growing rich! As
having nothing, yet possessing everything!

Paul may have been accused by his opponents of being a
deceiver but proved himself to be true and trustworthy in personal conduct. He may have been accused of being ignorant,
but he knew the things revealed to him by God (1 Corinthians
2:6–13). He was often near death but seemed to come out alive
each time because God delivered him (2 Corinthians 1:8–9). He
endured many sorrows in the course of his ministry, but he also
took great joy in doing God's will and in seeing people saved (1
Thessalonians 2:18–20). Paul was often physically poor, though
he was content in that condition (Philippians 4:11–13). Even at
his poorest, he was confident that he possessed all of the blessings
of the kingdom in Jesus Christ (Ephesians 1:3). In this diatribe
from 2 Corinthians 6:3–10, Paul was pouring out his heart, showing his intense feelings about ministry, about how he had been
treated, and about his joy in doing God's will.

Second Corinthians 6:11–13

Our mouth is open to you, O Corinthians,
our heart is wide open! You are not restricted in
us, but you are restricted in your own hearts! I
speak as to (my) children, pay us back in kind!
Open yourselves up to us!

This is a very emotional statement about the inequality Paul
sees in the relationship between himself and the Corinthians.
Paul is wide open in his communication and in his feelings. He is
open and transparent with them. They, in turn, are not so open
with Paul either in their communications or in their feelings. Paul

wants *antimisthian,* repayment in kind. He wants the Corinthians to love him and talk openly with him just as he does toward them. He feels toward them as if they were his children (1 Corinthians 4:15). He wishes they felt toward him more like they would feel toward a loving father! He described this kind of relationship when he was talking about how he dealt with the Christians in Thessalonica when he said, "You are witnesses, how holily, and righteously, and blamelessly we conducted ourselves toward you who believe, just as each one of you knows, like a father toward his own children, encouraging you and comforting you and testifying to you so that you may walk in a manner worthy of God" (1 Thessalonians 2:10–12).

Don't Tolerate Negative Influence of Unbelievers!

Second Corinthians 6:14–16a

> Do not be yoked together with unbelievers! For what share has righteousness with lawlessness? Or what fellowship has light with darkness? And what agreement has Christ with Beliar, and what part has a believer with an unbeliever? And what consensus is there between a temple of God and idols?

The unbelievers to which Paul has reference are those mentioned in 2 Corinthians 4:3–4. They are the ones who have a veil over their minds when the Old Testament Scriptures are read (2 Corinthians 3:14–15). They are the ones who are blinded by this veil to the gospel of Christ (2 Corinthians 4:3–4). These are the very ones who were working against Paul and his message among the Corinthians. Being yoked or tied to this kind of person would be like putting a donkey and an ox in the same yoke to work your field (Deuteronomy 22:10). This practice was forbidden in Moses' law. The donkey and the ox would work against one another, just as teachers who faithfully teach the gospel will be working against those whose teachings contradict the gospel. The rhetorical questions that follow Paul's admonition emphasize the fallacy of being "yoked together" with these Judaizing unbelievers. The word translated "yoked together" is *heterozugontes*, which means to be yoked with something of a completely different kind, like a donkey with an ox. Obviously, there is no fellowship or agreement between light and darkness, righteousness and lawlessness, Christ and Satan, or God and an idol's temple! Often, people who form close relationships with unbelievers and do not have God and his word at the center of those relationships run into great conflict because they think so differently, and their goals and priorities are so different. Preachers and elders who are not of one mind doctrinally often find themselves pulling in different directions in a congregation. It is difficult for people to walk together unless they both intend to travel in the same direction (Amos 3:3).

Second Corinthians 6:16b–18

> For we are a temple of the living God, just as God said, "I will dwell among them and walk among them, and I will be their God, and they shall be my people." Wherefore, the Lord says, "Come out from among them, and be separate, and do not touch anything unclean, and I will welcome you, and I will be to you as a father and you will be to me as sons and daughters," says the Lord almighty!

When Paul says, "We are a temple," he is referring to God's redeemed people in Christ, the New Testament church. He teaches this clearly in Ephesians 2:20–22 and 1 Corinthians 3:10–17. As God said to Israel, he chooses to dwell among his elect people in a very personal and proprietary manner. He seems to be at least alluding to Leviticus 26:11–12 where God promised to dwell with his people if they would separate themselves from the pagan people of the land and do his will. Because God associates with his elect in Christ today, he wants those people to separate themselves from the negative influence of those who do not belong to the elect. He wants them to understand that they are distinct in the relationship they have with God, and to separate themselves from any who would destroy or weaken that relationship.

Reflections on Chapter 6

1. Talk about 2 Corinthians 6:3 and how the ministry of Christ could possibly be blamed because of the conduct of his ministers.

2. Read 2 Corinthians 6:4–10 and talk about how Paul actually gained his credibility among the Corinthians as a sincere and genuine minister of Christ.

3. Talk about occasions when you have felt the same way about fellow Christians as Paul felt in 2 Corinthians 6:11–13.

4. Where else earlier in the letter does Paul talk about these "unbelievers" with whom the Corinthians seem to have been "yoked together"?

5. Why does Paul want the Corinthians to separate themselves from these unbelievers?

6. How does 2 Corinthians 7:1 help to answer the previous question?

7

S econd Corinthians 7:1

> Therefore, having these promises, let us cleanse ourselves from every defilement of flesh and spirit, completing sanctification in the fear of God.

Contextually, based on these passages cited above, Paul is saying that if we want God to dwell among us and walk among us, we need to cleanse ourselves of people like the "unbelievers" mentioned in 2 Corinthians 6:14–15. We need to rid ourselves of those things and people that would defile us spiritually. The "sanctification" or "holiness" we need to complete is being set apart or separated from those things, and people that would destroy our relationship with God. In this case, it was a group of people pulling the Corinthians away from the apostle and his inspired teaching.

Second Corinthians 7:2–4

> Make room for us! We wronged no one! We corrupted no one! We did not behave covetously toward anyone! I am not speaking to condemn you for you are in our hearts to die together and to live together! I have much boldness toward you! I have much to boast about regarding you! I

have been filled with encouragement, overflow-
ing with joy in all of our affliction!

Second Corinthians 6:11–13 combined with this passage
makes it pretty clear that Paul felt a lack of reciprocation for the love
he both felt and demonstrated toward the Corinthians. He is asking
them to open their hearts to him. He is appealing to his honorable
conduct among them. They knew he did not wrong any of them or
corrupt them in any way or pursue them for his own financial gain.
He is very confident in making these assertions, knowing that they
would have to acknowledge the truth of what he is saying.

This shows us how vitally important the conduct of an evangelist is. This is why Paul told young Timothy to be an example
to the believers (1 Timothy 4:12). When those among whom we
minister can testify that we conducted ourselves as sincere servants
of God, this gives us much credibility in their eyes and allows us
to speak to them much more confidently about spiritual things.
Do the people among whom we serve truly believe us to be sincere
and genuine in our service to God and in our daily lives?

Paul thought and spoke fondly of the Corinthians often and
rejoiced over the good they did, even in dark times like those he
spoke about in 2 Corinthians 1:8–9. He was having a hard time
with the idea that some of the Corinthians did not feel the same
way about him. The call of the evangelist is to serve Christ regardless of the way people may treat him!

Second Corinthians 7:5

For even when we came to Macedonia,
our flesh had no rest, but we were afflicted in
every way, conflict on the outside, fears on the
inside! But God, who encourages the humble,
encouraged us by the arrival of Titus!

According to Acts 20:3ff, Paul left Greece (likely Corinth) and returned to Macedonia. He did not find Titus in Macedonia as stated in 2 Corinthians 7:5 and sailed from Philippi southward to Troas. He still did not find Titus in Troas as he had hoped and left to pursue another opportunity to spread the gospel (2 Corinthians 2:12–13). So finally, Titus had arrived with good news and bad news about the Corinthian church. In many ways, he had brought relief to Paul's worried mind, and in other ways, concerns.

Second Corinthians 7:7

> And not just by his arrival to us, but also because of the encouragement with which he was encouraged by you, bringing news to us of your longing for us, your mourning, your zeal for me, so that I am made to rejoice!

Obviously, Paul was relieved to know that his previous tearstained letter had not completely alienated the Corinthians (2 Corinthians 2:4ff). He was rejoicing that they had not only been led to "mourn" or repent of things they had been doing wrong, but that many of them still had good feelings toward Paul. The rest of the letter shows that the news was not all good. Paul came to understand from Titus that his influence was not dead among the Corinthians but still very much alive, though under attack by the Judaizing teachers among them.

Second Corinthians 7:8–9

> Because even if I caused you sorrow by the epistle, I do not regret it. But even if I did regret it, I see (now) that the epistle caused you sorrow only for a short time. But now I rejoice not

because you were caused sorrow, but because
you were made sorry resulting in repentance.

Paul did not enjoy causing grief or sorrow to anyone, but he
was willing to cause the Corinthians temporary sorrow when he
wrote the tearstained letter in order to accomplish a good result.
Sin needs to be confronted and corrected with love by the word
of God. Paul certainly did this in his first epistle (2 Corinthians
2:4–11). Too many preachers of the word today are so afraid of
causing grief to their listeners they never really confront sin in a
direct manner. We must call people to repentance if we are to be
true preachers of God's word.

Second Corinthians 7:10

For godly sorrow produces repentance
without regret that leads to salvation, but the
sorrow of the world produces death.

Repentance, *metanoia*, is a change of mind. This change of
mind is brought about when one allows the word of God to be
planted in the mind and allows the word to work. The word works
by convicting people of the truth of the message, and through
genuine conviction, changing the attitudes and commitments of
the person. The result is a change of both attitude and action.
Sorrow is not the same thing as repentance. Judas was sorrowful
and killed himself rather than allowing God's word to change him.
Worldly sorrow causes people to feel sorry for themselves, but does
not produce a directional change. Peter was sorrowful after denying Jesus, and eventually, he changed his attitude and became a
great preacher of the gospel of Christ! He was led to change his
mind and his direction in life!

Second Corinthians 7:11

> For behold what a result this godly sor-
> row has caused in you, what diligence, what a
> desire to clear yourselves, what a compulsion,
> what fear, what longing, what zeal, what indig-
> nation! In everything you showed yourselves to
> be sincere in the matter!

All of these words are descriptive of the change brought about
in the Corinthians as a result of the word communicated by Paul.
The word *diligence* signifies great effort and eagerness to make
things right. The word *apologia* usually means an explanation or a
defense, but that meaning doesn't suit the context here. They were
not defending themselves for wrong conduct, but were eager to put
themselves in a defensible position by changing what needed to be
changed. They feared God enough to repent, being persuaded by
the word (see 2 Corinthians 5:9). They were zealous to do what
was right. They were longing to please God. They demonstrated
themselves to have "pure" or sincere motives by their willingness
to make corrections where the inspired apostle called for them to
be made. All of these were attitudinal changes brought about by
accepting the word of God.

Second Corinthians 7:12–13

> So then, even when I wrote to you, it was
> not *just* for the sake of the one who had done
> the wrong, or for the sake of the one who had
> suffered the wrong, but in order that your dil-
> igence toward us might be made plain before
> God. Because of this we are greatly encouraged!

Here, Paul is reflecting, after hearing good news about the Corinthians from Titus, on what he had been feeling when he wrote 1 Corinthians. He did not just write the letter because of the man who had been living with his father's wife or because of the man who had been wronged by his wife's adultery (1 Corinthians 5). Paul wrote to the church in general in order to ascertain whether they were still diligently desiring to conform to the instruction of God's ambassador. To find out that they did still care about the teaching of Christ through his apostles was a source of great relief to Paul's anxiety over his spiritual children. So he was greatly encouraged by their response to his letter!

Second Corinthians 7:14–16

> And in the midst of our encouragement, we rejoiced even more abundantly at the joy of Titus because his spirit was refreshed by all of you! Because if I have boasted to him regarding you in any way, I was not put to shame, but just as we have spoken all things in truth regarding you, so our boasting to Titus proved to be true. And his tender feelings toward you overflowed abundantly when he recalled all of your obedience, how with fear and trembling you welcomed him. So with good courage I rejoice in every way about you!

One of the things that made Paul so happy when Titus returned was to see how positive Titus was about the response of the Corinthians. They had not only welcomed Paul's emissary with open arms, but had encouraged Titus by their attitudes and their response to Paul's letter. To see the effect the Corinthians had on Paul's trusted protégé was greatly encouraging to Paul.

Preachers love to receive good news about the spiritual condition of those in whom they have invested time, effort, love, and teaching. Preachers love to see people they trust speak well of the spiritual progress of their converts!

Reflections on Chapter 7

1. How does the statement of 2 Corinthians 7:1 refer to the discussion of the previous chapter?
2. What do you think was hindering the Corinthians from opening their hearts more toward Paul?
3. Why was Paul so greatly encouraged and relieved by the coming of Titus (2 Corinthians 7:5–7)?
4. Though Paul knew his first epistle to the Corinthians was somewhat upsetting to them, why did he not regret writing it?
5. Talk about the difference between godly sorrow and worldly sorrow.
6. If repentance is not sorrow, what is it?
7. Discuss the attitude of the Corinthians described in verse 11.
8. Why do you think Paul was so encouraged by the positive attitude of Titus regarding the Corinthians?

8

Second Corinthians 8:1

> We make known to you, brothers, the grace of God which has been given in the assemblies of Macedonia because in much testing of affliction, the abundance of their joy, and the depth of their poverty abounded resulting in the riches of their generosity!

When people have been struggling, one way to get them to move forward in their spiritual life is to involve them in a good, positive work for the Lord. In this section of the letter, Paul is encouraging the Corinthians to follow through on a project to help their poor brethren in Judea. As an example for the Corinthians, he speaks of "the grace of God which has been given among the assemblies of Macedonia." This phrase usually has the flavor of some spiritual gift that has been given to people. In speaking of the spiritual gift of his apostleship, Paul talks about "the gift of God's grace which has been given to me" (Romans 12:3, 6; Ephesians 3:2, 7, 8; 4:7). He speaks of the spiritual gifts given to each Christian when he says, "To each one was this grace given, according to the measure of the gift of Christ" (Ephesians 4:7). As he enumerates some of the gifts possessed by different members of the Roman church, he says, "having gifts differing according to the grace that has been given to us" (Romans 12:6). One of those spiritual gifts listed in Romans 12 is the gift of giving (Romans 12:8). In that passage, he also uses the same word for "generosity" or "liberality" that is used in 2 Corinthians 8:2, *aplotetos*. So Paul seems to be saying that the poor Macedonian Christians have been given the gift of "giving" by God, and it is manifesting itself in their generosity. Their desire to give was in them not only in prosperity but also in want!

Second Corinthians 8:3–4

> Because according to their ability, I bear witness, and even beyond their ability, of their own accord, *they were* begging us with much entreaty to share in the grace of this ministry toward the saints.

When one observed the Christians in the Macedonian churches, one would not perceive them to be people of wealth. Their desire to take part in this work of love went beyond their obvious resources. Their giving was not simply giving from the overflow, but it was sacrificial giving because of the desire to give. It was the desire to do something for God and for others that compelled the Macedonians to give. They wanted to share or participate in showing the love of Christ to others!

Second Corinthians 8:5

> And not as we had hoped, but they first gave themselves to the Lord and to us through the will of God.

The Macedonian brethren exceeded Paul's expectations in regard to their giving. But Paul reveals the reason that proved true.

It was because they had first truly given themselves to the Lord Jesus. When we give ourselves to Christ, we give what we have to Christ. We realize that everything we own is not ours, but his. We realize that "one died for all so that all died, and they that live should no longer live for themselves, but for him, who for their sakes died and rose again" (2 Corinthians 5:14–15). Our possessions are like the "talents" of gold or silver entrusted to the servants in Matthew 25:14ff. God wants to make sure we are using those possessions for him and his mission.

Second Corinthians 8:6

> So that we encouraged Titus, that just as
> he made a beginning, so also he might bring
> this grace to completion in you.

Evidently, it was through the encouragement of Titus that the Corinthians began to think about participating in the contribution. The beginning point for giving is in the mind. It begins when we are challenged by God to use what he has given us to help the Lord's work or to help others. The grace of giving, however, is not completed until the actual gift is given. It is not just the promise of a gift or the intent to give that God wants, but the actual gift itself. It is in the act of giving that the grace is completed!

2 Corinthians 8:7

> But just as you abound in everything, in
> faith, and in word, and in knowledge, and in all
> diligence, and in the love which is from us and
> among you all, so (we desire that) you abound
> in this grace also!

Paul knew many good qualities of the Corinthians. They were gifted and eager to do good things. To grow in the grace of giving would help them advance to another level in their spiritual growth. Perhaps, unlike the Macedonians, they were not yet as eager to give of their money and property for the Lord's work. Remember that even supporting Paul as a preacher seems to have been somewhat of an issue for them at Corinth (1 Corinthians 9:14–18). Paul wants these people to grow in their giving from the commitment made in their hearts to its completion in the act of giving!

Second Corinthians 8:8

> I am not speaking as if giving a command,
> but as a result of the diligence of others (I am)
> testing the authenticity of your love.

To command the Corinthians would remove the key element of free will and choice. Giving is about choosing to give because one wants to do so. Choosing to give the best or choosing to give sacrificially is the essence of freewill offering. It is that unselfish decision that smells sweet as an offering to God! The questions are "Do you love God?" and "Do you love Christ?" We love by doing (1 John 3:18). The Macedonians had provided this kind of example through their extreme diligence in giving because they first gave themselves. Would the Corinthians demonstrate a similar authenticity in their love for God?

Second Corinthians 8:9–10

> You know the grace of our Lord Jesus
> Christ, that though he was rich, for your sakes
> he became poor, so that you, by his poverty,

COMMENTARY ON SECOND CORINTHIANS

might be made rich! And I give my judgment
in this, for this is better for you who made a
beginning a year ago, not only to do but also
to desire (to give). So now, also to complete the
doing of it, so that just as you had the willingness to desire (to participate), so also you might
have the willingness to complete (the gift).

Jesus is the consummate example of unselfish giving. He
left equality with God in heaven to enter incomparable poverty
(Philippians 2:6). He did this for us so that we might be enriched
by saving grace (1 Peter 3:18)! He did not just think about doing
this; he actually did it. He followed through to the very end! Paul
did not want the Corinthians to just talk about giving or plan to
give. He wanted them to actually come up with the money and
contribute. The follow-through in giving is where we act by faith.
We trust God to bless us as we decide to give! God is not just inter-
ested in our intentions but in our actions!

Second Corinthians 8:12

For if the willingness is present, it is
acceptable when one actually has (the gift), not
when one does not have it!

Paul is saying that God is not pleased if we do not follow
good intentions with actions. God is pleased when we exhibit the
discipline and planning to give the actual contribution. God is
pleased with the process that goes on in an individual. First, there
is the conviction that a good work needs to be done in the name
of God. That is followed by the decision to take part in that good
work. After that comes the precise planning and discipline necessary to set aside the money for the contribution. This involves

saying no to other things in order to set the money aside. Finally, the money is actually given, the fruit of conviction, commitment, and discipline. These unselfish qualities and actions make the gift pleasing in the sight of God. After all, our ultimate purpose is to please God with our actions, including our giving to his church (2 Corinthians 5:9).

If an evangelist or an elder is going to appeal to others on the basis of God's word to purpose, plan, discipline themselves, and give, then the spiritual leader must clearly exemplify this behavior in his own life. Among other things, this means that we must exercise financial discipline, ridding ourselves of as much debt as possible and saying no to purchases when they hinder our freedom to give. This is a process that often takes years, but the church needs to know that we are struggling sincerely to do the very thing we are asking others to do in the name of Jesus. Giving toward good works is a very positive activity for the church, especially when the leaders keep the church informed about the progress and results of the contribution.

Second Corinthians 8:13–15

> This is not so that relief for others might cause you hardship, but it is for the sake of equality! For at present your surplus makes up for their shortfall, so that their surplus may (one day) make up for your shortfall, so there might be equality! As it is written, "He that had much had none left over, and he that had little had no lack."

The quotation comes from Exodus 16:18 regarding the gathering of manna in the wilderness. God made sure that each had as much as they needed and that nobody was lacking. Paul is saying that when we help others today, they may well be helping us tomorrow as the circumstances demand. There must be an attitude of unselfishness among God's people (1 Timothy 6:17–18). We must be ready to share. John the Baptizer told the crowds coming to his baptism, "He that has two tunics, let him give to him who has none" (Luke 3:10). Benevolence is more complicated than this. Paul told the Thessalonians not to reward laziness and that each one should earn his own bread (2 Thessalonians 3:10ff). The focus in 2 Corinthians is the generosity that should characterize the hearts of God's people.

Second Corinthians 8:16

> Thanks be to God who put the same earnestness in the heart of Titus! Because he welcomed our exhortation, and being even more earnest, he voluntarily went forth to you!

The "earnestness" or "diligence," *spouden*, in Titus was his shared zeal to reach out to the poor saints in Jerusalem and to involve the Corinthian church in this good work! Titus was eagerly going to the Corinthians and eagerly encouraging them to finish what they started! He was not being forced to do this, but wanted to do this because of his own zeal for God!

Second Corinthians 8:18–20

> And we have sent with him the brother whose praise in the gospel is (heard) in all of the churches, and not only that but he was ordained by all of the churches to travel with this gift that is ministered by us, for the glory of the Lord and because of our willingness!

> Avoiding this, that no one should criticize the
> way this generous gift is administered by us!

Along with Titus, who had already built a rapport with the Corinthian church, Paul was sending this unnamed brother who was beloved and praised by the church for his work "in the gospel." This likely meant that he was a trusted preacher, teacher, or evangelist who was highly trusted by the people in the congregations participating in this contribution. One might speculate that this brother was someone like Apollos who was a powerful preacher/teacher and with whom the people in Corinth were familiar (Acts 18:27–28). At any rate, the reason for the presence of this man was to assure the minds of the participating churches that the contribution was being handled in an honest and transparent manner.

Second Corinthians 8:21–22

> For we are thinking beforehand, not only
> about what is good in the sight of the Lord, but
> also in the sight of man. And we have sent with
> them the brother whose earnestness has often
> been tested in many ways, and now he is even
> more earnest because of his confidence in you.

Verses 16–17 mentions Titus who was beloved by both Paul and the Corinthians. This is followed by another brother who was praised in all the churches who would be sent to travel "with him" or with Titus (2 Corinthians 8:18). Now it seems that Paul is sending a third brother who has been well tested in many ways and proven to be earnest and sincere (2 Corinthians 8:22). In this way, by having all of these trusted brothers accompany the contribution and oversee its safety, they could avoid any hint of impropriety in their handling of the contribution.

Second Corinthians 8:23–24

> So then, not only regarding Titus, my partner and fellow worker in your interests, but also regarding our brothers, the representatives of the churches, they bring glory to Christ! Moreover, the demonstration of your love, and our boasting about you to them is being openly declared in the presence of the churches!

Paul is praising all who are involved in this great demonstration of love and unity. Titus and the other brothers are bringing glory to God through their support and participation. When the Corinthians follow through with their gift, their obvious love will magnify the good things Paul has said about them to the other churches! Praising people for the good they are doing is now and has always been a great motivator for good!

Reflections on Chapter 8

1. What was the gift seemingly given to the Macedonian churches according to vv. 1–2?
2. What did the Macedonians give to Christ first?
3. What does Paul mean by the principle of equality voiced in vv. 13–15?
4. Why did Paul and Titus take such care to send a group of respected men along with the contribution to Jerusalem?
5. What was "the demonstration of your love" mentioned in verse 24?

9

Second Corinthians 9:1–2

> For about this ministry, which is for the saints, it is superfluous for me to write to you. For I know your willingness for which I boast to the Macedonians that Achaia has been preparing for a year, and your zeal has inspired many.

The Macedonian Christians begged to be a part of this "ministry to the saints" (2 Corinthians 8:4). This ministry was an outward overture by predominately Gentile churches toward predominately Jewish churches. It was a willing display of unity and compassion. The Corinthians had been enthusiastic about this work, and Paul is urging them to carry through with what they have planned.

Second Corinthians 9:3

> And I have sent the brothers so that our boasting about you in this matter might not be in vain, so that you might be prepared, just as I said, lest the Macedonians should come with me and find you unprepared and we should

be ashamed, or I should say you (would be ashamed), in this condition.

Paul knew that people sometimes needed to be reminded and encouraged to follow through. He was making sure that the Corinthians did this by telling them that not only had he been bragging on them to the Macedonians, but he would be bringing some of them with him when he came to Corinth and he wanted these brethren from the northern cities to see the fidelity and dependability of the Corinthians. This was all the more motivation for the Corinthians to have the money ready.

Second Corinthians 9:5–6

> Therefore, we thought it necessary to encourage the brothers, that they might come to you before us, and make up beforehand your already promised blessing, that it might be ready as a matter of bountiful blessing and not as a matter of (reluctant) greed. And this, the one who sows sparingly shall also reap sparingly, and the one who sows bountifully shall also reap bountifully.

Paul did not want to leave this important contribution to chance. He wanted to make sure the money was gathered in a timely fashion. The word *eulogia*, as used twice in verse 5, seems to mean an act done out of willingness and generosity as opposed to an act done under compulsion. The word *pleonexia*, greed or covetousness, conveys the reluctant spirit of a selfish person wanting to hang on to what he considers his own wealth. Verse 6 seems to be an allusion to the truths expressed in Proverbs 11:24 and

Proverbs 22:9. The point of this allusion is that generosity results in receiving the bountiful blessings of God.

Second Corinthians 9:7–8

> Just as each one has purposed in his heart (so let him give), not out of grief or of necessity. For God loves a cheerful giver. And God is able to make all grace abound toward you, so that always, having all sufficiency, you may abound unto every good deed.

The verb in verse 7 is understood from the previous context. "Just as each one has purposed in his heart" is an adverbial phrase and demands a verb, which must be supplied., The verb must be something like *do* or *give*. The word *lupe* means grief or sadness or sorrow. It complements the word *greed* or *covetousness* from verse 5. One is sad or grieved to let go of one's possessions if one is greedy in one's heart. In contrast, God loves a willing, cheerful giver. Paul reminds his readers that God is a generous giver and he is eager to reward generous givers with his own generosity! Our giving should be planned, "as he purposed in his heart," and it should be cheerful!

Second Corinthians 9:9–10

> Just as it is written, "He scattered, he gave to the poor people! His righteousness remains forever!" And the one who supplies seed to the sower and bread for food, shall supply and multiply your seed, and shall grow the results of your righteousness.

The citation is from Psalm 112:9 and is one among many descriptions of the man who fears the Lord. Such a man reaps from the Lord the reward of his generosity because God opens the "windows of heaven" and pours forth his blessings upon him (Malachi 3:10). Not only will God give such a giver more blessings, but he will multiply the results of his generous giving in the lives of others. "Your righteousness" in verse 10 is the righteous act of giving to others.

Second Corinthians 9:11–12

> Being enriched in every way resulting in all generosity which produces through us thanksgiving to God. Because the ministry of this holy service, not only fills up what is lacking for the saints, but also overflows through many thanksgivings to God!

There are several results that will come from the Corinthians' righteous act of giving. They themselves will be blessed by God for giving. Because of the godly character and spiritual growth they exhibit by their giving, Paul and his company will give thanks to God. The poor saints in Judea will have their needs supplied. The saints in Judea will then send thanksgiving and praise up to God, and their lives will be changed by the love and generosity of their Gentile brethren.

Second Corinthians 9:13–15

> Through the proving of this ministry, having glorified God for the steadfastness of your confession of the gospel of Christ and the generosity of your sharing toward them and

> toward all, and their prayer (will be) for you,
> as they long for you because of the overflow-
> ing abundance of the grace of God upon you!
> Thanks be to God for his indescribable gift!

This is one of Paul's famous long sentences. He is still talking about the far-reaching results of the Corinthians' giving. The "proving of this ministry" is speaking of the Corinthians actually following through with their gift. The Judean saints will not only glorify God for the gift, but they will see how sincere the Corinthians are in their confession of Jesus as Lord because they are following his example of unselfish giving. As a result, says the apostle, the Jewish brethren who are blessed by the gift will pray for the Corinthians and long for them because they will see God working in their generosity. When Paul thanks God for his "indescribable gift," it is a bit difficult to ascertain his meaning. Surely, the gift of the crucified Christ is the greatest gift ever given. But his mention of "the grace of God upon you" is characteristic of Paul's terminology for spiritual gifts of various kinds, including his own gift of apostleship (Romans 12:3, 6; Galatians 2:9; Ephesians 3:2, 7, 8; 4:7). The same phrase is used in 2 Corinthians 8:1 when Paul speaks of the "grace of God which was given in the churches of Macedonia." It may be that Paul is talking about the wonderful spiritual gift of "giving" which is mentioned in Romans 12:8 and is accompanied by "generosity," *aplotetos*, which is mentioned repeatedly in 2 Corinthians 8–9 (see 2 Corinthians 8:2; 9:11, 13).

Reflections on Chapter Nine

1. Discuss the meaning of the word translated as "willingness" in 2 Corinthians 8:10–12 and 9:1.
2. Paul says the Achaians had been preparing for a year for this contribution. What do you think is involved in this kind of preparation?
3. Describe the difference between giving as a matter of bounty and giving as a reluctant act of greed.
4. In 2 Corinthians 9:7, Paul talks about purposing in one's heart. What does that look like? Discuss.
5. Talk about the promises that are attached to our giving in 2 Corinthians 9:10–11. What can we depend on as we give?
6. Talk about the chain reaction that our giving creates according to 2 Corinthians 9:13ff.

10

Second Corinthians 10:1–2

> I, Paul, myself, who am "humble when present with you," and "courageous towards you when absent," urge you by the gentleness and kindness of Christ, even I, beg you, I who though not present am emboldened with confidence, to dare to consider some who regard us as though we are living according to the flesh.

The parts of the translation which I have placed in quotes represent what the unwanted teachers were saying about Paul in his absence. Paul is talking about the group of Judaizing teachers that were now among the Corinthians. He mentioned these in 2 Corinthians 2:17, 3:1, 4:3, and 6:14. These troublemaking teachers were speaking against Paul, trying to alienate the Corinthians from him so they could turn them to their point of view. Paul's methods were not "according to the flesh" like the methods of his Judaizing competitors. He tried to deal, even with those who opposed his inspired teaching, in a manner that was in accordance with God's will.

Second Corinthians 10:3

> For though we are living in the flesh, we do not make war according to the flesh, for the weapons of our warfare are not fleshly, but are powerful through God for the casting down of fortresses, casting down reasoning and every high thing raised up against the knowledge of God, capturing every thought unto the obedience of Christ!

The preacher or teacher of the gospel uses the sword of the Spirit and the power of a godly example to break down the fortresses Satan builds around the minds and hearts of people. Satan helps us construct barriers. These are attitudes, ideas, feelings, and misunderstandings that keep God and his word from taking over. When the gospel is preached and understood by an honest person, the truth of God's great love and his redemptive work will break down those walls. An honest heart will be convicted by the word. An honest person will allow the word to change his/her thinking and lead him/her to commitment and obedience. Gentle and respectful speech and kind acts of service on the part of Christians can certainly help penetrate Satan's walls as well. God's goal is to capture the mind and bring people to the obedience of Christ in every aspect of their lives (Romans 12:2; Ephesians 4:21–24). As preachers and teachers, we should, like Paul, pray that we can proclaim the gospel clearly and plainly so that people can readily understand it, be convicted by it, and be persuaded to obey it (Colossians 4:4).

Second Corinthians 10:6

> And whenever your obedience is fulfilled, we stand ready to punish any disobedience.

The troublemakers' sarcastic statements about Paul being courageous when absent but humble when present seem to be answered here. Paul does not now, nor will he when present, shrink from telling the church God's will and demanding that they conform to it. He will take disciplinary action, if need be, to enforce compliance to God's commands, much as he did in the matter of the man who was living with his father's wife (1 Corinthians 5; 2 Corinthians 2:5–11). Paul returned once again to the matter of the man who had been living with his father's wife in 2 Corinthians 7:7–12. Paul's commitment to the word of Christ had not wavered.

Second Corinthians 10:7

> You (Corinthians) see only what is on the surface. If anyone is convinced that he belongs to Christ, let he himself consider also that just as he belongs to Christ, so do we. For even if I should boast more abundantly about our authority which the Lord gave us for building you up and not for tearing you down, I will not be ashamed. So that I might not glory as if "making you afraid through letters."

The Corinthians were not very discerning when it came to the teachers that came to them. They were not doing as John later called his readers to do when he urged, "Test the spirits to see if they are from God because many false prophets have gone out into the world" (1 John 4:1). Paul is being dragged into comparing himself with these troubling teachers, those he later calls "false apostles" and "ministers of Satan" (2 Corinthians 11:13–15). Paul has been given authority as an apostle by Jesus Christ himself, something his opponents could not claim (Acts 9:15ff; Galatians

1:1, 10–12). Having claimed apostolic authority, Paul was still trying not to live up to the charge that he was bold in his letters yet timid when present in person. These teachers were making things personal, and though we must strive to rise above this kind of comparing, it is very difficult sometimes.

Second Corinthians 10:11

> Because "His letters," they say, "are burdensome and strong, but his bodily presence is weak, and his speech is despised." Let such a one consider this, that what we are in word through letters, we are the same in deed when present!

He is simply assuring his readers that he will follow through with whatever action is needed when he meets them face-to-face. The Judaizing teachers were evidently trained in rhetoric and used the kind of speech respected in Corinthian circles. They thought Paul's way of speaking, which did not match the kind of speech employed by Greek rhetorical debaters, did not inspire confidence in his message. Paul acknowledged this in 1 Corinthians 2:1–5. Though not trained in Greek rhetoric, he was not inferior to those teachers in his divinely revealed knowledge!

Second Corinthians 10:12

> For we do not dare to judge or compare ourselves with those who commend themselves. But they themselves, measuring themselves by themselves and comparing themselves with themselves are without understanding.

Paul's opponents were in the habit of comparing themselves with others. Paul himself was "circumcised the eighth day, of the people of Israel, of the tribe of Benjamin, a Hebrew of Hebrews, in regard to the law, a Pharisee" (Philippians 3:4–6). He had been schooled at the feet of Gamaliel (Acts 22:3). He had advanced in Judaism beyond the majority of his countrymen because he had been very zealous for the traditions of his forefathers (Galatians 1:13–14).

Today, we also can get into the fruitless business of comparing ourselves with others. We compare our education, our work experience, our publications, and our capabilities, and do this so that we can feel good about ourselves and so that others will accept us. Paul says, "It is not the one who commends himself, but the one whom the Lord commends who is approved" (2 Corinthians 10:17). Today's obsession with social media profiles and postings fosters this kind of continual comparison with others. A much better question for God's ministers is "Does God approve of what I am doing?" If we strive to gain God's approval, we will be much better off than if we worry about the approval and esteem of other people.

Second Corinthians 10:13–15

> But we will not boast without measure, but according to the measure of the standard which God apportioned to us, and we extend that even to you! For even if we extend our boasting unto you we do not overextend ourselves, for we actually came to you with the gospel of Christ! For we do not boast in the labors of others without due cause, but we have the hope that as your faith grows, we will be magnified by you according to our own area of work.

Paul clearly implies that his opponents were boasting about things for which they were not responsible. They were boasting about their letters of commendation and about the work that other people actually accomplished. This would be like a brand-new minister coming to a congregation filled with excited young couples and lots of visitors and bragging as if all of these were the result of his own labors. Our own resume as ministers is based, in God's eyes, on what we ourselves have done through his power. The things people have experienced from us are the things which make our reputation as ministers and gain the respect of others. A good minister should let his own actions speak for themselves as he strives to please God (2 Corinthians 5:9, 14–15). Paul was able to boast about the spiritual progress in the lives of the Corinthians because he was the one who actually brought the gospel to them, the gospel that changed their lives for the better!

Second Corinthians 10:16–18

> So that we might preach the gospel even (in areas) beyond you, so that we might not be ready to boast about the efforts of another, but, 'Let the one who boasts, boast in the Lord!' For it is not the one who commends himself that is approved, but the one whom the Lord commends!

Paul was weary of the bragging and posturing of his opponents in Corinth. He resolved that he would never take credit for the work of other people nor would he fail to give credit to the Lord who worked through him and all true ministers of Christ. Paul believed that God was working through him everywhere he went. He reported to the church at Antioch after the Galatian mission about "what God had done through them and how he opened a door of faith unto the Gentiles" (Acts 14:27). Paul was ever conscious that God was working through the people who trusted in him (Galatians 2:9–10; Philippians 2:13). Our boasting should be in this form: "Look what God has done through the efforts of these servants!" The approval we seek is the approval of God. We want God to say, "Well done, good and faithful servant!" Paul saw boasting in one's self as a negative thing, something that focused man on self instead of the work of God. Boasting in one's own goodness or one's fleshly accomplishments was against the mindset of a Christian (Romans 2:17, 23; 3:27; 4:2; 11:18; 12:3; 1 Corinthians 1:29, 31; 2 Corinthians 10:17–18; 12:7–8). The only good kind of boasting is boasting in the loving redemptive work of God or boasting about God's transforming work in the lives of others (Romans 5:2–3, 11; 2 Corinthians 10:18).

Reflections on Chapter 10

1. According to 2 Corinthians 10:1–3, what kind of accusations were being made by Paul's opponents against him?
2. Paul said the weapons he used were designed for the casting down of fortresses. Read 2 Corinthians 10:3–5 and talk about the kind of fortresses that Satan builds around people's hearts and minds to keep God out.
3. Why did God give his ministers authority according to 2 Corinthians 10:7–10?
4. What standards were Paul's opponents using to judge themselves according to 2 Corinthians 10:12? Why is this standard invalid?
5. In what did Paul say it is right to boast?
6. Whose approval was Paul seeking?

11

Second Corinthians 11:1

> You should put up with a little bit of my
> foolishness, but you are already putting up with
> me! I am jealous over you with a godly jealousy!
> For I espoused you to one husband that I might
> present you as a pure virgin to Christ! I am
> afraid, lest by any means, like Satan deceived
> Eve by his craftiness, your minds should be cor-
> rupted from the generosity and sincerity that is
> (directed) toward Christ.

Paul is ashamed of himself for getting caught up in the boasting of his opponents and is trying to explain that his feelings arise
from godly motives. There is selfish jealousy and there is godly jealousy. God himself is a jealous God when it comes to his relationship with his people (Exodus 20:5). Paul wanted the Corinthians
to be saved, to maintain their relationship with God. By leading them to Christ, Paul had betrothed these people to Christ,
to be presented to him on the day of judgment (Ephesians 5:26;
Revelation 19:6; 21:1–3). He wanted to present them in purity,
not as spiritual adulterers! Satan is the deceiver of the whole world
(John 8:44; Revelation 12:9). Paul was afraid that through the
deception of these Judaizing teachers, the Corinthian Christians
could be led away from their dedication to Christ. The word *aplo-*

teti is translated "generosity" or "liberality" in other places in the book (2 Corinthians 8:2; 9:11, 13). This word describes the willingness to freely give of one's self in service of another as well as the willingness to freely give one's money. This sincere devotion in our souls should belong only to Christ and should not be given to any other being. These false teachers were trying to change this giving, devoted mindset that was directed toward Christ and turn it elsewhere!

Second Corinthians 11:4

> For if someone who comes preaches another Jesus whom we did not preach, or if you receive a different spirit which you did not receive, or a different gospel which you did not welcome, you put up with that very well!

Many in ancient times tried to change the nature of the claims about Jesus. Paul uses the word *heteron,* "different," to describe the content of his opponents' teaching, much as he does in Galatians 1:7. Jews ultimately denied Jesus's divine origin! They could not confess with Paul that Jesus is "God over all blessed forever" (Romans 9:5). The Jesus they preached did not make the Mosaic law obsolete by his death and resurrection. The Jesus whom the Judaizers preached was not crucified for the sins of man, nor did he rise from the dead, nor would he be coming again to judge the world. Like the Muslims who came later, and other groups after them, they saw Jesus as only a man who was not the bringer of a totally New Covenant between God and sinful man! Unfortunately, the Corinthians seemed a bit too tolerant of those who preached a different Jesus and a different gospel. Paul had already pleaded with them not to be yoked together with such unbelievers and to come out from among them and be separate

(2 Corinthians 6:14–17). If Paul's terminology is similar here to his terminology in Galatians 1:6–7, the gospel of these interlopers was different because it was not firmly rooted in the redemptive work of Christ and the resultant "grace of Christ."

Second Corinthians 11:5–8

> For I consider myself in no way inferior to the super apostles! For even if I am unlearned in speech, yet I am not in knowledge, but I made things clear in every way to all of you! Did I commit a sin by humbling myself so that you might be exalted because I preached the gospel to you without charge? I robbed other churches, taking wages from them so I could minister to you.

Paul had been chosen by Christ himself, just as the other apostles had been chosen (Acts 9:15; Galatians 1:1f). He had received his gospel directly from Christ (Galatians 1:11–12, 14–20). Paul was well-educated in the things of Judaism, a member of its highest circles (Galatians 1:13–14; Philippians 3:5ff). The mystery of Christ was revealed to him directly by the Holy Spirit (Ephesians 3:3–5). God was working through Paul just as he worked through Peter, James, and John, the leading apostles (Galatians 2:8–10). Paul had made the gospel of Christ clear to the Corinthians, not hindered by any lack of ability to share what had been revealed to him. He had chosen not to avail himself of the right of financial support from the Corinthian church because he perceived it to be an impediment to them in hearing the gospel (1 Corinthians 9:1–16). Other churches, like the church at Philippi, had supported Paul and supplied his needs when Corinth did not (Philippians 1:5; 4:15f).

Second Corinthians 11:9

> And even when I was with you and was
> in need, I did not burden anyone, for what I
> lacked was fully supplied by the brothers from
> Macedonia, and I made sure that I was never a
> burden to you, and I will keep it that way!

Paul would not be accused of peddling the gospel like his opponents did (2 Corinthians 2:17). He had chosen to refuse the right of support in Corinth and was determined that he would continue to do that in that particular location because he thought it best (1 Corinthians 9:1–16). There was something about the Corinthians' point of view that made it necessary for Paul to choose this path (1 Corinthians 9:22).

Second Corinthians 11:10

> This is the truth of Christ regarding
> me, that this matter of boasting will not be
> kept from me in the regions of Achaia. Why?
> Because I do not love you? God knows! But
> what I do, I will do so that I might cut off the
> opportunity for those who wish an opportu-
> nity (to accuse me), so that they might find
> something to boast about just as I boast in you.

Paul's boasting was about what God had done through the Corinthians. His boasting about preaching the gospel for free was only to show his sincerity and his genuine love for their souls. He would not take pay from this group of people because he did not want to give his detractors a chance to question his sincerity. Paul just wished the Corinthians would brag about him as much as he bragged about them to others!

Second Corinthians 11:13–15

> For these people are false apostles, deceitful workers, disguised as apostles of Christ. And no marvel, for Satan himself masquerades as an angel of light. It is no great thing, then, if his ministers masquerade as ministers of righteousness. Whose end will be according to their deeds!

Just as there are true ministers of the New Covenant and sincere ministers of reconciliation, there are also deceptive ministers of Satan. These men and women, in the guise of Christian ministry, work to turn people away from the truth. Paul said his opponents were false apostles. Does this mean they were actually claiming to be apostles like Peter and Paul were apostles? That is possible. Paul indicated to the Thessalonians that some circulated oral and written messages that claimed to be from apostles when they were not (2 Thessalonians 2:1–3). It may be that Paul's opponents claimed to be sent out by church leaders like James or Peter when they really did not speak for them. Perhaps they were like those brothers who came "from James" in Galatians 2:11–14. In any case, they were masquerading. They were fakes.

Satan masquerades as an angel of light when he is really an angel of darkness (Revelation 12:7–9). God sees through the masks that people wear. God rewards all people, including ministers, for their deeds. James warned people about claiming to be teachers, "for theirs is the heavier judgment" (James 3:1). At this point in his letter, Paul spares no words to call these teachers what they really are!

Second Corinthians 11:16–21

> I say again, lest anyone should think I am
> being foolish, if indeed you also think me to
> be acting like a fool, that I also might boast
> a little, though many are boasting in a fleshly
> manner! I also will boast, for you gladly put up
> with fools since you are so wise, for you put
> up with anyone who enslaves you, if anyone
> devours you, if anyone praises you, if anyone
> slaps you in the face! I speak in a dishonor-
> able way because we have been made weak!
> Insomuch as anyone dares (to boast), I speak
> foolishness, I also dare!

Paul has been driven to act in a way he considers foolish
(2 Corinthians 10:12). Because the false teachers were comparing themselves to Paul so as to discredit him, Paul was play-
ing their game in a way. He was saying things about himself
that were true and honorable, but he didn't like having to stick
up for himself in this way. He asks the Corinthians to put up
with a little foolishness from him because they were obviously
putting up with fools (Paul's opponents). Paul sarcastically calls
the Corinthians "wise" because they were not wise. In fact, says
Paul, the people they were allowing to work among them were
trying to enslave them to the law and trying to spiritually devour
them. These fools the Corinthians tolerated would praise them,
then slap them in the face, taking advantage of them because
their motives were not pure (2 Corinthians 2:17). This is why
Paul was engaging in this desperate attempt to make them wake
up before it was too late!

Second Corinthians 11:22–23

> Are they Hebrews? I am also! Are they
> Israelites? I am also! Are they the seed of
> Abraham? I am too! Are they ministers of
> Christ? I speak as one who is out of his mind,
> I am more so! In labors more abundantly, in
> imprisonments more abundantly, in wounds
> more abundantly, in (threat of) deaths often.

Paul is now responding in frustration to the empty claims of his opponents in Corinth. They claimed to be Hebrews and Israelites. Paul was more so because he had trained at the feet of Gamaliel, had advanced in Judaism to the level of the Sanhedrin, and had reached high levels of recognition among the Jewish leaders (Acts 22:1–2; Galatians 1:13–14; Philippians 3:5–6). The fact that his opponents were claiming to be ministers of Christ is interesting because he has already said that they are preaching a different Jesus, perhaps a more Jewish Jesus and a different gospel (2 Corinthians 11:4). Paul has made it clear that he has worked hard to support himself so that he might not hinder the gospel (1 Corinthians 9:1–16). He was imprisoned at different times in Jerusalem, in Caesarea, perhaps in Ephesus, and certainly in Rome (Acts 22–26; Ephesians 4:1; 1 Corinthians 15:32). Paul had been beaten many times and bore on his body the *stigmata,* the wounds he had received for the sake of Jesus (Galatians 6:17). He had faced death at sea, death from wild beasts, and death by stoning (Acts 14:19; 27:39ff; 2 Corinthians 1:8–9). His opponents could not claim a similar dedication.

Second Corinthians 11:24–26

> From the Jews, five times I received forty
> lashes minus one. Three times I was beaten

with rods. Once I was stoned. Three times I was shipwrecked, having spent a night and day in the deep. In journeys often, in danger from rivers, in danger from robbers, in danger from countrymen, in danger from Gentiles, in danger in cities, in danger in desert places, in danger at sea, in danger from false brethren.

This is quite a litany of suffering. Paul had lived his life as an apostle in peril from different things. Many of these things are natural dangers that everyone in that time experienced. The repeated beatings and imprisonments were all related to his proclamation of the gospel as was the stoning at Lystra and at least one instance of shipwreck in Acts 27. Paul was often persecuted by the Jewish population as he was at Thessalonica in Acts 17. Among all of these other dangers was Paul's peril from false brethren. This is the kind of peril he was in at the moment from those false brothers, those false apostles, those ministers of Satan who were trying to sabotage his relationship with the Corinthian church. The fact that Paul endured all of these perils and continued to be a faithful minister stood in great contrast with these peddlers of the gospel who were troubling the Corinthians (2 Corinthians 2:17).

Second Corinthians 11:27

In labor and hardship, in many sleepless nights, in hunger and thirst, in fasting often, in cold and nakedness, in addition to all of these daily pressures, there is my anxiety for the churches! Who is weak and I am not made weak? Who is caused to stumble and I do not burn?

In addition to the list of hardships, Paul finally comes to the one that is closest to his heart. Along with all of the other troubles and hardships of his life, he had continual anxiety for the churches! The word translated concern or anxiety is *merimna,* the same root word that is used in other passages regarding worry. Jesus used the same terminology when he told his disciples not to worry about what they would eat or drink or what they would wear (Matthew 6:24–33). He told them to trust God for the necessities of life and God would provide! Paul told the Philippian church to "be anxious in nothing, but in everything, through prayer, and supplication, with thanksgiving, let your requests be made known unto God" (Philippians 4:6). In that passage, he seems to be telling them not to be overcome by anxiety but to ask God for what they need and thank God for their blessings at the same time. Still, in this passage, Paul acknowledges his own worry or anxiety for the souls of God's redeemed people. A good minister cares about the souls of the people with whom he works. Paul did not just worry about the Corinthians, but also about the souls in Antioch, Lystra, Derbe, Iconium, Philippi, Thessalonica, Berea, Troas, Ephesus, Colossae, Hierapolis, Laodicea, Rome, and a host of other places. They were not just faces but precious souls to him. When he told the Romans that "all the churches of Christ greet you," he saw faces in his mind, not just places (Romans 16:16). Not all anxiety can be avoided, but we should at least spend some of that on spiritual matters related to the salvation of souls! Paul was saddened and often terribly distressed when he heard of his converts turning away from God or falling into sin. Do we care as much as Paul cared?

Second Corinthians 11:30

> If it is necessary to boast, I will boast in my
> weaknesses! The God and Father of the Lord

Jesus Christ knows, I do not lie! In Damascus,
the Ethnarch, Aretas the king, set a watch on
the city of Damascus in order to arrest me! But
I was lowered in a basket through a hole in the
wall and I escaped his hands!

Perhaps Paul is boasting in this great list of trials from which
God delivered him, giving glory to God for his grace! Paul's desire
was not to exalt himself. Even in Damascus, God delivered him
when he could easily have been killed. One can read about the
Jewish conspiracy to kill Paul in Damascus and his escape through
the city wall in Acts 9:23–25. God also delivered Paul in Ephesus
when he despaired about possibly losing his life (2 Corinthians
1:8–10).

Reflections on Chapter 11

1. Talk about how our relationship with Christ is compared to that of a betrothed couple in 2 Corinthians 11:1–3.

2. How does Paul describe the Jesus, the spirit, and the gospel that was being presented by his opponents in Corinth (2 Corinthians 11:4)?

3. In 2 Corinthians 11:5–8, Paul's opponents were arguing that Paul was inferior to them for what reason?

4. According to 2 Corinthians 11:13–15, _____ masquerades as an angel of _____, and his ministers masquerade as _____ of righteousness.

5. In 2 Corinthians 11:16–21, what were some of the means the false teachers were using so that they could deceive the Corinthians? What does Paul say they were actually doing?

6. What kinds of things does Paul list in this chapter that actually enhanced his credibility as a sincere minister of Christ?

12

Second Corinthians 12:1

> It is necessary to boast, though there is no
> profit in it, so I will come to dreams and reve-
> lations from the Lord. I know a man in Christ
> who fourteen years ago (whether in the body I
> do not know, or out of the body I do not know.
> God knows), such a man was caught up to the
> third heaven! And I know this man, (whether
> in the body or apart from the body, I do not
> know. God knows). And he was caught up
> into paradise, and he heard unspeakable words,
> which it is not lawful for a man to speak.

Having earlier said that he would commend himself to the
conscience of the Corinthians based on his own behavior among
them, Paul has now been drawn into comparing himself with his
opponents (2 Corinthians 3:1; 6:3ff; 7:2ff). He even said that
people who compare themselves with other people are without
understanding (2 Corinthians 10:12), and further, that it is not
the one who commends himself but the one whom the Lord commends that is truly approved (2 Corinthians 10:17–18). Having
said all of this, Paul has argued that his own willingness to suffer
for the gospel, his behavior among the Corinthians, and his persistence in working for their souls while refusing to be paid shows

that his Christianity is real and his motives are pure as a minister of Christ. In addition, he wants the Corinthians to know again, as he explained to them in his first letter, that Paul has been given visions and revelations directly from God (1 Corinthians 2:6–13).

Paul boasts of a profound experience he had fourteen years earlier when he was "caught up" to the third heaven, otherwise called paradise. The word *harpazo*, to be seized or snatched or taken away, is used in verse 2 and again in verse 4. This is the same term Paul uses in 1 Thessalonians 4:16 where he said the living Christians would be "caught up" into the clouds along with the Christians who were raised from the dead to meet Jesus in the air on the day of his *Parousia*. The Jews envisioned several different levels of the heavenly realm, inhabited by both angels and demons, one of which was called the "garden" or "paradise." Jesus told the thief that he would be with him in paradise that very day (Luke 23:43). John told the Asian Christians that those who overcome would eat from the tree of life, which is in the paradise of God (Revelation 2:7).

The Jewish people believed Paradise, the Garden of God, was the destination of the righteous, and there was much religious speculation about it. One intertestamental Jewish writer said, "But they who honor the true and everlasting God inherit life throughout the ages of time, dwelling in the fertile garden of Paradise, feasting on sweet bread from the starry heaven" (*Sibylline Oracles*, II. 46–49). The intertestamental author of the Secrets of Enoch describes ten levels of heaven in which dwell a variety of both good and evil spiritual beings, much as Paul describes the "heavenly realms" as containing both angels and demons in Ephesians. This Jewish writer describes the "third heaven," saying:

> I saw all of the sweet flowering trees and
> beheld their fruits, which were sweet smelling,
> and all the foods borne by them bubbling with

fragrant exhalation. And in the midst of the trees, the tree of life, in that place whereon the Lord rests, when he goes up into Paradise. And this tree is of ineffable goodness and fragrance, and adored more than every existing thing… and Paradise is between corruptibility and incorruptibility. And two springs come out which send forth honey and milk, and their springs send forth oil and wine…and go down into the Paradise of Eden. (Secrets of Enoch VIII. 2–6).

Paul claims to have seen paradise or the "third heaven;" whether in a vision or bodily, he is not sure. He claimed that there he heard things which no man is permitted to speak. Not only had he seen the risen Christ, but he had been transported to see into "the heavenly realms." Surely, these revelations were beyond the realm of human experience for all but a very select few (Revelation 4:2ff).

Second Corinthians 12:5–7a

I will boast on behalf of such a man, but on behalf of myself I will not boast except in weaknesses! For if I wish to boast, I will not be foolish, for I speak the truth! But I refrain, lest anyone should think of me in a way that goes beyond what he sees in me or hears from me, even in view of the surpassing greatness of the revelations!

Paul is still trying to be modest and is embarrassed to mention this incredible experience, yet it is true. He is a prophet of the highest order in the company of the great biblical prophets. Yet, he does not want people to form an opinion of him based on an experience he had fourteen years earlier but based on what they themselves have seen and heard in interactions with him (2 Corinthians 6:3ff). He believes what he said in 2 Corinthians 11:18, "It is not the one who commends himself that is approved, but the one whom the Lord commends."

2 Corinthians 12:7b–9

> Wherefore, so that I might not become overly arrogant, there was given to me a thorn in the flesh, a messenger of Satan, so that it might beat me, so that I might not become arrogant. About this I begged the Lord three times, that it should be taken away from me. And he said to me, "My grace is sufficient for you, for power is made complete in weakness." Therefore, I will more gladly boast in my weaknesses, so that the power of Christ might dwell with me!

God knew Paul well enough to know that he had the potential to be arrogant, and if he was arrogant and puffed up, he would not be nearly as useful to God. This very business of boasting and comparing himself with his opponents in Corinth went against what he knew to be good conduct. Paul said it all in 2 Corinthians 11:17–18. Paul knew that few people could ever claim what he had been permitted to experience in paradise. God allowed Satan to strike Paul with some sort of physical malady in order to remind him that he was weak, helpless, and dependent on God. When one reads between the lines, especially in his letter to the Galatian churches, it seems that this may have been some kind of rather offensive illness of the eyes (Galatians 4:14–15). In any case, it served to keep Paul from becoming arrogant, so God chose to allow Paul to continue in his physical suffering. Remember, God works all things, the suffering and the joy, together for the good of his purpose (Romans 8:28). As he had done in Asia (2 Corinthians 1:8–9), God wanted Paul to trust God, not himself. Paul prayed earnestly to be relieved of his illness, and God gave him a "no" answer because God knew it was best for Paul and for the cause of Christ! We are actually most powerful sometimes when we are weakest because we are trusting in the power of Christ (Ephesians 1:19ff; 3:16, 20).

Second Corinthians 12:10

> Wherefore, I take pleasure in weaknesses,
> in insults, in necessities, in persecutions, and
> hardships for Christ's sake, for when I am weak,
> then I am strong!

Paul urged the Ephesians to "be strong in the Lord and in the strength of his might" (Ephesians 6:10). When God works through feeble human beings, great things are often done! God can work through seemingly impossible circumstances to accomplish his will! When Paul was arrested in Jerusalem and taken to Caesarea, and ultimately, to Rome, countless people heard the gospel. During his imprisonment, people heard the gospel, from the lowliest servants and soldiers to the highest officials in government (Acts 22–28). God does not need our strength. He only needs our willingness to do what is needed in the moment of opportunity!

Second Corinthians 12:11

> I have become foolish! You drove me to it!
> For I ought to have been commended by you!
> For in no way am I inferior to the greatest of the
> apostles! For I worked the signs of an apostle

> among you with steadfastness, signs and won-
> ders and miracles! For in what way were you
> made to feel inferior to the rest of the churches,
> except that I did not become a burden to you?
> Forgive me this unrighteousness!

Paul is ashamed of himself for doing what he himself said one should not do in 2 Corinthians 10:12. Though he was trying not to be a self-promoter and an arrogant person, he had been pointing out ways in which he was better than his opponents as a spiritual leader. He was a true minister of Christ! His conduct among the Corinthians was sincere and honest. He was not peddling the gospel! He was a genuine recipient of divine revelation from Christ himself! He was a true apostle of Jesus! The fact that Paul mentions "the signs of an apostle" seems to indicate that apostles had a demonstrably greater ability to do signs and wonders than others with spiritual gifts. This seems to also be indicated in Hebrews 2:3–4 and Mark 16:20. He said in the first letter that he came to the Corinthians in demonstration of the Spirit and power (1 Corinthians 2:3–5). Though his aim was not selfish, he had been drawn into this game of boasting and comparisons which he despised. They had forced him into it because he cared so deeply for their souls. The fact that he had not taken financial support from them was now being used against him! He is both hurt and sarcastic when he says, "Forgive me this unrighteousness!"

Second Corinthians 12:14–15

> Behold, this is the third time that I am
> ready to come to you, and I will not be a bur-
> den! For I do not seek what is yours, but you!
> For it is not for the children to save for the par-
> ents, but the parents to save for the children!

> But I will most gladly spend and be spent for
> your souls. If I love you more abundantly, shall
> I be loved less?

He says this was the third time he was preparing to come to them. Surely, he came to them in Acts 18 when he established the church. He spent three months in Greece, likely in Corinth in Acts 20:3. He had planned another visit but was not able to come at that time (2 Corinthians 1:12–16). He wanted to come again for a third visit. Paul told the Corinthians earlier that they may have many different teachers, but they only had one father in the gospel (1 Corinthians 4:14–16). He bares his soul when he says that he does not seek their money or their possessions but their very souls! He sees himself as the loving parent who only cares about the interests of his children. Paul's altruism was beyond what many of us who are more selfish will ever realize! He was determined to continue to minister to the Corinthians without compensation. Paul was willing to spend his own money and spend his own physical and emotional energy in order to accomplish the salvation of souls! We often ask, "What is in it for me?" Paul was selfless in his quest to win the lost!

Second Corinthians 12:16–17

> But whatever the case may be, I have not
> been a burden to you! But being such a crafty
> fellow, I took you by deceit! Did any of those
> I sent wrong you? By which of them did I
> defraud you?

Paul could be honest in saying that he had not taken any money from the Corinthians nor did he or those he sent to them take advantage of them in any way. This was a mark of his unselfish

COMMENTARY ON SECOND CORINTHIANS

integrity in dealing with the Corinthians, unlike those interlopers who were "peddling the word of God" (2 Corinthians 2:17).

Second Corinthians 12:18

> I have encouraged Titus and have sent the brother along with him. Titus never defrauded you, did he? Have we not conducted ourselves in the same spirit? Have we not walked in the same footprints (as he)?

As mentioned in 2 Corinthians 8:16–19, Titus and another well-loved brother were going to visit the Corinthians again and encourage them about their contribution. Titus had been unselfish and giving among them as was Paul. Titus, Paul, and those associated with him followed the same unselfish methods in their ministry. The Corinthians could not point to a single instance of fraud or deceit or covetousness when it concerned Paul and his circle (2 Corinthians 7:2).

Second Corinthians 12:19–20

> Do you think that in the past we have defended ourselves to you? Before God, we speak in Christ! Everything (we do), beloved, is for your edification! For I am afraid, lest when I come to you I might not find you as I want to, but I also might be found (in a state) in which you do not want me to be. Lest by any means (I should find that there is) strife, jealousy, angry outbursts, divisions, slanderers, gossips, arrogance, and disorderly conduct!

As all of this comparing and defending comes to an end, Paul asks the Corinthians once again to look back on his time with them. Was he ever one to brag or defend himself? They know the answer is no! Paul's authority as an apostle was given to him so that he could build people up spiritually, not tear them down (2 Corinthians 10:8; 13:10). The word translated "edification" is *oikodomeo,* meaning to build or build up. Paul's mission was spiritual construction, not spiritual destruction! The same is true of our mission. His long diatribe about his behavior, his sufferings, and his unquestionable qualifications as an apostle of Christ is only designed to help the Corinthians understand what they must do. They must separate themselves from the bad influence of the false teachers! Paul is afraid to have to come again to Corinth and find them in need of pervasive correction and discipline. But if they allow the interlopers to continue to seduce their minds, such might be the case, and it would be most unpleasant. Many of the things Paul is afraid to find are things he wrote about in his first letter to the Corinthians.

Second Corinthians 12:21

> Lest when I come again to you my God should humble me before you, and I shall be made sorry before many of those who have sinned before, who have not repented of their uncleanness and fornication and lasciviousness which they have practiced!

As Paul made clear earlier in the letter (2 Corinthians 2:1–4), he did not want to come again to the Corinthians with the sad task of rebuking them and correcting them for their sinful behavior. He had been accused by his opponents of being forceful and decisive in his letters but weak in his bodily presence (2

Corinthians 10:10–11). He even commended the Corinthians for their compliance to the instructions he had given in his first letter (2 Corinthians 7:10–13). Now, however, due to the negative influence Paul perceives as coming from his opponents, Paul fears he might have to make another unpleasant visit to his spiritual children in Corinth.

Reflections on Chapter 12

1. What is Paul actually boasting about in 2 Corinthians 12:1–5?
2. What information do we have in other places about the place Paul calls paradise or the third heaven?
3. How do Paul's statements in 2 Corinthians 12:7–9 help us with the identity of this man who saw such astounding visions of the heavenly realm?
4. When Paul begged God to remove his thorn in the flesh, what was God's answer to Paul?
5. How does this help us understand that our suffering can be for our good?
6. According to 2 Corinthians 12:14–15, how did Paul see his relationship with the Corinthians?
7. What did Paul maintain about the moral quality of his behavior among the Corinthians?

13

Second Corinthians 13:1–2

> This is now the third time I am coming
> to you! At the mouth of two or three witnesses
> every word shall be established! I said before
> and I now say, as when present the second time,
> and now as absent, to those who have sinned
> before, and to all the rest, that when I come
> again I will not spare you!

Paul was in Corinth when he established the church in
Acts 18. He was there again for a brief period of three months
in Acts 20:2–3. He probably wrote the book of Romans at that
time. Paul means to confront the false teachers, face those who
would accuse him of misconduct, and deal with whatever needs
to be dealt with in the church there. He means to confront those
who may be involved in the kinds of things he mentions in 2
Corinthians 12:19–21 as well. The fact that he uses the language
of Deuteronomy 19:15 may indicate that he has in mind church
discipline of the kind described by Jesus (Matthew 18:15–18)
and by Paul when he wrote to Timothy (1 Timothy 5:19). Of
course, he hopes that necessary corrections will take place before
he arrives.

Second Corinthians 13:3

> Wherefore, seek approval from the Christ
> who is speaking in me, who is not weak among
> you, but is powerful among you! For he was
> crucified in weakness, but was raised in power.
> For even though we are weak in him, on the
> other hand we will live with him among you by
> the power of God!

Whose approval do we seek? Paul made it clear that it is not those who commend themselves that are approved but those whom the Lord approves (2 Corinthians 10:17–18). The Corinthians needed to stop seeking the approval of the false apostles who ministered among them as emissaries of Satan but the approval of the Lord himself! Paul had taught the Corinthians to trust in the power of God, though he himself was often weak among them (1 Corinthians 2:1–5). Paul was often physically weak because of his thorn in the flesh and often tried to be gentle in his dealings with people as well. Neither of these things should have been construed as spiritual weakness. Paul used the power of Christ, working through his own humble spirit and working through the power of God's word to convict and convert the hearts of people and to bring every thought into captivity unto the obedience of Christ (2 Corinthians 10:3–5). Paul wanted the Corinthians to look beyond the façade of the opponents and beyond the outward imperfections of Paul and to see how God had been working among them through the genuine teaching and example of true servants of God!

Second Corinthians 13:5

> Test yourselves, to see whether you are in
> the faith! Put yourselves to the test! Or do you
> not know yourselves, whether Christ is in you?
> Unless you are found to fail the test!

In the case of the Corinthians, this self-examination would involve a number of factors. Were they trusting in the wisdom of God or the wisdom of men? Did they accept that which had been revealed by God to his apostles or the worldly wisdom of puffed up human beings (1 Corinthians 2:6–3:1)? Were they listening to ministers of the New Covenant (2 Corinthians 3:6)? Were they reading the Hebrew Scriptures with a veil over their faces, preventing them from seeing Christ? Were they, with unveiled faces, seeing the glory of Jesus (2 Corinthians 3:14–4:4)? Were they living lives of repentance, having been convicted by the word they had heard from Paul and from Titus (2 Corinthians 7:10ff)? Were they separating themselves from unbelievers who were trying to derail their faith in Christ (2 Corinthians 6:14–18)? Were they trying to gain the approval of the Lord Jesus or of mortal men (2 Corinthians 10:17–18)? Were they trusting in human credentials or in the power of Christ? Were they trusting in the redemptive work of Christ or in the righteousness sought by keeping the Law? For them, these were some of the questions involved in their self-examination. When we examine ourselves, we must ask whether we are New Testament Christians or not. We must ask whether we have heard and obeyed the gospel and whether we are striving to walk according to the instructions of Paul and the other inspired apostles or not!

Second Corinthians 13:6

> But I hope you know that we do not fail
> the test! And we pray to God that you might
> not do anything evil, not so that it will be obvi-
> ous that we are approved, but that you might
> do what is good, even though we might seem
> (to some) as if we had failed.

As Paul asked the Corinthians to test themselves, he asked them to acknowledge that Paul and his companions where servants approved by God. Paul's desire was that the Corinthians did what was right in God's sight, regardless of the opinions that some may have held about Paul, Silvanus, Timothy, or Titus. He acknowledged earlier that he served God both when people were saying good things about him and when they were saying bad things about him (2 Corinthians 6:8).

Second Corinthians 13:8–9

> For we are not able to do anything con-
> trary to the truth, but only to act on behalf of
> the truth. For we rejoice whenever we are weak
> and you are strong. And this we pray, that you
> might be made complete!

Paul's ministry of the New Covenant, his ministry of righteousness, his ministry of the spirit, his ministry of reconciliation was all dedicated to the truth of God and the salvation of souls (2 Corinthians 3:6, 8, 9; 5:18). He rejoiced in the spiritual progress of the Corinthians whenever they manifested it! He wanted for them what he wanted for the other Christians, that he might present every individual "complete in Christ" (Colossians 1:28). The

Corinthians had been converted by Paul but had a long way to go in order to be complete or mature Christians.

Second Corinthians 13:10

> For this reason I am writing these things to you while absent, so that when present I might not act harshly according to the authority which the Lord gave me for building (you) up, and not for tearing (you) down.

Paul made it plain to the Corinthians that he had delayed his visit to them in part, because he did not want to come to them again with harshness and sadness (2 Corinthians 2:1ff). God did not make Paul an apostle and give him the power to do miracles so that he might lord it over people or treat them harshly but so that he might build them up spiritually (2 Corinthians 10:8). Ministers of Christ are in a unique position of influence in people's lives. If we are thoughtless in the way we deal with people, we can tear down their self-worth, plunge them into depression, and cause them to give up on their commitment to Christ. We are in the business of spiritual construction, not spiritual destruction! Our goal through our teaching and our behavior is to strengthen people and deepen their commitment to God. We want to encourage, not discourage. We want to motivate, not decimate. We want to inspire hope, not despair. The Corinthians knew from their own past experience with Paul that this was true (2 Corinthians 6:3–10; 7:2).

Second Corinthians 13:11

> Finally, brothers, rejoice! Allow yourselves to be made complete! Be encouraged! Be of the same mind! Be at peace! And the God of love

and peace will be with you! Greet one another
with a kiss of brotherly love! All the saints greet
you!

This exhortation comes from Paul's heart. He wants joy for
these people who have been plagued with trouble, strife, and division. He wants them to accept his admonitions so that they can
become more mature and more complete in Christ. He wants
them to be at peace with each other and with their spiritual father,
Paul (1 Corinthians 4:15–16). He feels much affection toward
them, so he sends them warm and heartfelt greetings, hoping that
they will feel the same way about him (2 Corinthians 6:11–13).

Second Corinthians 13:13

May the grace of our Lord Jesus Christ,
and the love of God, and the fellowship of the
Holy Spirit be with all of you!

This is one of the great Trinitarian statements of the New
Testament (Matthew 28:19; 1 Corinthians 12:4–6; 2 Corinthians
13:14; Revelation 1:4–5). It is Jesus Christ who brought us the
grace of God (Titus 2:11). He is the one whose redemptive death
makes it possible for God to freely give us his righteousness
(Romans 5:17). The love of God, offered to all in the whole world,
is only truly experienced in Christ (Romans 8:39). All of us are
sealed with the Spirit when we come to Christ (Ephesians 1:13).
When we are baptized into the body, we are made to drink from
the reservoir of the Holy Spirit (1 Corinthians 12:13). The Spirit
dwells in each of our bodies (1 Corinthians 6:19). Collectively,
we make up the church, the spiritual temple of the Holy Spirit
(1 Corinthians 3:16–17; Ephesians 2:20–22). To each member
of the body, the Spirit gives gifts to be employed in ministry as he

decides (Romans 12:6; 1 Corinthians 12:7, 11, 18, 28; Ephesians 4:7–12). We share in the Spirit's indwelling, in his intercession, and in the strengthening power he provides in our inner being. We share in the Spirit's shaping of our characters as he produces his fruit in our lives (Galatians 5:22–23). What a magnificent prayer that we should all participate in the grace of Jesus, in the love of God that passes knowledge, and in the incredible blessings of the Holy Spirit in our lives!

Reflections on Chapter 13

1. In 2 Corinthians 13:5, what does Paul urge the Corinthians to do?
2. According to 2 Corinthians 13:10, why was Paul writing this letter to the Corinthians at that particular time?
3. For what reason did Paul receive authority as an apostle according to 2 Corinthians 13:10?
4. Where else in the Corinthian letters do we find an admonition similar to that of 2 Corinthians 13:11?
5. How does this letter inform the expectations of ministers today about their long-term relationships with congregations of God's people?

APPENDIX

Practical Ministry Handbook

This is an appendix to Paul's emotional letter, 2 Corinthians. It is included here especially for those who have committed themselves to the ministry of being an evangelist, a minister of the new covenant, a minister of reconciliation. It is my hope that it will provide a tiny bit of guidance for these young soldiers of Christ. I pray that you will go forth and do the work of evangelists. May God work mightily through you for the salvation of souls!

Determining Compatibility

Before making an employment agreement, a wise evangelist will not only visit with a congregation but will have a frank discussion with the church leaders about the basic nature of what he will be preaching. If you intend to preach biblical doctrine about salvation, the New Testament church, marriage and divorce, sexual conduct, fellowship, the mission of the church, and a host of other things, you should give the leaders a good feel for what you will preach and invite them to ask any questions they would like to ask. It is certainly vital to find out if the preacher is doctrinally and philosophically compatible with the group with which he will be working. This discussion is a must before completing any employment agreement! It is also vitally important to make sure the leadership of the church is on the same page as the evangelist regarding what they expect him to do. What are their expectations regarding hospital visitation, home visitation, study time, time devoted to lessons, how often he will be teaching class, how he will spend his evenings, etc.?

Included in this discussion should be expectations regarding the role of the preacher's wife. Not every woman has the same gifts or the same kind of personality. Some are more suited to working behind the scenes in quiet ways, and others are more suited to leading publicly in the ladies' programs. Some preachers' wives have careers outside the home and others do not. The preacher should openly communicate the kinds of things his wife will likely be doing and the kinds of things they should not expect her to do. Preachers should not commit their wives to do things they are not comfortable doing. Regarding expectations of the preacher and expectations of his family, any differences should be openly expressed and discussed before making any kind of agreement.

Making an Initial Agreement

When a preacher interviews with a congregation and is ready to accept the work as an evangelist, it is vital to make a clear and comprehensive agreement with the elders or church leaders. This will help to ensure that both preacher and elders begin the work on the same page with similar expectations of one another. There is much work to be done after this agreement is completed in building good relationships between the preacher and the other leaders, but this written agreement is a good beginning point.

- Both leaders and preacher should get a dated written copy of the agreement. The agreement should include a basic ministry description, detailing what the congregation expects the minister to do. The reality is that the job will always evolve into what is most needed by that congregation, but it is good to have a record of expectations to which both church leaders and preacher can refer. If the leaders later want to change the job description, then a new updated document should be generated and agreed upon by all parties.

- The written agreement should clearly spell out all areas of compensation for the preacher. This should include regular salary, whether it will be paid weekly, every two weeks, monthly, etc. It is recommended that the preacher have part of his compensation designated as housing allowance, especially if he buys his own home. Even if he does not purchase his own home, the money he spends on yard work, any home maintenance expenses, utilities, etc., can be paid in the form of housing allowance and it will not be subject to Federal Income Tax. In the agreement should be whether or not the church will provide health insurance and whether or not they will pay into a retirement fund of some sort for the minister. The written agreement should also spell out how much vacation time the minister gets, how many days for meetings, lectureships, etc., so that all parties are on the same page. All of this should be established before work ever begins.

- The agreement should also include conditions under which the elders would be justified in discharging the preacher as well as expectations of the preacher should he decide to voluntarily choose another work.

Relationship Building Time!

When the preacher first arrives at a new congregation or a new city in which he wants to plant a church, the first step is building relationships! A wise evangelist will visit the members of his congregation in their homes or have them into his home or invite them out to coffee and desert or find some other way to personally interact so that he might get to know each family to some degree. This will take a considerable investment of time during the beginning period of his ministry. One of the most important groups with which to build relationships is the elder-ship. A wise preacher will ask each elder to go with him to visit different members in homes or hospitals and will spend time getting to know each leader. Praying together with individual leaders is a great way to build spiritual relationships. When developing individual relationships, it will help bring more understanding and communication into meetings when the preacher is discussing things with the elders because both elders and preacher will know one another better and understand one another better. This builds trust. The preacher should work at encouraging the elders, expressing appreciation for the good things they do, and should do this both publicly and privately. The more the preacher builds relationships with the people in his congregation through some kind of personal interaction, the more effective he will be in leading them spiritually.

Visiting members and their families in the hospital when they are sick is also a great way to build relationships. Ministers of smaller congregations may be able to do this more often for each member than ministers with larger congregations. My rule of thumb has been to try to visit each member who is admitted to the hospital at least once during their stay there. Hospital visits should be kept relatively short because people are sick or in pain and often do not feel like entertaining guests. The purpose of the hospital visit is to convey our concerns, pray with and for those who are sick, and inquire how we might serve the family of the sick. Five or ten minutes is usually plenty of time for a good hospital visit. The fact that the preacher has shown love and concern and has been a part of that vulnerable time in a person's life helps to build a spiritual bond.

Another great purpose for hospital visits is to build positive spiritual relationships with the friends and family who are not members of the church. Relationships begun at this critical time can continue later with visits to church services or Bible studies that lead people to become members of God's church.

Visiting guests who visit our church services is another great way to begin to build relationships. This may involve nothing more than an early evening knock on someone's door to deliver a gift like a loaf of banana bread or a pie and tell them how much we appreciated having them visit our services. We don't need to be intrusive or insist on going in and sitting down. We just need to convey our interest and let them know of our desire to be of service. Many guests will be positively impressed that we remembered them and cared enough to acknowledge them.

Whether it is having people in our home, visiting people in their homes, visiting people in the hospital, or visiting with people over coffee, the wise preacher is always working to build relationships with the people he wants to influence for the gospel of Christ!

BECOMING A BETTER PREACHER!

The preacher of God's Word must use a significant amount of his time working on his primary duty, the teaching and preaching of God's Word. This means he must block off a considerable amount of time to study, prepare lessons, find practical illustrations, and improve as a presenter.

- Personal study time is vital. I have found that taking a particular book and devoting myself to the deep study of that book over the course of six months or a year yields great benefits. If it is a New Testament book, I try to carefully translate the book from the Greek text and work through the book in a very painstaking way. If you can't deal with the language, just get a more literal translation and carefully study. I read and reread the book, underlining words and phrases and ideas that recur in the text. I make sure and note connections between the passages where words and key phrases are repeated. I ascertain the great principles and themes in the book and use those themes to formulate sermons. This kind of study is careful spadework that yields great personal growth and builds a base of preaching material. This kind of study is the most vital aspect of a preacher's long-term growth! Early morning hours or late evening hours are often most productive for study of this kind without interruptions.

- Preparing lessons is another important pursuit of a good preacher's time. This means that one should find a major idea in a passage of Scripture, formulate a thesis statement, which expresses that idea, and organize clear points that support that thesis statement. This part of sermon preparation is the basic organization of the sermon in a clear, logical form.

   In addition to organizing the lesson, one should give considerable thought to illustrating the major points of the lesson. The best illustrations are real-life stories of people who have experienced something you are talking about or events where the principle you are emphasizing was demonstrated. Illustration gives people an idea of what happens in real life when people follow or refuse to follow the principle being taught.

   Then good preaching needs a clear and simple application. What does the lesson call us to do? How can we live out a response to the lesson this week? Preparing good lessons involves using the biblical principles one has found in personal study, organizing those principles into a logical form, illustrating those principles with real-world illustrations, and applying those principles to the lives of your listeners. Listen to two or three good preachers on a regular basis and see what they do best so you can learn from them. Pay attention to their basic ideas, their organization, their illustration, and their application! The preparation of good lessons will take a great deal of work on the part of a dedicated preacher!

- If you use Keynote or PowerPoint presentations, be sure that they clearly state your main idea, your main points, and perhaps strongly emphasize your applications. Make the slides simple and professional looking. Keep slides to a minimum, and if you put Scripture passages on slides, clearly emphasize the portions of passages you wish to highlight. Very often, with these presentations, less is more. The simpler, the better!

- Good preachers need to work on their speech as well. One of the great ways to do this is to listen to your own lessons each week critically! Learn to pronounce your words clearly and with sufficient emphasis and volume. Learn to use proper grammar and subject verb agreement. Learn how to read or quote passages so that the parts of the passage you want to emphasize stand out clearly. Practice out loud, saying what you want to say so that it sounds right to you. Especially for beginning preachers, this is a technique that is very helpful for self-improvement!

- A good preacher needs to go to a couple of good lectureships or workshops each year and learn from other good preachers. Listening to the presentations of others is a great way to gain ideas for better ways of presenting our own lessons!

A preacher who is a valuable long-term asset to a congregation is a man who is always learning, always trying to improve, and always honing his skills to make himself better! This is a lifetime endeavor!

BEING A SOUL-WINNER!

If we want other people to share the gospel, preachers need to be soul-winners as well! Soul-winning is all about building relationships with people who are not members, asking people to study God's word, and leading them to obey the gospel. In order to be a soul-winner, one needs to always be looking for people who need to obey the gospel.

There are several places a preacher can find these people. The easiest contacts are guests that attend services. Look for guests! Greet them and welcome them. Find out their names! Greet them again after services. Invite them to your class or to a small group meeting. Try to remember their names so that you can call them by name if they come back again! Each time they come, talk with them a little more. Ask about their religious background and what brought them to your congregation. Invite them to a social event. The first goal is to build a relationship.

The preacher also finds souls in his recreational activities, at the health clubs, on the golf course, among the families of his children's friends, and in many other places. We develop spiritual contacts when we are sensitive to the needs and struggles of others, when we are willing to visit people in the hospital and pray with them, and when we offer other help when people are in need.

Sooner or later, when we have developed a good relationship with someone and have prayed with them or offered comfort from the Scriptures, it is time to ask our friend if he/she would study the Bible with us. "Why don't we get together one afternoon this week and spend an hour studying the Bible together? How about Tuesday at 4:30?" Many times, people will accept such an invitation, and then it is up to the preacher to patiently, lovingly, and clearly teach the gospel with the purpose of leading the person to a decision about obeying the gospel of Christ. When we teach people, we need to take them where they are and lead them to where they need to be. This means finding out about their religious backgrounds, establishing some basic Bible facts and principles, and building a foundation for them to properly understand God's word. It might take months or even years to lead some people to Christ, but leading people to Christ is the greatest work in the entire world!

HELPING PEOPLE THROUGH DEATH

When one of your church members dies or when one of their immediate family members dies, you have a great opportunity to have a positive influence. When you learn of the death, you should go immediately to see the family and communicate your love and concern. At the very least, you should call if it is very late at night and should inform the family of your intent to drop by in the morning. When you arrive to visit with the family, you sincerely express how very sorry you are for their loss. You might bring a dish of food or simply offer to serve the family in some way. When you feel that your visit is coming to an end, suggest having a prayer for the family members. Ask God to give them comfort and strength and to help them get through the funeral.

The family may ask if you can do the funeral. If they do ask, tell them yes or no and tell them if there are any times when you are unable to do the funeral. The main thing you want to do is be a support to the family in any way you can. Funerals are all different, and the best funerals are prepared for each individual based on your experience with them. Of course, the basic truths of the gospel are applicable to all.

There are many other things that could be said about being successful as a minister. The most important thing is one's commitment to Christ and his word! Let us be faithful servants of Jesus and faithful proclaimers of the message he entrusted to his apostles and prophets! As Paul wrote in 1 Corinthians 4:1–5, we will one day give an account to the Lord Jesus Christ for our stewardship of the gospel!

WORKS CITED

Behr, C. A. *Aelius Aristides, The Complete Works, Vol. II: Orations XVII–LIII*. Leiden, 1981.

Brown, F., Driver, S.R., Briggs, C. *A Hebrew and English Lexicon of the Old Testament*, Oxford: Clarendon Press, 1976 (pp. 296–297).

Buschsel, Friedrich. *Theological Dictionary of the New Testament, Vol. VII*. Edited by Gerhard Kittel. Grand Rapids, Michigan: W. B. Eerdmans, 1967.

Charles, R.H. and N. Forbes. "The Book of the Secrets of Enoch." In The Apocrypha and Pseudepigrapha of the Old Testament, Volume 2, New York: Oxford University Press, 1993. Page 434.

———. "The Sibylline Oracles." In The Apocrypha and Pseudepigrapha of the Old Testament, Volume 2, New York: Oxford University Press, 1993. Page 378.

———. "The Testaments of the Twelve Patriarchs." In The Apocrypha and Pseudepigrapha of the Old Testament, Volume 2, New York: Oxford University Press, 1993. Page 299.

Colson, F.H., Translator, Philo, *The Contemplative Life*, in Loeb Classical Library, Cambridge, Mass.: Harvard University Press, 1967. P. 163.

Conybeare, W.J., and Howson, J.S. The Life and Epistles of St. Paul, Grand Rapids, Mich.: 1962.

Danby, Herbert, trans. *The Mishnah*. London: Oxford Universit Press, 1974.

Delling, Gerhart. *Thriambeuo,* in Theological Dictionary c the New Testament, Volume III, ed. Gerhard Kittel, W.B Eerdmans, Grand Rapids. Mich. 1967. P. 160.

Kuhn, K. G. "Maranatha" in *Theological Dictionary of the Neu Testament, Vol. IV.* Edited by Gerhard Kittel. Grand Rapids, Michigan: W. B. Eerdmans, 1967.

Lake, Kirsopp, translator, *The Didache,* in The Apostolic Fathers, Loeb Classical Library, Cambridge, Mass.: Harvard University Press, 1977, p. 331.

Marlowe, Michael. *Head-Covering Customs of the Ancient World.* Bible Researcher, February 2005.

Metzger, Bruce. *A Textual Commentary on the Greek New Testament.* New York: United Bible Society, 1975.

Murphy-O'Connor, Jerome. *St. Paul's Corinth: Text and Archaeology.* Liturgical Press, p.161, 2002.

Pausanias. *Descriptions of Greece* on Theoi.com, Theoi Project, Aaron J. Atsma. New Zealand, copyright 2000–2017.

Philo. *The Contemplative Life.* Translated by F. H. Colson. Loeb Classical Library, London: Harvard University Press, 1967.

Pliny the Younger. *Letters and Panegyricus, Vol. 2.* Translated by Betty Radice. Cambridge, Massachussetts: Harvard University Press, 1975.

Roberts, A. and Donaldson, J. translators, *Justin Martyr, Apology*, in The Ante-Nicene Fathers, Volume 1, Buffalo, N.Y: Christian Literature Company 1885, (pp. 185–186).

———. *Tertullian: On the Veiling of Virgins,* in The Ante-Nicene Fathers, Volume 1, Buffalo, N.Y: Christian Literature Company 1885, (p. 31).

Schaff, Phillip and Wace, Henry. "The Letters of Jerome," in Nicene and Post-Nicene Fathers, Series 2, Volume VII. New York: Christian Literature Company, 1893.

ABOUT THE AUTHOR

Dan R. Owen is a New Testament teacher at Bear Valley Bible Institute International of Denver, Colorado. He has a BA in Bible and biblical languages from Oklahoma Christian University, an MA in Greek New Testament from Harding Graduate School of Religion, and a PhD in ministerial education from Southern Illinois University. Dr. Owen has been preaching the Gospel for forty-five years and has been teaching both undergraduate and graduate Bible courses since 1981.